BOOK M: LIBER MUNDI

Atu House

Barre, Massachusetts

First Edition

Cover design by M. M. Meleen
Tarot illustrations and Tree of Life diagram by M. M. Meleen
Book design by Victoria Waters
Editing by M.M. Meleen and Peter Baker

ISBN: 978-0-9840010-1-9

All mail addressed to the author is forwarded, but the publisher will not give out an address or a phone number. Any internet references are current at publication time, but the publisher cannot guarantee that a specific location will continue to be maintained. For information on the Tabula Mundi Tarot, please refer to www.tabulamundi.com.

Atu House
P.O. Box 673
Barre, MA 01005

Printed in the United States of America

In Memory of M.S. Meleen
March 20, 1969 — May 25, 2015

Oh let the sun beat down upon my face, stars to fill my dream
I am a traveler of both time and space, to be where I have been
To sit with elders of the gentle race, this world has seldom seen
They talk of days for which they sit and wait and all will be revealed
. . . Let me take you there.

~ Led Zeppelin, "Kashmir"

Table of Contents

Preface

Do what thou wilt shall be the whole of the law.

The Fool of Tabula Mundi, rather than about to step off of a cliff or through a portal, is poised to step into a wormhole in the fabric of space-time. This sets the tone for the entire deck.

Tabula Mundi, which translates to "picture of the world," is my second tarot deck and my personal tarot *Magnum Opus*, so far anyway. The tarot illustrations in this book come from the Tabula Mundi Nox et Lux edition published in 2015. A color version is in progress.

The Major Arcana cards took time for meditation on the attributions and evocative formal Golden Dawn titles followed by time for the actual art. For the Minors just as with the Majors my intention was for each card to be a completely new image that still conveyed the underlying Golden Dawn teachings. I came up with a system for my process of image design from a method of contemplation described in *Liber Theta* (James Eshelman's updated and more Thelemic version of *Book T*). This conveys the decanic and qabalistic structure. While the artwork style for the Minors was the same as for the Majors, the meditative part of the process accelerated and the images formed in a creative flood, forming some interesting connections. What came first, the chicken or the egg? In this case, the images came first and the symbolic ideas in the text came after, thus in a sense I didn't consciously conceive of them. They came with the egg, which came first.

A tarot deck has to have an underlying tarot structure, so I chose the framework set forth by the Golden Dawn in Book T but with Thoth innovations. By framework, I mean things like the numbering and names of the cards, the planetary, zodiacal and elemental attributions, and the names and elements for the court cards and suits, and importantly, Aleister Crowley's Thelemic underpinnings. I chose the Thoth for the structure as it is the one that for me has the most resonant depth of meanings. As this is a Thoth based deck, I will quote Crowley liberally throughout the text. I'm not a Crowley or Thoth expert; I'm just a fan.

I am grateful for my exposure to Aleister Crowley's *Book of Thoth*, as it is what I consider the most profound and useful book on the tarot in existence. It is a truly magic book that continues to reward the reader with repeated readings, and the explorations it sometimes suggests. I am also grateful for the free availability of *Book T* and *Liber Theta*. I highly recommend that you consult these and the *Book of Thoth*. As they were primary source works for the deck's structure I consider them essential reading to understand this deck.

It is my hope that the images of Tabula Mundi endure and inspire, and that this book casts some light on your understanding of tarot. By entering the wormhole I have seen another perspective or picture of the world and for sure I stand upon the shoulders of giants.

Love is the law, love under will.

M.M. Meleen
June 20, 2015 (Anno Vi Sun in 28° Gemini, Moon in 13° Leo)
In the fabric of space-time

Reinventing the Wheel

Why make another Tarot? Why make a Tarot at all? Tarot encapsulates facets of the full human experience making it the perfect artistic vehicle. I've been asked why I did a second deck, Tabula Mundi, and how it differs from the first. If you can imagine how much work it is to create 79 cohesive images (seventy eight cards plus one for the card backs) and then write a book for them, you might also wonder why I chose to put myself through this process again, especially considering the first one accomplished the mission, and the financial rewards are not equivalent to the relationship to linear time.

Before Tabula Mundi, the Rosetta Tarot was my first deck creation. As such I was not going to try to reinvent the wheel. In my original conception the Rosetta was intended to be a deck combining the best traits of the classic RWS and my favorite deck, the Thoth. It became a definitely Thoth inspired pack. Though the Rosetta Tarot can't be thought exactly a clone due the many deviations, in the Rosetta there are many cards that are direct homage to their counterparts in the Thoth.

The initial inspiration for the Rosetta came after seeing Carl Jung's *Red Book*. The whole concept of a work done over several years, semi-secretly, that involved a beautiful illuminated book, occult knowledge, exploration of the subconscious, and travel in the imagination, lit up my desire to devote my life to creating something similar. Not because I think I am an artist or a scholar of that stature but because it seemed to be the only thing in life I both felt capable of and drawn to do. Of course the project morphed from the original idea of the images painted in a book to actually creating a deck.

When I did the Rosetta, I just wanted first to create an artistic creation in tribute to the decks I grew up with while adding my own personal touch. But before the ink was even dry on the Rosetta's printing and the first copies were rolling out, I knew that what I had really wanted to do was create a deck with images not like any other deck. I had to do it again, as I wanted to create a deck with every card having completely unique interpretations of the images yet still portraying the traditional archetypes without error. Whether or not I have done so with this deck is open to interpretation. It is my *Tabula Mundi*, or picture of the world and in the process there was a definite connection to a world current.

Like songs you remember forever, the images of the iconic tarots are consciously there if you call on them and maybe subconsciously there as well. I didn't want to draw on either of the two iconic tarot decks for my images, but just for invoking their force to tap into the stream for something etheric. The images had to tap into universal archetypes, and tune into the channel of the card, and not be randomly assigned artworks or evoke the feeling of wallowing in the detritus of my psyche. For the images, I wanted them to be generated and gestated within my own mind, though also drawing on the zeitgeist.

I also wanted a chance to do another deck to improve upon the art in the Rosetta. The Rosetta's original artwork images were made card sized with tiny paint brushes and different mediums for each suit, some of which I'd never used before. As a result of the small size and the unfamiliar media, it often was not possible to draw details I wanted or even to capture proportions accurately. (I've been told, due to my many rants of the time and after, that my autobiography of that period should be titled "Hand the size of a ****** sesame seed.") In Tabula Mundi, I work on images that are larger and then shrunk to card size after scanning. This has been a huge improvement, though there were new difficulties from the choice of permanent marker and India ink on frosted Mylar, which is unforgiving as a medium because both the color inks and black ink lines are permanent and cannot be erased. The artwork was all done by hand, and not manipulated digitally. They were drawn with pencil and pen and ruler and compass, and then painted with brushes and colored ink, so that each card is an original painting. The originals are approximately 7 x 11 inches.

It should be noted that conscious effort was taken while creating the Tabula Mundi artworks to utilize the principles of sacred geometry. Sometimes this was as simple as dividing the plane first by the phi ratio. Other times, the image was drawn over an elaborate geometrical grid that fit the meaning of the card. Some of these underlying structures became part of the images; others did not and were only used as a guide. This not only gives pleasing form but also animation. The Hermetic text the *Asclepius* was the theoretical basis of talismanic magic that described the magical religion of the Egyptians. The *Asclepius* maintained that the Egyptians knew how to infuse the statues of their gods with talismanic powers, giving life to the statues and making them into actual gods. They used celestial rites and proportions reflecting the harmony of heaven, imparting magical animation. Giulio Camillo, in a speech about his own Memory Theatre (similar to the Memory Palace) interprets the magic of the Egyptian statues in an artistic sense, asserting that a perfectly proportioned statue becomes animated with a spirit, becoming a magical statue. He thus applied it to his occult memory system, insisting that the magical power of the images were a result of perfect proportions.

My greatest strength is that I can and do conceive of pretty far out and yet valid ideas; my weakness is that often I don't have the skill or artistic chops to manifest them. In my head I see the elephant (and I see a lot of elephants); on the page I am the blind man drawing the elephant's foot. I'm not a writer by predilection either, and words do not come naturally to me but I have things to share here that I hope you will find interesting. I'm writing about the one thing I am qualified to write about, and that is this pack of cards. Time stopped the book from being longer. While I have few words I have a lot of ideas that I hope are expressed in the artwork.

Introduction to a Picture of the World

> It has always been said that initiation occurs "by and in itself." One cannot explain the life of things; one can only merge oneself with it and thus feel it. In every epoch, therefore, the goal of all initiatory institutions was to give whoever asked for it the means of self initiation. Among those called in this way were sometimes found those who were chosen.
>
> ~ R.A. Schwaller de Lubicz, *A Study of Numbers*

This book is intended as the primary companion book for the tarot deck called Tabula Mundi, which translates to *world slate*, "a picture of the world." By seeing a different picture of the same archetypes, one gets new understandings. So *Book M: Liber Mundi* may provide some insight useful with most Golden Dawn based decks and thus be also applicable to the iconic decks such as the Thoth and the Rider Waite-Smith, and to their derivatives.

The Tabula Mundi tarot images are not based on any other deck, but they incorporate the traditional Golden Dawn structure and Crowley's revisions to the names, attributions and meanings of the cards. Thus, the cards are based on the following framework:

- The formal titles of the Lord of each of the 78 cards
- 22 letters of the Hebrew alphabet mapped to the 22 trumps, or Keys
- 10 *sephiroth*, or categories of manifestation, existing in four Worlds mapped to the suits
- The color scales of the four worlds
- The 36 decans of the Zodiac and their Chaldean rulers
- The four classical elements
- The three alchemical elements
- The Divine Name Yod-Hé-Vau-Hé, and the Qabalistic idea of Father-Mother-Son-Daughter, mapped to the four suits and the Knight, Queen, Prince, Princess

When creating the Major Arcana, the traditional Golden Dawn descriptions were contemplated, but not followed directly. They were combined with an understanding of the Atu, or Key, and the attributions. They are meant to hold to the Thoth meanings. The Minors take the Thoth and Golden Dawn meanings as well, but are not pip cards consisting of celestial hands holding the required number of suit elements, nor do they clone the Thoth images. Instead they were created based on a meditation described in *Liber Theta*; a process which will be explained in full in the relevant part of the text. For the court cards, a similar process was used to incorporate the court's associated minor cards. Rather than following the Golden Dawn court card armor and equipment descriptions to the letter, care was taken to include the traditional court crests. The meaning of these crests is explained in the text.

There are other books that can be consulted for more information about tarot history and western occultism history. Because others have covered the subject so thoroughly you won't find that here. Nor will there be an attempt to write a comprehensive treatise on any of the hermetic teachings. That would just be reinventing the wheel. What you will find are basic explanations of each sephira of the Tree of Life and the decans of the astrological signs as they play a part in the underlying structure of this deck and other Golden Dawn and Thoth based decks. There is also commentary on each card and an explanation of how it fits within the deck's structure. Each discourse contains descriptions and stories about the symbolism in the image of the card, in very basic form and as they apply to and appear in this deck and some of these types of decks. The symbolism covers a wide range of topics relating to mythology, religion, history, alchemy, Qabalah, Thelema and astrology.

For the Major Arcana there is a brief section called "Random Artist Notes" that is just an informal aside on things like the inspiration or model for the card or more personal commentary. It isn't all that relevant for divinatory or study purposes as it isn't directly related to the card meaning, but at times it may be interesting or at least amusing.

The Tabula Mundi images were formed through contemplation of the card's formal title combined with the Hebrew letter, the related attributions, and position on the Tree of Life. By holding all those things in mind consciously, constantly and somewhat obsessively, and then letting go of holding them, eventually the image or at least the idea of the image would present itself. It took a month or more for each of the Major Arcana. The actual drawing and painting took an average of forty hours each but the other weeks were for the ineffable fertilization period. They are complex ideas and require images with a lot of interlocking meanings, and you can't rush the muse. (The muse however, can *occasionally* be coaxed.)

Also included is a brief comparison of the Tabula Mundi minors to the imagery of the minors of the Rider Waite-Smith, the Thoth, and the Rosetta. In comparing the minors of Tabula Mundi to its predecessor the Rosetta, and those to the ancestral Thoth and Rider Waite-Smith, via the descriptions of the images you may see the similarities and differences and how they illustrate an underlying shared structure. Including pictures of those would only have been possible for my own deck, the Rosetta, without a lot of trouble getting permissions, and so they have been omitted. Readers are probably extremely familiar with the RWS and Thoth, and some of you with the Rosetta. All three decks have readily available images online. The advantage to taking the time to envision them in your head instead of having a visual presented to you is that it mirrors somewhat the process used to create the Tabula Mundi cards, both the Majors and especially the decanic lesser arcana. It is very good practice to strengthen your abilities to hold images in your mind this way for other work with visualization.

When contemplating the Majors, simultaneously reflect on their evocative formal titles, their Hebrew letter and its meaning, and the elemental or astrological attribution of the card as well as its path on the Tree of Life. If all that is new to you, begin with the ceremonial titles listed in the chapter headings, as contemplating the poetry of those illustrious and suggestive phrasings is most illuminating and in itself contains layers of meaning.

When contemplating the thirty six decanic Minors, it will prove useful to compare them to their two related Majors, one of which is the card of their zodiacal sign and the other is the card of the planet that rules the decan of that sign. As well one can reflect upon the sephira and the element. The Aces should be considered with the Princesses of their suit.

The entire Tarot is a Memory Palace, as every card connects to every other. This is especially evident when considering the court cards. When exploring the courts, for the Knights, Queens, and Princes one should certainly consider the three associated Minor cards from the thirty degree span of the zodiac they rule. In addition, their primary zodiacal Major card should be kept in mind. For additional information one can also review the attributes of the "missing" minor card. Since they pick up only two decans of their primary sign, the missing card can shed some light on traits of their sign they don't pick up. The secondary Major associated with their shadow card can also be explored if desired. For additional research purposes, the associated hexagram of the I-Ching according to the *Book of Thoth* has been listed in court card headings.

The Princesses should always be contemplated with their Aces, as they are the thrones or fruition of the will of the element. The trump associated with the central sign of the three signs they span should be considered primarily but in combination with the two on either side. For additional information one can consider the related elemental trump, as well as the Princesses relationship to the other three courts. For maximum benefit, one can also reflect upon the appropriate one of the four powers of the Sphinx: To Will, To Dare, To Know, and To Keep Silent.

In the divine name IAO, I invoke thee, thou Great Angel HRU,
who art set over the operations of this Secret Wisdom.
Lay thine hand invisibly on these consecrated cards of art,
that thereby I may obtain true knowledge of hidden things,
to the glory of the ineffable Name. Amen.

A Journey through the Wormhole

The Major Arcana

I could be bounded in a nutshell and count myself a king of infinite space . . .

~ Shakespeare, *Hamlet*, Act 2, Scene 2

In the universe, there are things that are known,
and things that are unknown, and in between, there are doors.

~ William Blake

For doors, one needs keys. The Major Arcana or keys of Tabula Mundi were created by meditation on the card's formal title, the Hebrew letter, its zodiacal or elemental attribution, and its path on the Tree of Life. Tarot truly is a *Universe in a Nutshell.* In his book of that title Steven Hawking says to "watch out for wormholes: you never know what may come out of them." Personally I'd also watch out for falling into one!

"The truth is wormholes are all around us, only they're too small to see. They occur in nooks and crannies in space and time," Hawking writes. "Nothing is flat or solid. If you look closely enough at anything you'll find holes and wrinkles in it. It's a basic physical principle, and it even applies to time. Even something as smooth as a pool ball has tiny crevices, wrinkles and voids. Down at the smallest of scales, smaller even than molecules, smaller than atoms, we get to a place called the quantum foam. This is where wormholes exist. Tiny tunnels or shortcuts through space and time constantly form, disappear, and reform within this quantum world. And they actually link two separate places and two different times."

The Major Arcana of Tabula Mundi attempts to show the Fool's Journey as a passage through a wormhole, exiting at the tube torus of the Universe. The Fool, card Zero, rather than containing Nothing, actually contains infinite possibilities, and can thus link to any other card in the deck. When encountering a wormhole, one never knows what may come out of it, or where it may lead.

Lady Frieda Harris, artist of the Thoth deck, once said "The Tarot could be described as God's Picture Book, or it could be likened to a celestial game of chess, the Trumps being the piece to be moved according to the law of their own order over a checkered board of the four elements." In this deck the Fool's journey begins with a step into a wormhole in the fabric of space-time. Along the way the whole of creation is witnessed and a never-ending panorama of cognitive imagery is encountered: the Tabula Mundi or "picture of the world"; the Universe (or a Universe) in a nutshell. Watch out for wormholes, and let the journey begin!

This leads us to the revolving story of the Fool's Journey . . .

Once there was Nothing, a nothing that was not even the concept of Nothing; it was the Nothing that was nought. This Nothing was limitless, yet numinous. This Nothing was luminous, and the luminosity was directed towards the center of itself until it condensed at the center into a single infinitely contracted point. This Point was called "I Am." It wore a Crown of nine points.

From this timeless beginning through the three veils of Nothing strolled a Fool. He wore a Jester's cap of nine points and carried a bag containing the four winds. He drew in breath and was about to say "I will be," as he fell through a wormhole at the infinitely contracted center of this resplendent Nothing. Things started to get interesting.

The Fool heard Something. Perhaps it was the music of the spheres. He found himself in the center of a spinning galaxy. He felt himself transmute from the androgynous being in the center of the galaxy into a man holding a galaxy, wearing a belt that reminded him of Nothing. He said "Abrahadabra." His bag with the four winds disappeared, but he knew its contents were before him on a table. He touched the disk of earth as he gazed upon the waters of the cup before him. He saw the moon's reflection. The Moon grew in brilliance until it was concealed. He closed his eyes.

She opened her eyes. She was standing like a column in a shaft of moonlight between two pillars. One was made of darkness and one of light. She was draped in heavy waters that condensed in swirling forms. She stood upon the ground, and tasted of the seeds within her heart.

The seeds quickened and became sweet. Grasses grew around her and doves sang. The waters within her grew salty. A door within her opened and bees flew from out her heart. In their swarming flight they traced the Fibonacci spiral as they began their scouting. The bees found a home and entered the willow basket.

Now this skep or basket was tended by a mighty king. Bees and keeper have a symbiotic mental relationship, and they became one. He consulted them after battle. He kept the bees to remind him of the necessity of order to rule his kingdom. They spoke to him of chaos and entropy and told him that nature was red in tooth and claw. He sat and pondered this.

He became wise. He brought down the celestial fire. He was the law that affixed the above to the below, and was a priest of the mysteries. He learned and taught until his soul became divided, as if cleaved by a sword. He passed through the keyhole and became two.

He was male, he was the red lion. She was female and was the white eagle. The two were separate and yet the higher self of that being that they once were united them in marriage. In the sweetness of tantric embrace they made the honey elixir. They dissolved into red blood and white gluten, which spiraled together into a mighty cup.

Two in one they were conveyed. This cup was a grail born along on a chariot riding a great wall of water. The charioteer was skillful and did not intend to spill a drop. This required tremendous balance and control. He sought advice from the oracles black and white, and they told him to drink deeply. He drained the cup within. He closed his eyes and began to concentrate on balance, and then began to transform.

She found she was wearing a blindfold, and was balanced on a sword. She was not just balancing, but had metamorphosed into balance itself. She became the dance and was a woman satisfied. Within her was a seed, a point of fire. This spark triggered a descent into matter, and she found herself changing in an elemental way, becoming a wandering man of earth.

This man was a hooded prophet. He was the flame within the virgin. He carried a lamp containing the sun as he descended into a passage in the earth. In the darkness this sun began to glow brightly. Rays of light shot off in all directions and expanded into a great wheel.

The wheel turned. Feeling, thought and ecstasy revolved. He lusted after ecstasy, and was drawn toward a reddish-amber light.

She found herself astride a leonine beast; a great serpent. She drank from the cup of ecstasy and became strong. The beast was hers, and she felt the joy of her passion and vigor. Her kundalini was awakened, and the transfiguration began.

He found himself inverted upon a great tree above the Well of Memory. He gazed with one eye upon a closed eye within the pool. The eye opened, and his closed.

Upon death he found himself now a skeleton astride an eagle-serpent, flying past the Great Pyramids and above the Nile. He took his scythe and began to stir the muck up from the waters. Bubbles arose and he watched one become an egg, and then become a great alchemical vessel. Once again he became a being divided, and yet united.

The green lion found itself before the vessel. Her bow was of the moon; his arrow was of the sun. The vessel brought forth life through the art of alchemy.

They found themselves at the gates of matter, drawn to the light of incarnation. This was earthly life and the forces of time. This was the thrust of a mighty phallus.

The phallus grew larger and became a massive tower. This tower was surmounted with a crown and an eye. This was the House of God. Its entrance was the mouth of Hell. Lightning struck, the eye opened, and the tower crumbled. The edifice was destroyed. The dust settled and the sky cleared.

Behold the firmament; an infinite vista of stars and the celestial river of the Milky Way. Between the waters and the celestial river, our lady of the stars sits upon the horizon. She is the blue lidded daughter of sunset, and the naked brilliance of the voluptuous night sky. She is infinite and there is nothing more beautiful. She washes herself with starlight poured from the cup of the moon and pours the cup of the sun upon the waters. All is ecstasy until you can hold no more. You become a star.

You find yourself at the prow of a ghostly ship at midnight. You are not awake, you are dreaming. Strange phantoms beckon as you pass through the gates of horn and ivory. Flux and reflux, you pass through the dark night of the midnight sun.

Dawn breaks and the sun rises. The solar barge on its passage through the zodiac arrives in glory. The fire of the world has awakened, and so have you.

You are standing in front of a keyhole filled with primal fire. In the east the solar disk rises; you hail your father, the point in the center of the circle. This is the flame that burns in every heart of man, and in the core of every star. Around the disk is the goddess of the infinite starry sky, your mother, the queen of heaven. At the rapture of their union, you enter the chemical retort to be consumed and reborn.

At birth you exit a portal that looks familiar, and yet changed. This is the other side of the wormhole, and you are the holy maiden, the great one of the night of time. The Aeons are the pulsing of your blood. This is the circle squared; the Great Work accomplished. This is Nothing in its complete expansion.

And then the Nothing was nought, and the journey begins again.

Know Naught!

The place where he was, was absolutely flat. In the human world we seldom
see flatness, for the trees and houses and hedges give a serrated edge
to the landscape: even the grass sticks up with its myriad blades.
But here, in the belly of the night, the illimitable, flat, wet mud was
as featureless as a dark junket. If it had been wet sand, even,
it would have had those little wave marks, like the palate of one's mouth.

And, in this enormous flatness, there lived one element: the wind.
For it was an element: it was a dimension, a power of darkness. In the human
world, the wind comes from somewhere, and goes somewhere, and, as it goes,
it passes through somewhere: through trees or streets or hedgerows.
This wind came from nowhere. It was going through the flatness of nowhere,
to no place. Horizontal, soundless except for a peculiar boom, tangible,
infinite, the astounding dimensional weight of it streamed across
the mud. You could have ruled it with a straight-edge. The titanic
grey line of it was unwavering and solid. You could have hooked the
crook of your umbrella over it, and it would have hung there.

The king, facing into this wind, felt that he was uncreated.
Except for the wet solidity under his webbed feet, he was living in nothing:
a solid nothing, like chaos. His were the feelings of a point in geometry,
existing mysteriously on the shortest distance between two points: or of a
line, drawn on a plane surface which had length, breadth but no magnitude.
No magnitude! It was the very self of magnitude. It was power, current, force,
direction, a pulseless world-stream steady in limbo."

~ T. H. White, *The Once and Future King, The Book of Merlyn*

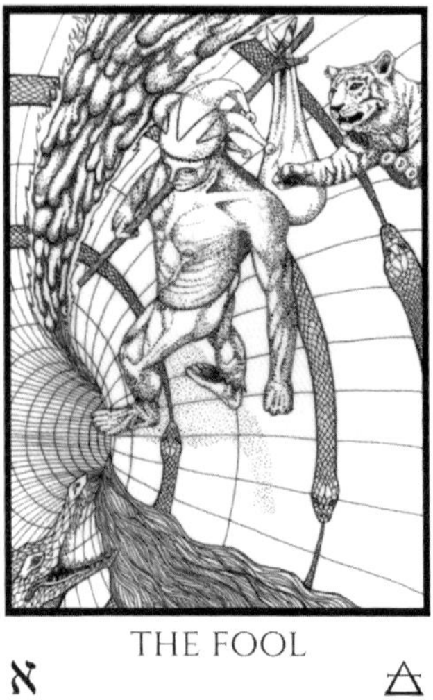

0 – THE FOOL

Spirit of the Aether

Elemental Trump of Air

Hebrew letter: Aleph (ox)

Tree of Life: Path 11 from [1] Kether (Crown) to [2] Chokmah (Wisdom)

Color Scales: Bright Pale Yellow, Sky Blue, Blue-Emerald Green, Emerald Flecked Gold

0 = 1 + (- 1)

I am the Lord of the Double Wand of Power; the wand of the Force of Coph Nia— but my left hand is empty, for I have crushed an Universe; & nought remains.

~ *Liber AL vel Legis III* 72

A*nd then the Nothing was nought, and nought remains.* It is neither day nor night but some point in time between; a moment pregnant with possibility. This is the void before the beginning, or the re-beginning. This is the nascent state of pre-existence. The three ouroboros rings the Fool crosses on his descent into Kether represent the three negative veils of Ain (Nothing that is Not), Ain-Soph (Nothing without Limit), and Ain-Soph-Aur (Limitless Light). Crowley refers to Ain-Soph-Aur as potentially meaning the space-time continuum,[1] a model joining space and time to a single idea, space being three dimensional and time playing the role of the fourth dimension. Threes and fours; this is a model that repeats throughout the tarot in the zodiacal groupings and the triplicities and quadruplicity of sephiroth groupings on the Tree of Life, as well as in the structure of the arrangement of minors and courts.

Mighty was the draught of Voidness to draw Existence in.[2] From the initial nothingness of Ain comes potential for thought, which leads to the

1 Aleister Crowley, *The Book of Thoth*, pg 13

2 William Blake, *Vala, or the Four Zoas, Night the Second* in which Albion, the primeval man, falls and is divided into four emanations.

possibility of vibration, which leads to thought, which leads to the mind which contains thought. Kether, the source, leads to Chokmah as it heads towards manifestation. +1 (male) -1 (female) = 0 (androgynous). Thus is the Fool an androgyne, though usually viewed as "male" in sense of *puer aeternis* or eternal boy. On the Tree of Life, the Fool corresponds to the sephira of Kether, the primal fount and source of all emanation, as it leads down the first path to Chokmah.

The Fool says "I will be." He stands suspended in mid air, poised at the brink of an intra-universe wormhole in space and time, seemingly oblivious to the step he is about to take which will propel him within and through. *The Physics of Stargates* defines a wormhole as "a region of space-time containing a "world tube" (the time evolution of a closed surface) that cannot be continuously deformed (shrunk) to a "world line" (the time evolution of a point). This is the Fool's Journey; the beginning of a passage ending, or re-beginning, in the tube torus of The Universe.

A wormhole is a hypothetical topological feature of space-time, like a tunnel connecting two universes. Traversable wormholes allow for travel in both directions from one part of the universe to another, or from one universe to another. Since they connect two points in space-time, theoretically they also allow for travel in time. Meditation on this in relation to The Fool will shed insight on its position and significance in the Tarot. The Fool can take you anywhere, to any point on the Fool's Journey or all the way to the end. When you enter, there is no telling where you may end up. Or is there? Though the two ends of the wormhole may be in different areas of space and/or time, the inside, as a single piece of space-time, stays the same.

This is the card numbered zero. Zero is shaped like a portal, and represents a vacuum; the source of all things in the known universe. In the zodiac, the "zero point" is 0 degrees Aries, or the vernal equinox. The figure is clothed in vernal green and yellow, wearing a jesters cap like the horns of Bacchus. He is tattooed with symbols of the Sun, the Moon, and the three alchemical symbols. The Fool is Harpocrates or Heru, accompanied by Sebek and a tiger, or water and fire. This is the trump of the element Air or Aether. Aether differs from the pure elemental air of the Ace of Swords. This is the "air" of the vacuum, just before the first motion of Kether. Beside the Fool, twin streams of water and fire precede him into the vortex. Somewhere within when they combine symbolically air is formed.

From the Spirit, the archangel Metatron produced Air, and formed the 22 sounds, the letters, of which the Fool's letter Aleph is the first. Aleph is the indrawn breath "ahhh-lef" and is constructed of two Yods joined by a diagonal

Vau. This is a glyph of the first emanation, as Yod, the primal point, reflects itself. If one adds the numeric value of two Yods and a Vau, one gets 26, which is also the value of YHVH. Aleph's meaning is ox, yet the ox can refer to the earth plane. This upholds the maxim that Kether is in Malkuth, or that the alpha and omega are conjoined. The ox is poised, awaiting the goad. This is the essence of "about to."

All cards of the tarot are derived from the Fool and thus are inherent in Aether. Just as the Aces are the roots of the elements, the Fool is as one aspect of the angel HRU of tarot; the root of the Major Arcana. The Fool is connected to all. A portal opens and there is an original impulse and unexpected doorway, that leads anywhere in the Universe. "All such impulses are right if rightly received."[3]

KNOW NAUGHT!
ALL WAYS ARE LAWFUL TO INNOCENCE.
PURE FOLLY IS THE KEY TO INITIATION.
SILENCE BREAKS INTO RAPTURE.
BE NEITHER MAN NOR WOMAN, BUT BOTH IN ONE. BE SILENT, BABE
IN THE EGG OF BLUE, THAT THOU MAYEST GROW TO BEAR THE LANCE
AND GRAAL! WANDER ALONE, AND SING! IN THE KING'S PALACE HIS
DAUGHTER AWAITS THEE.

~ Aleister Crowley, *The Book of Thoth*

The Oracle

The fabric of space-time has curved inward and a portal is revealed. All things are possible; and naught is known. O Fool, as you cross the veils towards manifestation, take heed. The portal leads somewhere new. The right attitude is all. Inhale. This is an original idea; wisdom and folly are but two possibilities.

3   *Book of Thoth* pg 254

I – THE MAGUS

The Magus of Power

Planetary Trump of Mercury

Hebrew letter: Beth (house)

Tree of Life: Path 12, from [1] Kether (Crown) to [3] Binah (Understanding)

Color Scales: Yellow, Purple, Grey, Indigo Flecked Violet

THE MAGUS

ב ☿

> With the Wand createth He.
> With the Cup preserveth He.
> With the Dagger destroyeth He.
> With the Coin redeemeth He.
>
> ~ *Liber Magi* vv. 7-10

As above, so below. The mixmaster of the cosmic turntable is bringing down the house; his letter is Beth. Here the Magus is portrayed as the galactic DJ, the elemental juggler as a disk jockey mixing recorded music for an audience of dancers. He plays the music of the spheres. He pulls down a universe, a spiral disk, with one hand; the other hand rests on the turntable pentacle, thus connecting the above to the below. This is the cosmos manifesting in the material world. Here is the celestial spark of creation. Mercury is the first positive manifestation and as such is both the will, and the substance of the universe. He is both planetary and alchemical Mercury, and the first of the alchemical trumps. He is on the path between Godhead and Form.

Mercury is associated with communication and discourse. The DJ's equipment includes headphones, or earphones. These are used to listen to one recording while the other recording is being played to the audience, or to listen to both recordings simultaneously. But misunderstanding is inherent in the act of confining a concept to words. When moving from the realm of the divine to the mundane, things can get lost in translation, modulation with distortion. The same things come with mixing music. Sometimes the distortion is noise and sometimes it is intentional. The key to harmonic ratios is hidden in the famous Pythagorean tetractys, made up of the first four numbers—1, 2, 3, and 4—which in their proportions reveal the intervals. Music, with all its passion and emotion, is based upon mathematical relationships. Such musical notions as octaves, chords, scales, and keys can be understood logically using mathematics. The most harmonic and magically effective music was said to use the golden ratio. The golden ratio is the most irrational of irrational numbers, an infinite series of ever diminishing fractions. This "divine proportion" was said to transmit the incomprehensibility of God. Thoth is the god associated with Mercury and was said to be the inventor of music, as well as mathematics, geometry, astronomy, astrology, oratory, writing, botany, medicine, theology —he pretty much is credited with every branch of knowledge, human and divine.

The golden ratio is also evident in the physics of black holes. Black holes, and suns, have a "negative specific heat." This means they get hotter as they lose heat. Basically, loss of heat robs the gas of a body such as the sun of internal pressure, enabling gravity to squeeze it into a smaller volume. The gas then heats up. But for a spinning black hole, there is an outward "centrifugal force" acting to prevent any shrinkage of the hole. The force depends on how fast the hole is spinning. It turns out that at a critical value of the spin, a black hole flips from negative to positive specific heat—that is, from growing hotter as it loses heat to growing colder. The critical value is determined by the mass of the black hole and the golden ratio. Black holes and wormholes are similar and show the connection between the Fool and the Magus. But only wormholes are traversable. Black holes are tricksters, and unless you can travel faster than light, you just encounter a singularity.

The Magus wears the belt of the ouroboros portal from the Fool. The Magus is the first masculine emanation, as the androgynous Fool is separated into Magus and Priestess. The Fool has fallen through the wormhole and landed in the spiral galaxy in the Magus' hand. Where the Fool was silence, the indrawn breath before speech, the Magus is sound, the Logos. As breath activates words, the Fool activates Magus. The glyph of the planet Mercury has antennae, or horns. Mercury the figure wears the winged helm with a similar shape. With his antennae, Mercury transmits and receives transmission through the airwaves.

Magus is Mercury, never found more than 28 degrees from the Sun. He is connected with the Sun also because Magus I=one and Sun XIX=19=1+9=10 which reduces to one. The DJ mixer is adorned with the Sun and the solar lemniscate, and has four trees of life made from different colored lights for each world which flash in time with the music in the colors of the four scales. Wires transmit to and from, serving as a conduit.

Many portrayals of the Magus card show a magician with the four implements of the suits on a table before him. Here the DJ's equipment includes the four implements instead. The Disk is shown as a turntable. This is the Ace of Disks; the element of Earth and root of the material world all the way to Universe, connecting Kether to Malkuth. The spiral galaxy disk that he pulls down from Above will ultimately be placed on the Disk of Below which serves as the turntable. The caduceus Wand is shown as a controlling lever of the music mixer, and is for the element of Fire. The crystal at the top of the Wand is the spark of life, or manifestation of matter through will. The Sword is rising out of a Cup on the table. This is the mind inherent in emotions; both idea and desire are needed to manifest, and to separate the good from the evil. An all seeing eye as a spotlight connects the three Supernals.

The Oracle

Magus, listen to the music of the spheres. There is a message for you if you can decipher it. Bring the above to the below, and manifest your idea. Open your mind—the divine consciousness has a transmission. Translate the message and build a house of form. All the elements are at your fingertips. Create freely and manifest your Will. Beware deception or misinterpretation.

THE PRIESTESS

ב   ☽

II – THE PRIESTESS

The Priestess of the Silver Star

Planetary Trump of the Moon

Hebrew letter: Gimel (camel)

Tree of Life: Path 13, from [1] Kether (Crown) to [6] Tiphareth (Beauty)

Color Scales: Blue, Silver, Cold Pale Blue, Silver Rayed Sky Blue

I would lead you and bring you to my mother's house — she who has taught me.
I would give you spiced wine to drink, the nectar of my pomegranates.

~ Song of Songs 8:2

The Priestess is an archetype of Sophia, the Gnostic goddess of wisdom. Roman Catholics call her Hagia Sophia, or Holy Wisdom, as an expression of the feminine aspect of the Holy Trinity. Pythagoras taught Socrates, who taught Plato, the subject of philosophy as *philo-sophia*, meaning "friend of wisdom." In most if not all versions of the Gnostic myth, Sophia brings about instability in the Pleroma, in turn bringing about the creation of materiality. *Pleroma* means fullness or abundance and refers to it in the sense of the fullness of existence or the totality of divine powers. The Priestess is the first feminine manifestation, the anima, the Shekinah or dwelling of God, at once an expression of Binah the Mother in the supernal world and Malkuth the Bride in the mundane. She is on the middle pillar path between Kether, the source of divinity, and Tiphareth, man's inner personality and wisdom. Thus she represents initiation; to "know" her is to love her, and connect to the Godhead.

She stands between the pillars of light and darkness, divine and earthly, yin and yang, and represents the personification of the middle pillar, her path reaching from the crown of Kether to the beauty of Tiphareth. Boaz, meaning *strength*, is the black pillar, and Jachin, meaning *he establishes*, is the white pillar. These pillars represent the forces of polarity or the negative and positive in equilibrium. They also stand in for the two sides of the tree of life, the Pillar of Severity and the Pillar of Mercy. In the center, the Priestess is the embodiment of the Pillar of Equilibrium.

The card portrays her cloaked in heavy waters that swirl and coagulate at the stations of the Tree of Life. Her lunar headdress is comprised of both the full moon and the crescent in the position of Chokmah (Wisdom). The Moon is full and in the position of Kether as she is the reflected light of Kether acting through the Moon on the Sun (Tiphareth). This astral light can reveal or conceal by its very brilliance. Her six pointed Star of David necklace falls in Tiphareth. Her Yoni falls in the position of Yesod, sephira of the Moon. Her lyre has eight vibrating strings for the eight lunar phases, and is the bow that launches the arrow of Art. The lyre is also associated with Apollo and the Sun, referencing her path to Tiphareth. She herself is Apollo's sister Artemis, the virgin huntress and moon maiden who, with her silver bow, "hunts by enchantment." The strings on her bow here may not be visible at first glance, due their vibration. The bow also hints at the path of Art below her on the Tree of Life.

Her letter is Gimel, meaning Camel, and she is the camel crossing the desert of the Abyss, the sea behind the veil and source of all waters. This is the step between the ideal and the actual. Her body is said to be the great cup or grail of legend. To drink from the grail is the experience of initiation, to glimpse the Torah scroll of Wisdom she carries.

On many portrayals of the High Priestess pomegranates are featured. They tie in with the mythological stories of Koré and Persephone and may be associated with the tarot Priestesses due her attribution of the Moon, and Persephone's story of transience. Here the pomegranates are shown as seeds within writhing and vine-like hearts. Pomegranates seeds symbolize the beginning stirrings of life and death. The seeds of the greater mysteries reside in her transformed heart.

The Oracle

The Priestess initiates you to the higher mysteries, revealing the holy of holies. She offers the scroll of wisdom, and a glimpse beneath the veil. Be receptive to her feminine guidance. The mists part and secrets are revealed. The Eternal makes a connection, and the unconscious contacts consciousness. The lunar forces surround you; the light of the Moon conceals by its brilliance. Avoid becoming moonstruck; flow with fluctuation.

III – THE Empress

Daughter of the Mighty Ones

Planetary Trump of Venus

Hebrew letter: Daleth (door)

Tree of Life: Path 14, from [2] Chokmah (Wisdom) to [3] Binah (Understanding)

Color Scales: Emerald Green, Sky Blue, Spring Green, Rose Rayed Pale Green

THE EMPRESS

♉   ♀

Who trusted God was love indeed
And love Creation's final law
Tho' Nature, red in tooth and claw
With ravine, shriek'd against his creed

~ Alfred, Lord Tennyson

This is the Gate of Heaven, the path between the supernal parents Chokmah and Binah. Here they are united and balanced, opening the gate. Daleth, or door, is the symbolic passageway of the womb and the Empress is Mitochondrial Eve, the matrilineal common ancestor, the great Mother of all. Alchemically, she is Salt, the amniotic fluids of the womb, and this is reflected in her posture which mimics the alchemical glyph of salt. The glyph also decorates her bracelet. Where the Priestess is the virgin grail, the Empress is the grail fertilized. Her nature is devotion, and her instinct is to open to penetration and fertilization. This does not have to be in the literal sense, as it can also be symbolic of creative formation.

The Empress creates and gestates what the Emperor seeks to order. The door over her heart opens to reveal a heart full of honeycomb. In the foreground is a blown up diagram of the heart door to show the detail of the image. We see the progression from the virgin pomegranate heart of the Priestess as Koré to the fertile honeycombed hive heart of the Empress as Demeter. "Honey in the heart" is an expression which means the power of Love, the power of

Venus. From out this door of her heart hive worker bees fly, the females of the hive, in an ever-outward Golden spiral. The Golden spiral is a logarithmic spiral whose growth factor equals the golden ratio, in art and nature leading to ordered forms that are aesthetically pleasing, appropriate for Venus. This pattern is seen in nature in everything from plant growth to honeybees. If you divide the number of female bees by the number of male bees in a hive you get 1.618, the golden ratio.

Left to its own devices, a growing hive will swarm. A swarm lands in a cluster of bees that is in the shape of a human heart. If you have ever seen a bee hive swarm, you will recognize its awe inducing majesty. The bees exit the hive and spiral out in a grand tornado-like shape, and the noise is deafening. The beginning of the spiral is shown here with eight bees, a hint of the feminine lunar influence also shown by her position between the lunar crescents. These revolving crescents are in opposition, but there is no contradiction as it is the duality that is needed for balance.

She is shown with three distinct wheat stalks; in the mythology of the triple goddess, she is the mother or Demeter. She sits in a field of grasses echoing the themes of creative growth and nurturing.

Yet her archetype is also well represented by the line "Nature, red in tooth and claw"—the fierce regenerative powers of Nature and the perils of chaos and formlessness inherent therein. Bees are a traditional symbol of Venus as the majority of the hive is female, and it is ruled by a Queen. The beehives, full of female workers who protect the honey and brood savagely, are not always easily controlled by a keeper. The combination of black and yellow in nature indicates an element of danger, and the red, black and yellow in this card though not traditional, indicate the Empress' ties with the Emperor. Traditional depictions of the Empress show her with a starry headdress; here she is given a more modern starry kerchief in those colors. She is shown with the wings of the white eagle of alchemy, and carries the Lotus wand which is one of the attributes of Isis, that gives the feminine "power that contains."

The Oracle

Let yourself be penetrated; let yourself be fertile. There is honey in the heart. The power of the Mother is to create and to love with devotion. She does not seek to order. Nature is beautiful and chaotic. Creativity is love—birth your creation with sensual joy. Beware dormancy and self indulgence.

IV – THE Emperor

THE EMPEROR

ℵ   ♈

Son of the Morning; Chief among the Mighty

Zodiacal Trump of Aries; Mars rules, Sun exalted

Hebrew letter: Tzaddi (fish hook)

Tree of Life: Path 28, from [7] Netzach (Victory) to [9] Yesod (Foundation)

Color Scales: Scarlet, Red, Brilliant Flame, Glowing Red

King of Kings Ozymandias am I.

If any want to know how great I am and where I lie, let him outdo me in my work.

~ Inscription, statue of Ramses the Great

The Emperor completes the alchemical triad, taking the shape and form of sulfur in his posture. He is the trump of the first sign Aries the Ram, ruled by Mars. His footgear shows a helmeted warrior like the face on Mars, or an Egyptian pharaoh. He is the spiritual and creative Father as the Empress is the divine Mother. Aries is the sign of selfhood, and in men, this nature is expressed as authority while in women, as the animus. While Mars rules Aries, the Sun is exalted here emphasizing the positive masculinity of the card, and the Emperor is shown between two solar symbols. He is on the path between Netzach and Yesod—attaining *Victory* through a firm *Foundation*, and the desire to rule and order the chaotic subconscious forces.

The Emperor seeks to order what the Empress creates. Nature creates the honeybee, man seeks to hive it and tame it with sacred fire. This compulsion to order from chaos and the rule of mind over nature is represented by the compass and square, symbols of the Grand Architect of the Universe and his desire for structure. The compass is shown fashioned with a design of the red eagle of alchemy, symbolic of the red tincture and the solar forces, and surmounted by the Eye of God, the all seeing and omniscient completion of the holy trinity. This red tincture is the equivalent of the guna Rajas of Hindu philosophy, or alchemical sulfur. It is a force of motion and action, initiative swiftly expended and followed by creation and preservation. This is the complement to the Empress' white eagle or white tincture, the lunar forces and alchemical salt.

Behind the Emperor, the bricks are patterned in the Fibonacci sequence. The Fibonacci sequence begins with 0 and 1, and each following integer is the sum of the two preceding it, thusly 0, 1,1,2,3,5,8,13,21... It is often seen in patterns of growth in nature. The Fibonacci sequence mathematically is the rational form of the irrational Golden ratio of the Empress, and the fish hook of Tzaddi is shaped in the same spiral form that growth occurs in. This sequence is found in everything from the shape of a pinecone to the ratios inherent in the birth rate of bees.

Where the Emperor is portrayed between twin suns, the Empress sits between opposing moons. Notably the Empress gazes toward the Emperor, while he gazes towards the hive she symbolically represents. Thus they are a thematic pair, both through the color symbolism of yellow and black in each card in the card and the bee theme in both cards. The eagle and the bee were emblems of the Emperor Napoleon and the Empress Josephine, with the eagle signifying might and military victory and the bee symbolic of immortality and resurrection. In heraldry and Freemasonry the beehive is used as a symbol of industry, and a caution against laziness.

The poem by Percy Bysshe Shelley *Ozymandias* has a line "And on the pedestal these words appear: 'My name is Ozymandias, king of kings: Look on my works, ye Mighty, and despair!' Nothing beside remains."

This is a comment on the dangers of hubris applied to the establishment of order and the inevitable decline of empires and those who build them. The Emperor is shown post-victory in a contemplative stance more symbolic of the restful phase after the initial action normally indicated by the Emperor and Knight cards. Though Emperors and Knights are cards of great swiftness and masculine force, it is not a lasting state. Of note is the connection between the Emperor as card 4 and Death (13 which reduces to 4) symbolic of the King's sexual expenditure, much like the drone of the hive, who expends his force and usefulness to the hive in the act of mating and fertilizing the Queen.

The Oracle

King of Kings, seek order from chaos, and act to build a firm foundation for your kingdom. Send forth your seed. Ambition and power are qualities of rulership. The Grand Architect reminds you that planning is necessary. Be not rash and beware arrogance; it leads to the decline of empires and their builders.

V – THE HIEROPHANT

Magus of the Eternal Gods

Zodiacal Trump of Taurus; Venus rules, Moon exalted

Hebrew letter: Vau (nail)

Tree of Life: Path 16, from [2] Chokmah (Wisdom) to [4] Chesed (Mercy)

Color Scales: Red Orange, Deep Indigo, Deep Warm Olive, Rich Brown

THE HIEROPHANT

ו   ♉

V.V.V.V.V.
VI VERUM VNIVERSUM VIVUS VICI,
I, by the force of truth, have conquered the Universe in my lifetime.
. . . and his name shall be called Vir [man], and Vis [power], and Virus [poison], and Virtus [manliness], and Viridis [green], in one name that is all these, and above all these. ~ *The Vision and the Voice*

The five letter V's are shown on the tasseled implement in the Hierophant's hand. This brocade tail is often attached to the Tibetan damaru drum used to generate spiritual energy. This is said to dispel negative forces that arise from fear, and is used to make the sound of Sunyata or complete openness, the bridge connecting us to the basis of being beyond name and form. The brocaded tail here is decorated with a peacock tail design, for the alchemical stage of *Cauda Pavonis*, or rainbow colors and the peacock's eye which is the stage of truth or deceit. One works upon the inner being, and with success the third eye opens. The Hierophant also has a numerological connection with the alchemical Art card through reduction.

The five V's arranged symmetrically rotated in a circle form the shape of the pentagram, symbol of the four elements united by the fifth element of spirit. Crowley refers to the five V's elsewhere as the footprints of a camel, in reference to Gimel and the High Priestess, the female counterpart to the Hierophant as the Moon is exalted in Taurus, the Hierophant's sign. Both wear a crescent shaped headdress, hers as a lunar crescent and his as the horns of Taurus the bull. Both cards are initiators and keepers of wisdom and both are portrayed on their tarot card as positioned between two pillars. The pillars of the Hierophant are adorned with elephants, which like the bull are strong, solid and enduring.

In this card a Tibetan Rinpoche sits in a keyhole between two pillars adorned with the four Kerubic beasts of the fixed signs. These are also in living form on the Universe card, symbolic of the four elements. Hierophant on the spiritual path is both acolyte and teacher; student and master of the elemental forces as he has united the four elements within. The four elements or Kerubic beasts also represent the four powers of the Sphinx: To Know, to Will, to Dare, and to Keep Silent. Of these, the power of the Bull is to Keep Silent. Yet there is a fifth power, that of Spirit, the god within and the power To Go. By uniting the four elements the adept acquires the fifth virtue and realizes the reconciliation of the lowest with the highest to become God.

The Rinpoche holds the bell and dorje. The Dorje or Vajra is a masculine symbol representing the skillful means of transforming the mundane experience to the spiritual path. It has five extraordinary characteristics: it is impenetrable, immovable, immutable, indivisible, and indestructible. Vajra means "like a diamond" the hard brilliance that destroys ignorance and reveals Truth. The bell in his other hand is a feminine implement that represents Wisdom. The hollow of the bell is the void from which phenomena arises, while the clapper represents form. Together these objects signify the connection of wisdom and compassion in the enlightened mind. This path is the fire of Chokmah descending. The first manifestation becomes real.

His letter is Vau, meaning the nail that connects the smaller five pointed star above him to the large six pointed star of blue flame that he sits within; the earthly Microcosm nailed to the divine Macrocosm. He is the Vau of YHVH, our Holy Guardian Angel. On the nail above are the crossed keys of silver and gold, symbols associated with both the Hierophant and the High Priestess as insignias of office. The keys of silver and gold are said to show the balance between the subconscious and conscious and are the keys of earth and heaven, or the keys of Solomon's temple. He shows the way and unlocks the doors.

The Oracle

Listen to the guidance of the wise one that holds the keys. Endure and keep silence for in silence you will receive wisdom. Bring down the celestial fire and become an initiated priest of the mysteries. Invoke occult forces and receive teachings. Seek higher purpose. Wisdom and compassion bring enlightenment, the diamond light that destroys ignorance and reveals Truth. Beware intolerant doctrine.

VI – THE LOVERS

Children of the Voice Divine;
Oracles of the Mighty Gods

Zodiacal Trump of Gemini; Mercury
rules, Dragon's Head (Rahu or North
Node) exalted

Hebrew letter: Zain (sword)

Tree of Life: Path 17, from [3] Binah
(Understanding) to [6] Tiphareth (Beauty)

Color Scales: Orange, Pale Mauve, New
Yellow Leather, Reddish Grey inclined
to Mauve

THE LOVERS

ᚦ   ∐

And as all things have been & arose from one by the mediation of one:
so all things have their birth from this one thing by adaptation.
The Sun is its father, the moon its mother, the wind hath carried it in its
belly, the earth is its nurse. ~ *Emerald Tablet*, translation Isaac Newton

The twins Sun and Moon are united by the conjunction
which seems to be death.

This is a quote from Valentinus, an early Gnostic philosopher whose works
have mainly only survived in fragments. But he was on to something here.
The consummation of the alchemical marriage of the red lion and white eagle
requires a death of sorts, dissolution. *Solve et Coagula*, means "to separate and
to join together." The Sword of Zain separates, and the separate elements are
recombined. This implies a death of the ego on the path across the Abyss, from
Binah to Tiphareth. Binah compels form. In one sense the reintegration of
forms requires a choice, a union of opposites into something new. The *Book
of Thoth* calls this card Analysis, followed by Synthesis.[4] This is the trump of
Gemini, and where the Solve, or dissolution happens. We will see in the card
of Gemini's opposite sign Sagittarius, where the Coagula or combination
happens. The Hebrew letter for the card is Zain, meaning *sword*. In the card
the sword symbol is present as the motif of the sword in the stone as in legend.
The sword in the stone is also symbolic of the cleaving and then union of the

4   *Book of Thoth* pg 82

male with the female. The molecules of the two opposites are dissolved and then fused into one. In the legends, the sword can only be removed from the stone by a true king. But in the stories of old the king was a sacrificial king, and pulling the sword from the stone was an act of choice, which always indicates a sacrifice, as when one door opens another closes. The Sun's solar shape and Moon's crescent shape unite in the sword hilt and handle in silver and gold, for the male and the female, the Emperor and Empress.

The figures in the card represent the Emperor as the red lion and the Empress as the white eagle, sharing a Tantric kiss with their lower halves transformed per their animal nature. The woman is white eagle on her lower half while the man is red lion on his lower half. This is the red and the white tincture, or the sword and the grail. Above them, there is a robed figure in the shape of an Orphic egg overseeing the marriage or alchemical conjunction of the King and Queen. The robe or the body of the egg is colored grey, commingling the colors of the Supernals. The figure is making a gesture of arm folded in an X shape; "A prophet young, and in the sign of Osiris Risen." The figure is the young Hermit, himself a form of Mercury as is the Magus.

The first being said to be born or emanated from this Orphic egg was Phanes-Dionysus, or light personified. Thus the light is born out of the egg of darkness. *Phanes* means "light bringer" and was considered a god of the unity of opposites. Aion, the deity of Time, created a silver egg from which Phanes was born in combination with Nyx, the black wind goddess of Necessity. Around this egg, six concentric ovals radiate.

This is trump VI. Bees are both solar and lunar and build their cells in a six sided polygon shape or hexagon, a most efficient and harmonic structure. In this card the bees (the Empress) combined with the organizational structure of honeycomb (the Emperor) are transformed into a chalice filled with the elixir of honey. Around the lovers, the background shows a frame of honeycomb. In its center a portal or window has opened. Perhaps the alchemical reaction made heat, and in the melting formed an opening or window. Things seen through a window, like a mirror, can sometimes indicate projection. Between two things engaged in this dissolution process the boundaries between the two things get blurred.

The Oracle

The sword separates, yet two dissolve and recombine to form a sweet elixir. There is a choice to be made. Pull the sword from the stone and make the sacrifice of one option, as when one door opens, another closes. The choice should be made with devotion and avowal. Open yourself to second sight; the choice is yours. Be not frivolous or trivial.

VII – THE CHARIOT

Child of the Power of the Waters;
Lord of the Triumph of Light

Zodiacal Trump of Cancer; Moon rules, Jupiter exalted

Hebrew letter: Cheth (fence)

Tree of Life: Path 18, from [3] Binah (Understanding) to [5] Geburah (Severity)

Color Scales: Amber, Maroon, Rich Bright Russet, Dark Greenish Brown

THE CHARIOT

ה

♋

When in the height heaven was not named,
And the earth beneath did not yet bear a name,
And the primeval Apsu, who begat them,
And chaos, Tiamut, the mother of them both
Their waters were mingled together,
And no field was formed, no marsh was to be seen;
When of the gods none had been called into being,
And none bore a name, and no destinies were ordained;
Then were created the gods in the midst of heaven,   *~ Enûma Eliš*

From the waters of the Great Sea of Binah the waters descend upon Man, just as on the other side of the tree, the supernal fire descends from Chokmah with the Hierophant. Cancer, the sign of the cardinal inrush of water is tied to the Hebrew letter Cheth, meaning fence or enclosure. In this card the Charioteer is portrayed as a surfer riding the pipeline, enclosed within a wall of water. The great wave forms the starry canopy of the Chariot, with the spray birthing new stars along the way. The path leads from Binah to Geburah, bringing the influence of the supernals down in an influx of water. This links intuition with strength.

His board or Chariot is pulled by a black and a white hippocampus. Interestingly, hippocampi are often paired with the sea-goats of Capricorn, Cancer's opposite sign. The hippocampi are the combination of a land animal and a sea animal, as while they are horses above, below the waters they have the tail of a dolphin. In this way, land and sea, dark and light, they mingle and combine all of the elements. A sea-horse shaped portion of the brain is also named the hippocampus, and there is one on each side of the brain so they too are a matched pair. This part of the brain is said to regulate spatial navigation and memory. We see only the top half of the hippocampi creatures, the horses. Horses are animals symbolic of victory. White horses specifically represent heroic purity, while black horses represent power and mystery. Together they are yin and yang and a reconciliation of inner and outer balanced forces.

Yet beneath the waters is the submerged half of their beings, the dolphin portion. In Greek mythology dolphins have a special meaning, and are mentioned as companions of many deities, the solar and masculine and also the lunar and feminine. The Greek word for dolphin comes from the word for womb, appropriate for Cancer, a maternal sign, and for the Charioteer, bearer of the Grail or fertile elixir. Celtic mythology calls the dolphin the watcher or protector of the waters and pirate lore hails the dolphin as a symbol of protection.

The sign Cancer is associated with the Moon and the tides. The hippocampi are each wearing a lunar bit, one of the waxing moon and one of the waning. These represent Urin and Thummin, two divinatory objects used to determine God's will. The tides go in and they recede. While the horses may struggle, the Charioteer goes with the flow, with perfect balance enthroned rather than conducting[5]. He goes forward; he rides the momentum, in complete absorption. He wears the golden armor of the crab of Cancer as he protects and conveys the Grail. The Chariot follows the Lovers, and carries their dissolved and recombined solution. The Grail he carries is filled with a spiral galaxy of blood and gluten of the Lovers, the "two-in-one conveyed."

It should be mentioned that Cheth (spelled Cheth-Yod-Tau) has the value of 418 in Gematria. This is also the value of Abrahadabra, the word of the Aeon and cipher of the Great Work in communion with the higher self. Crowley refers to it as the establishment of the pillar of the Macrocosm in the void of the Microcosm, another sexual reference to the result of the alchemy of the Lovers. The Charioteer's primary function is to be the holy warrior and bring forth and protect the Chalice.

The Oracle

Ride the pipeline, in perfect balance, for the oracles of black and white determine God's will. Achieve the highest good and convey the Grail. Quest and seek, move forward with victory in mind. Protect the precious object and triumph, for you are armored and protected. Drink deep. While you ride in the Chariot of Power, ride the wave.

5   *Book of Thoth* pg 85

VIII – ADJUSTMENT

ADJUSTMENT

ל   Ω

Daughter of the Lord of Truth; Ruler of the Balance

Zodiacal trump of Libra; Venus rules, Saturn exalted

Hebrew letter: Lamed (ox goad)

Tree of Life: Path 22, from [5] Geburah (Severity) to [6] Tiphareth (Beauty)

Color Scales: Emerald, Blue, Deep Blue Green, Pale Green

I am the power of equilibration
Which holdeth Ruach in balance
Between formation and destruction,
As a driver with his goad
Keepeth his ox from straying off the highway.
Yet is this directive power inherent in Ruach itself,
For I myself am that great Breath of Life.

~ Book of Tokens

M a'at, goddess of truth and the administration of law, here is the living fulcrum. Balance is not standing still; it is the constant movement of minute adjustment. Balance is the adjustment of Karma, and how we learn about what is right. It is a cool calibration; it is exact but not emotional. It is perception and understanding of destiny, and the equilibration of opposites. Ma'at here holds the scales, with a feather in one pan, and a heart-jar in the other. The pans of the scale are formed by twin ouroboros spiraling in opposite directions, for the beginning and the end, and the cause and effect. Crowley calls the chains that the scales hang from the "chains of cause."[6] This concept of every action having a balance and a motion is reminiscent of the "butterfly effect," a theory that every small change can have an unknown effect on something. Thus he says that "every form of energy must be directed, must

---

6   *Book of Thoth* pg 87

32

be applied with integrity, to the full satisfaction of its destiny."[7] The path leads from Geburah to Tipareth; love is the law under will, or volition connected with the higher self.

The word *ma'at* means a rule, a measure, a law or a truth, justice; "that which is straight." The goddess Ma'at was symbolized by a feather, against which the heart of the deceased was weighed in the underworld. If the heart was lighter or equal in weight, then the deceased was determined to have led a virtuous life. If the heart was heavier, then it gets devoured. In Greek mythology this principle was one divided into the goddesses Nemesis and Themis. Nemesis had a vengeful and wrathful aspect of divine retribution while Themis was more benign in nature and in line with the concept of divine law and order. Themis also had the ability of prophecy and became one of the Oracles of Delphi.

She balances on a skate blade as a sword, adorned with Saturn as a symbol of corrective restriction over time. Saturn is exalted in Libra and thus Time has influence here. Thus is this the equilibrium of the dance of space-time. All takes place within the concept of the phenomena of time. The Fool enters the wormhole and exits as the Universe, but Adjustment is his prompt and correction in between. The Fool's letter Aleph, meaning ox, and Adjustment's letter of Lamed, meaning *ox-goad* (the ox-goad used "to teach"), links them together in partnership. Aleph-Lamed is the name of God, and Lamed-Aleph means "Not." Like the Fool, she bears tattoos. Adjustment's tattoos of Alpha and Omega are in acknowledgement of her relationship with the Fool and the Universe. Nothing is everything, all is revolving and everything has its equal and opposite reaction. All is truth because it all cancels out, and o=2. Love is the law; love under will.

The hilt of the sword she balances in is decorated with the representation of Saturn and a spiral curve on the hilt for Venus and Libra. This is the sword's edge of truth. This interplay of Venus and Saturn is the dance of life. Here, rather than balancing on her toes and the tip of the sword, she skates lightly on the sword's blade across the ice of Time, dancing to music only she can hear. This music is seen on the surface within the s-curves, in the notes of medieval chant. Music itself is symbolic of the measures of time and of balance, and the control of precise movements. She is constantly whirling where all is possible, and every beat is measured and adjusted for. Life is the dance, and existence is joy!

Her costume shows her ties to the Fool; her peacock feather to the Hierophant through Venus. Yet she also has ties to the Star. Adjustment is the card VIII, the sideways eight of the lemniscate of eternity. Likewise there is a message in that the Star card also reduces to eight, showing Adjustment's connection to Babalon the beautiful. The daughter becomes the mother, and a woman satisfied.

The Oracle

The balance of Adjustment is a dance. It depends upon minute movements; it is not still. Karma creates equality. Direct your destiny with integrity and master reality. Weigh your heart against Truth. Use discernment to make minute corrections. Adjustment is coming, and she assesses every act. The law compensates for imbalances. Nature is exact and unyielding yet not moralistic. Be fair and avoid hypocrisy, as one gets what one deserves.

IX – THE HERMIT

THE HERMIT

Magus of the Voice of Light; Prophet of the Gods

Zodiacal Trump of Virgo; Mercury rules

Hebrew letter: Yod (hand)

Tree of Life: Path 20, from [4] Chesed (Mercy) to [6] Tiphareth (Beauty)

Color Scales: Yellow Green, Indigo, Greenish Grey, Plum

> Wouldst thou go into isolation, my brother?
> Wouldst thou seek the way unto thyself?
>
> ~ Friedrich Nietzsche, *Thus Spake Zarathustra*

The Hermit is the trump of the earth sign Virgo, ruled by Mercury, and the letter Yod, the first letter of the Tetragrammaton, and thus the Logos or Creator, the male Fire of YHVH. This combination of fire and earth, the masculine Yod of the Hermit in the feminine sign of the Virgin is regenerative. Virgo is mutable earth, the "lowest" or most degenerated form of the element, and the most feminine and receptive. Creation is descent into matter.

The Path of Yod leads between the framework of manifestation (Chesed) and the central source of the higher self (Tiphareth). The Hermit, modeled here on Merlin, Jung's senex, or wise old man, is a masculine initiator and guardian, and an evolution of the Fool. His connection with the Fool is shown by the path opposite, that of Lamed/Adjustment, the Fool's counterpart. Like the Fool, he is portrayed headed downward towards an opening, but the Hermit has come down the mountain path and headed into a shamanic portal. In his role as Psychopompos, guide of the lower regions and guardian of the threshold, he carries the sacred fire below, followed by the hell hound Cerberus.

He is also an incarnation of the Magus, due the rulership of Mercury. Mercury in astronomy is never found far from the Sun, and the Hermit carries the fire of the Sun in his lantern, giving light to the world. Just as the Magus' number is the reduction of the number of the Sun's trump, the Hermit's numeral is the reduction of the Moon. Here the sky is shown in that violet color of the "between" time, that magical time neither night nor day when the portals are open and the veils are thin. In the sky is a Balsamic moon glowing with earthshine. The Balsamic moon is an introspective phase, and a time when physical energy is low but psychic energy is high. It is the time between endings and beginnings, an intuitive time and considered a seed state. In astrology it is considered the mark of an old soul to be born during this phase. This is a transitive time of contemplation and the journey inwards.

There are nine wheat shafts on the card. Wheat shafts always indicate fertility, and the number nine is a number of completions and wisdom, of wrapping up. It is a number of patience and meditation, and the nine months of gestation. The Hermit has both the feminine qualities of the Vestal Virgin of Earth and the womb, and the masculine qualities of the Yod. The Yod is the seed of all other letters, and from it all descends. It is also the "secret seed" of the process of fertilization.

The wanderer, with bent back and hood in the shape of a Yod, carries the Asclepius staff of a healer, of an arch-mage, of Moses; wound with the serpent of kundalini and topped by an orphic egg of light. Crowley says in the Book of Thoth that the Hermit's wand "is actually growing out of the Abyss, and is the spermatozoon developed as a poison, and manifesting the foetus." The Hermit as the Hebrew letter Yod is the equivalent of the spermatozoa, and this is represented symbolically by the staff as egg and sperm combined. The letter Yod means hand, and the egg here is marked with the hand of blessing and healing, and the hand as a tool of creation.

The Oracle

Seek yourself. Wander alone with the sun and moon to guide you. Carry the staff of wisdom, descend within and seek the secret seed. Illumination comes with solitude and prudent introspection.

X – Fortune

The Lord of the Forces of Life

Planetary Trump of Jupiter

Hebrew letter: Kaph (palm of hand, and fist)

Tree of Life: Path 21, from [4] Chesed (Mercy) to [7] Netzach (Victory)

Color Scales: Violet, Purple Tinged Blue, Bright Purple, Blue Rayed Yellow

FORTUNE

 כ   ♃

No single thing abides; but all things flow.
Fragment to fragment clings-the things thus grow
Until we know and name them. By degrees
They melt, and are no more the things we know.

Globed from the atoms falling slow or swift
I see the suns, I see the systems lift
Their forms; and even the systems and the suns
Shall go back slowly to the eternal drift.
~Lucretius, *On the Nature of Things*

The Wheel of Fortune in this card is shown as a great spinning wheel weaving the warps and wefts of life, with the Vajra as a shuttle. The Vajra is known as the thunderbolt, weapon of Jupiter. The four-arms of the Vajra symbolize the four immeasurables (compassion, love, sympathetic joy and equanimity;) the four doors of liberation (emptiness, signlessness, wishlessness and lack of composition;) the conquest of the four Maras (emotional defilements, passion, death, divine pride and lust) the four activities or karmas; and the four joys (joy, supreme joy, the joy of cessation and innate joy); all around a central point of *dharmata* (reality).

The Thoth deck has the three Hindu Gunas revolving around the Wheel. The three Gunas, or attributes in Vedic philosophy, are present in everything in the world. *Sattva* is balance, intelligence and purity, and corresponds to alchemical Mercury. *Rajas* is energy, motion, and passion, and corresponds to alchemical Sulfur. *Tamas* is inertia, darkness, and death, and corresponds to Salt. The Gunas are continually revolving. Nothing can remain in the same state for long. Fortune changes. Jupiter is primarily a beneficial influence, so most often this is a card of luck. Usually it implies a turn for the better, though luck is unpredictable. All three gunas ride the rim of the wheel, seeking the center. Feeling, thought, and ecstasy each revolve around the wheel. As the Rites of Jupiter proclaim "Free a million million mortals on the wheel of being tossed! Open wide the mystic portals, and be altogether lost!"

The Wheel here has as the Guna trinity a crowned three-eyed barn owl clutching a sword, in the position of the Sphinx (Vishnu/Sulfur). At the top of the Wheel the owl stands elevated, at least for now. The ring-tailed lemur clutching a carpenter's square climbs the wheel as a stand in for Hermanubis (Brahma/Mercury). Hermanubis, the dog-monkey god combining the attributes of Hermes and Anubis, both with similar roles as conductors of souls, is the messenger of Jupiter. The hand-serpent writing the zero to complete the phi symbol is the Typhonic beast (Shiva/Salt), wrapped around and counterbalancing the other side. This symbol is itself a wheel; an axle within a circle, or nothing split by unity. Typhon writes out the equation and opens the eye of Shiva. The mythology of the story of the battle of Zeus, Typhon and Hermes seems to have some parallels.

The spinning wheel itself has ten spokes, for the ten sephira on the tree of life, the numeral ten of the card, and the binary one and zero combining to make phi. Crowley says of the ten that as the sphere of Malkuth, it indicates this card governs material affairs. The wheel is also the iris of a great eye, the eye of Shiva that creates and destroys the universe. On the right, the planetary warps and wefts of life are woven, while on the left we see the firmament of stars. Above, Zeus' thunder bolts of lightning strike, initiating change. The letter for this card is Kaph, which means both palm and fist. Is your hand open to receive?

The Oracle

The Wheel revolves, only the axle at the center is still. Fortune changes, usually for the better. There is constant transformation. The shuttle weaves your fortune; be willing to see the pattern in the warps and wefts. There is always the element of luck, the incalculable factor.

XI – LUST

Daughter of the Flaming Sword; Leader of the Lion

Zodiacal Trump of Leo; Sun rules

Hebrew letter: Teth (serpent)

Tree of Life: Path 19, from [4] Chesed (Mercy) to [5] Geburah (Severity)

Color Scales: Greenish Yellow, Deep Purple, Grey, Reddish Yellow

LUST

Remember all ye that existence is pure joy; that all the sorrows are but as shadows; they pass & are done; but there is that which remains.

Now think not to find them in the forest or on the mountain; but in beds of purple, caressed by magnificent beasts of women with large limbs, and fire and light in their eyes, and masses of flaming hair about them; there shall ye find them. Ye shall see them at rule, at victorious armies, at all the joy; and there shall be in them a joy a million times greater than this.

~The Book of the Law

The lion-serpent is firmly grasped by the hand of a goddess. There are many goddess archetypes associated with lions or large cats. In Babylonia, Gilgamesh says of Ishtar "thou has loved the lion, mighty in strength." In Hinduism, there is Durga, the invincible, a form of Shakti often shown riding on a tiger. In Egypt, there is Sekhmet, lion-headed warrior goddess and solar deity. The Sumerian Inanna, tamer of lions and goddess of love, fertility, sacred prostitution, and warfare, has the lion as a totem and is often depicted standing on the backs of two lions. All have in common vigor, fierceness and an association with the *hieros gamos*, a sexual ritual between the god and the goddess, a Great Rite. These women arouse and channel the lower nature, that of the beast.

Leo is ruled by the Sun and thus is the most powerful of all the zodiac signs. This is the Red Lion of alchemy, nature under control or willpower directing vitality, to joyously integrate and thus transform the animal nature. In this depiction a woman of strength holds the lion firmly and rather erotically by its serpent-tail, awakening dormant kundalini. In her other hand, she holds aloft the Grail containing the elemental sacrament. This is the same Grail carried by the Charioteer, the two in one conveyed, but here is the alchemical process of distillation of self into godhead. The cup is marked with the emblem of the Sun and above it floats the solar analemma.

The woman in the card is the Moon illuminated by the lion Sun. Eleven rays crown her. She is a woman clothed with the sun of Revelations, Babalon and the Beast who opens the seven seals. In this card is a statement of the Aeon of Horus, which according to the precession of the equinoxes is the Age of Aquarius. Since every sign is on an axis of polarity, this is the axis of Aquarius and Leo, or the wo(man) and the lion. This is the Aeon of Lust, or the rapture of vigor and the joy of strength exercised.

In the background of the card is a dark volcano, behind which rises the sun and moon conjoined with seven stars. A great red rose blooms on the card, red for the red chakra of the base of the forces of kundalini, and a rose as a symbol of the goddess and her spiritual vortices. In the foreground are three wheat shafts and three sunflowers, a subtle reminder of the solar trinity of the spiritual sun, the intellectual sun and the material sun, or spirit, soul and body. All three must be harnessed with passion and vigor. Lust can open the levels above the Sun (Tiphareth) through the seven chakras. This is the path between Chesed and Geburah, perfectly balanced on the Tree both horizontally and vertically. It is the profound and powerful path of the light of the fire of the sun, where base matter is transformed into gold.

The Oracle

Be eager; be wanton. Grasp the lion by the tail and enjoy the rapture of vigor. Abandon yourself to passion, indulge your magick. Go forth with courage and joy in desire and ecstatic abandon.

XII – THE HANGED MAN

THE HANGED MAN

מ ▽

The Spirit of the Mighty Waters

Elemental Trump of Water

Hebrew letter: Mem (water)

Tree of Life: Path 23, from [5] Geburah (Severity) to [8] Hod (Splendor)

Color Scales: Deep Blue, Sea Green, Deep Olive Green, White Flecked Purple

> It was a terrible price that Mimir would ask for a draught from the Well of Wisdom, and very troubled was Odin All-Father when it was revealed to him. His right eye! For all time to be without the sight of his right eye! Almost he would have turned back to Asgard, giving up his quest for wisdom.
>
> ~ Padraic Colum, *The Children of Odin*

The Hanged Man is associated with resurrected gods and heroes suspended on trees: Odin on the world tree Yggdrasil, Attis on the Pine, Osiris who washed ashore and was enclosed in the roots of the Acacia. Odin sacrificed his eye for a drink from Mimir's Well, the fountain of wisdom at the foot of Yggdrasil, the world ash tree. Odin hung on the tree Yggdrasil for "nine long nights" pierced by his own spear in order to gain power in the nine worlds and learn the wisdom of the runes. Mimir filled a horn with water and gave it to Odin to drink. The future became clear to Odin, and all the sorrows and troubles of men, and how nobility could defeat them. He then plucked out his eye, and handed it to Mimir, who dropped it into the Well of Wisdom, where it sank deep into the waters. It shines up through the pool like the sun reflected upon the water.

From the waters of the pool a water dragon or sea serpent rises, wearing the face of a man wearing the mask of a dragon. The horns of the mask form the shape of the trident of Neptune, as does one of the hands of the figure. The sea dragon is Necksa, the elemental king of the Undines. Neptune is a god of the waters, and Neptune the planet is a nebulous force with many masks. Neptune's father Saturn swallowed his children whole to prevent them from overthrowing his rule. Neptune spent his time while in Saturn's belly introspectively, in dreamy isolation, seeing a different world view. He eventually was released by his brother Jupiter, and became the god of the sea, with a trident that gave him power over the waters. This message is echoed by the Orphic egg, which hangs suspended from the branches of the tree as if treasure guarded by the dragon, and symbolizes the time of enclosed incubation.

The man has one eye closed, or missing. The dragon also is missing an eye. The missing eye of the Hanged Man is on the right, the serpent's, on the left. The right eye is said to control the left brain, and vice versa. The sacrifice of his right eye deprived him of his left brain powers of logic and reason, and forced him to see through the other eye for a time, to suspend his other senses. Eventually one becomes like the philosopher in Plato's allegory of the cave, who upon release realizes the true form of reality as opposed to the shadows on the wall.

The Hanged Man is like Adam Kadmon inverted; the Tree of Life with its roots in heaven. Manly P. Hall, in *The Secret Teachings of All Ages* says "The mediæval Qabbalists represented creation as a tree with its roots in the reality of spirit and its branches in the illusion of tangible existence. The Sephirothic tree of the Qabbalah was therefore inverted, with its roots in heaven and its branches upon the earth. Madam Blavatsky notes that the Great Pyramid was considered to be a symbol of this inverted tree, with its root at the apex of the pyramid and its branches diverging in four streams towards the base. The Mysteries taught that the divine energies from the gods descended upon the top of the Pyramid, which was likened to an inverted tree with its branches below and its roots at the apex. From this inverted tree the divine wisdom is disseminated by streaming down the diverging sides and radiating throughout the world."

The posture of the Hanged Man is the inverted symbol of sulfur, and forms a cross as does the figure in the Universe. Tau, the letter of the Universe, is at the center of the cube of space, as is the final form of the letter Mem. Mem is the letter of the Hanged Man, and means Water, and the Hanged Man card is a baptism, purification by water rather than by fire. There is suffering and sacrifice, but what price is wisdom?

The Oracle

Surrender. For this is the sacrifice you offer the waters in return for wisdom. Turn things around, see another perspective. Suspend your senses and seek the sixth sense. Devote yourself to destiny. It may take time.

XIII – DEATH

The Child of the Great Transformers;
Lord of the Gates of Death

Zodiacal Trump of Scorpio; Mars (also Pluto) rules

Hebrew letter: Nun (fish)

Tree of Life: Path 24, from [6] Tiphareth (Beauty) to [7] Netzach (Victory)

Color Scales: Green Blue, Dull Brown, Very Dark Brown, Vivid Indigo Brown

DEATH

♏

♋

Have the gates of death been opened unto thee?
or hast thou seen the doors of the shadow of death?

~ Job 38:17

Nun is fish, a symbol of resurrection; death is the secret of creation. The fish in this case is a salmon, with its spawning representative of the cycle of life and death. It should be noted that Death and the Devil are opposites on the Tree of Life. Death is *Lord of the Gates of Death* while the Devil is *Lord of the Gates of Matter*, and death and life are intertwined.

They say Death rides a pale horse; I say Death rides a feathered serpent. The skeleton rides a composite creature that is comprised of the three aspects of the sign Scorpio, representing the three stages of putrefaction. The scorpion as the lowest form is the tail, the first stage or the beginning of the element's will to change. The mid part of the beast is the undulating serpent of the cycle of life and death. The upper body is the eagle, the gaseous or purest stage which rises in exaltation above matter.

This putrefaction is incubation. This is the raising of the Djed, symbolized by the haft of the scythe in the form of a Djed pillar. The Djed pillar represents the spine of Osiris, and spine is an anagram of penis. This ritual is the resurrection of Osiris. The skeleton wears the Atef crown, the feathered white crown worn by Osiris. This crown was also worn by Sobek the crocodile god and the Bennu bird associated with the phoenix. The Bennu was said to be associated with Osiris, and took part in the creation of the world by enabling the actions of the creator god Atum. The Bennu flew over the waters of Nun and issued a cry which determined creation. Yet Osiris wears the Atef in his role as the ruler of the Underworld.

The Great Pyramid is the tomb that is not a tomb. It has shafts aligned with several stars. The Kings Chamber is aligned with the belt of Orion/ Osiris, god of the netherworld. The northern shaft aligns with Thuban, in the constellation of Draco. In modern times Polaris marks our celestial north pole, but at the time of the ancient pyramid builders the star closest to the pole was Thuban. The north shaft of the Queens Chamber aligns with "Beta" in Ursa Minor, considered part of Draco by the Egyptians, while the south shaft is aligned with Sirius, star of Isis. Draco was in those times known as the Hippo goddess Tawaret, associated with birth. Draco is sometimes represented by Typhon, the demon son of two primordial deities: Gaia, the Earth as mother and Tartarus, the Deep Abyss of the Underworld as father. This is parallel to the deep abyss of creation, the watery chaos or cosmic abyss of creation and Tiamet, its personification as dragon. In the northern hemisphere Draco is circumpolar, or never setting. The skeleton points out our pole star as a symbol of immortality, never leaving the night sky.

In this card Death is the stag beetle pointing at the Pole Star. Part of the *Book of Lies* chapter called "The Stag Beetle" reads, "The birth of individuality is ecstasy; so also is its death. In love the individuality is slain; who loves not love? Love death therefore, and long eagerly for it." The chapter called "The Pole Star" says of love and death "The wings of love droop not with time, nor slacken for life or for death. Love destroyeth self, uniting self with that which is not-self, so that Love breedeth All and None in One."

At the bottom of the sea treasure is found. From the putrefaction of the waters gaseous bubbles rise, each bubble containing the small spiral form of a young serpent, the embryonic form of a dragon. Dragons are symbolic of DNA, the spiral chain of life.

The theme of snakes rising from the waters has a related connection with the pyramids. The stone at the top of the pyramid is called the Benben stone, named for the Benben mound in Egytian mythology. The Benben mound rose from the primordial watery abyss of Nu, and there Atum, the creator god, settled. In the *Book of the Dead*, Atum was said to rise from the chaos waters in the form of a snake renewing itself every morning. The stone at the top of the pyramid was considered the solidified seed of Atum.

Not to be overlooked is the solar barge silently passing behind the figure of Death and the fact that the shape of the solar barge is representative of a vertical slice of the wormhole[8] or a long view of one seen in totality from the side.

The Oracle

Life and death are each an illusion, each a part of the snake renewing itself. Shed your skin; transform. Though the change may be sudden, it is a necessary conclusion. From putrefaction comes new growth. Take the long view.

8   See Appendix for illustration

XIV – ArT

ART

Daughter of the Reconcilers; The Bringer Forth of Life

Zodiacal Trump of Sagittarius; Jupiter rules, Dragon's Tail exalted

Hebrew letter: Samekh (support, prop)

Tree of Life: Path 25, from [6] Tiphareth (Beauty) to [9] Yesod (Foundation)

Color Scales: Blue, Yellow, Green, Vivid Dark Blue

The moon waneth. The moon waneth. The moon waneth.
For in that arrow is the Light of Truth that overmastereth
the light of the sun, whereby she shines.

~ The Vision and the Voice

Spirit and soul should be added to the body and taken away (solve et coagula).
"It may be a great wonder that two lions turn into one."

~ De Lapide philosophico

The Art card is known as Temperance in most decks. Crowley renamed this card Art, for the art of alchemy. Whether called Temperance or Art, the meaning of temperance has more to do with tempering than with renunciation. Tempering is the process of perfecting with fire and water, like a blacksmith does with a sword. The Art card is the trump of Sagittarius, and it shows a further state of that which was begun in the card of Sagittarius' opposite sign Gemini, The Lovers. The Hebrew letter of the Lovers card is Zain, meaning sword, and the Art card furthers the process begun in the Lovers card, tempering and refining it. In most traditional renderings one sees an angelic being transferring water from a red cup to a blue, or mixing fire and water. The Lovers have coalesced into one being, here shown as a Dianic personification of the Green Lion of alchemy. Often depicted devouring the Sun, the Green Lion states "I am the true green and Golden Lion without cares. In me all the secrets of the Philosophers are hidden." The green lion is associated with the alchemical motto V.I.T.R.I.O.L. which stands for *Visita Interiora Terrae Rectificando Invenies Occultum Lapidem.* Here the Green Lion is winged and shown in its human Gryphon form as the Eagle and Lion combined. As it is winged and can ascend it marks the spiritualization of the Green Lion. This is a physical process whereby the balance of opposing energies works to strengthen the physical vessel to accommodate an influx of light.

Visit the interior of the earth and by rectifying (purifying) you will find the hidden stone. We see here again the Orphic egg first encountered in the Lovers card, and the White Eagle and Red Lion of the Lovers have combined. The Sun and the Moon have combined. Temperance is on the path between Yesod the Moon, and Tiphareth, the Sun. Artemis launches her flaming arrow from the bow, in the form of the crescent moon dripping water, upwards to the sun, passing upwards through the central pillar of the Tree of Life in an initiatory process. Fire and water combine to form air and a rainbow, which connects earth and heaven—all four elements present. The rainbow is a symbol of this card as the arrow of Sagittarius pierces the rainbow—the paths on the tree of life that spell QShTh, meaning bow or rainbow. Below is an alchemical vessel representing Yesod in which fire and water combine. Above they show the paths leading to and from Tiphareth. Around their conjunction is a crown of light. The arrow is "the force that through the green fuse drives the flower drives my red blood" (Dylan Thomas) and the blue and red serpents she wears are the colors of Chokmah and Binah, fire and water, and the twin channels of Kundalini.

The card is bright—but the path leading between Sun and Moon would be the brightest of all, at least at the end when the light is seen. In the crucible, in the interior, it might be quite dark. The sign of Sagittarius is ruled by Jupiter and in Sagittarius the Dragon's Tail is exalted. The Dragon's Tail is the South Node of the Moon. These two nodes, called the Dragon's Head and the Dragon's Tail, are not planets but the intersecting points of two orbits, that of the Ecliptic, or apparent path of the Sun from Earth, and the orbit of the Moon around the Earth. The Book of Thoth calls passage on this card the Arrow, and says of it "Now, then, behold how the head of the dragon is but the tail of the Aethyr!"

The Hebrew letter is Samekh, meaning "to support." Samekh is one of only two closed letters, the other being Mem final. The shape of the letter itself is an enclosed vessel, like a crucible or a womb, a circle or ouroboros. It has been referred to as related to anger, in the sense of the divine rage and passion that releases the arrow, and trial by fire or tempering. An alternate meaning is that of vibration or quivering. This is the card of Sagittarius, the Archer, located on the middle pillar joining the stations of the Sun and the Moon. Artemis releases the solar arrow with the lunar bow through the middle pillar. This arrow can be thought of as the support, or prop, of Samekh. Together the fire and water, the Sun and Moon, combine in the orphic egg, becoming each other and bringing forth life, and in the crucible, the "Womb preserving Life," they combine forming rainbows. This is the Daughter of the Reconcilers, the Bringer Forth of Life. We will see this vessel again in the Aeon, the card of Shin, the central letter of QShTh.

The Oracle

Unify and synthesize opposites. Temper with fire and water, dissolve and bind in the proper measure. The art of alchemy is to engender successful transmutation.

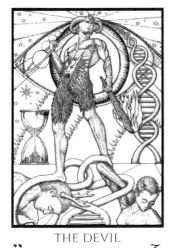

XV – THE DEVIL

Lord of the Gates of Matter; Child of the Forces of Time

Zodiacal Trump of Capricorn; Saturn rules, Mars exalted

Hebrew letter: Ayin (eye)

Tree of Life: Path 26, from [6] Tiphareth (Beauty) to [8] Hod (Splendor)

Color Scales: Indigo, Black, Blue Black, Cold Very Dark Grey

THE DEVIL

ע   ♑

> Calm is the bottom of my sea: who would guess that it hideth droll
> monsters! Unmoved is my depth: but it sparkleth
> with swimming enigmas and laughters.
>
> ~ Friedrich Nietzsche, *Thus Spake Zarathustra*

Some call him Lucifer, Son of the Morning. Others, Pan Pangenetor, the All-Begetter. Or maybe you call him Priapus, Set, Satan, Baal-Sebus, Beelzebub, Baphomet, Banebdjet or Ba 'Neb' Djedu. If you meet him, have some courtesy; he's in need of some restraint. He controls the gateway of the material world.

The Devil is on the path opposite the path of Death on the Tree, Lord of the Gates of Matter as opposed to the Gates of Death. This is the irrepressible and very male urge to life, the will to creation. Many medieval European portrayals of the Devil in tarot show the Devil with a voracious face on his belly. Here he is shown with the face of a Green Man there. The Green Man with mouth agape over his solar plexus chakra shows the craving for the world of matter. This craving is the force that leads souls to head down the path towards the light that results in rebirth. We see the figures from Lovers card ensnared and entangled below his lower half as DNA itself. This DNA also projects from his third eye.

Joseph Campbell said "Gods suppressed become devils, and often it is these devils whom we first encounter when we turn inward." The Sefer ha-Zohar says that the figure of God is twofold, with a head of light and a head of darkness. A sacred name of God, IAO, offers a threefold expression though. Yod-Aleph-Ayin are the three Atus of the Hermit, the Fool, and the Devil, so these three cards form the threefold expression of creative masculine force, and the Devil is the most masculine manifestation of the three. The Devil is a form of Pan, the son of Hermes and some call the Devil the son of the Fool. Yet he is the Demogorgon, the primordial supreme being of the threefold world. Demogorgon the name is said to be a variant or corruption of demiurge. The Devil and God are one, just as the Emerald Tablet states that all things are from One, by the meditation of One.

The Hebrew letter for the card Ayin means "eye" and its key is "mirth." This is the card of Capricorn, the Zenith of the horoscope; the goat climbing the mountain or energy in its most material form. The Goat was known in early Babylonian times as the God Enki, the Babylonian Satan. Whenever he roamed the Earth, he took the form of a goat, though he also took the form of a fish to roam the waters and Capricorn is sometimes shown as a fish-tailed sea-goat. Enki was known as 'He of Vast Intellect and Lord of the Sacred Eye'. He was the god who protected humanity and gave the gift of knowledge. He ended up represented as the snake in the Tree of Life in the Garden of Eden, offering learning. Enki was considered the "Father of Light" and his celebrants wore goat skins.

Capricorn is ruled by Saturn governing the forces of Time, and in this sign Mars is exalted, the fiery phallic initiative. The Devil is raw male power, Pan, the All-Begetter, Priapus and the unstoppable life urge. This is the light-bringer, and with light comes shadow, and yet unlived creative potential and possibility. Crowley says in *Book of Thoth* "The formula of this card is then the complete appreciation of all existing things."

The Oracle

Here is the blind impulse towards as yet unlived potential. This is irrepressible craving. Gods suppressed become devils. Awaken, and acknowledge the shadow within to master manifest form.

XVI – THE TOWER

THE TOWER

ד   ♂

Lord of the Hosts of the Mighty

Planetary Trump of Mars

Hebrew letter: Pè (mouth)

Tree of Life: Path 27, from [7] Netzach (Victory) to [8] Hod (Splendor)

Color Scales: Scarlet, Red, Venetian Red, Bright Red Rayed Azure and Emerald

> What use are fortress, trench, can moat or wall prevail
> Against the lightning hurled by Heaven's Lord and Master?
>
> ~ Hohberg, 1675

Crowley says this card may as well have been called War. The Tower, as the trump of Mars, usually is shown in a phallic manner and this card is no exception. The Hebrew letter Pè means "mouth" and at the base (or testicles) of the tower we see a great gaping Hell mouth surrounded by demons as seen on the medieval stage acts the tarot is said to have been associated with. This mouth is on the head of a boar, belching fire and roaring out a word of power that brings the lightning, aka the initiation, enlightenment, and the moment of orgasm. This is the Caledonian Boar of Greek legend, sent by Artemis against a king as revenge for slighting her. During the hunt to rid the countryside of the boar, several great warriors are killed, and in the aftermath of the affair many more are killed in arguments and vengeful killings.

Behind the tower is the glaring red pupil of an eye. This is the Eye of Shiva that can destroy the universe with an opening of its lid. Crowley says of this something that can be conveyed in the equation Ultimate Reality equals Perfection equals Nothingness, therefore all manifestations however delightful are stains so to obtain perfection all existing things must be annihilated.[9] Thus we are freed from our prisons, the prisons we cling to through lack of wisdom.

9   *Book of Thoth* pg 108

The *Book of the Law* refers directly to this card by its older title of the House of God. Nuith speaks "Invoke me under my stars! Love is the law, love under will. Nor let the fools mistake love; for there are love and love. There is the dove, and there is the serpent. Choose ye well! He, my prophet, hath chosen, knowing the law of the fortress, and the great mystery of the House of God." What would you get if you crossed a serpent and dove? Perhaps you would get an eagle or a hawk. For there is love and there is love.

The mouth is surrounded by a chimera, a dragon, and an bird that is both eagle and hawk. There is a story of Gilgamos (Gilgamesh) in *De Natura Animalium* (The Nature of Animals) in which the King of Babylon determines that his grandson Gilgamos is prophesied to kill him, and so he throws him from a high tower. But Gilgamos is rescued by an eagle and goes on to become king. Here we see the eagle struck and in free fall, temporality reversed. Temporality is humanity's experience of the linear progression of time. This is Mars' gift from its exaltation in Capricorn. At the moment of the lightning strike of the Tower, there is a reset of the progressions of the work of time. Zeus overthrows Chronos.

The figures that fall from the Tower are not human. Here the Tower is shown as Hellmouth, a part having a place in medieval stage sets. It is often shown with winged creatures and demons flying about. Likewise, Crowley refers the "Jaws of Dis" to the symbolism of the card. The brick foundations are cracking, and the red root chakra kicks in as the lightning of shamanic initiation flashes down the world axis.

The Oracle
Sudden and unforeseen, the lightning strikes, destroying outworn structures. What has been built up over time now crumbles into rubble. Yet we are enlightened, and freed from the prisons of our own making. The ground is cleared for new building.

XVII – THE STAR

THE STAR

ה   ♒

Daughter of the Firmament; Dweller between the Waters

Zodiacal Trump of Aquarius; Saturn (also Uranus) rules, Neptune exalted

Hebrew letter: Hè (window)

Tree of Life: Path 15, from [2] Chokmah (Wisdom) to [6] Tiphareth (Beauty)

Color Scales: Violet, Sky Blue, Bluish Mauve, White Faintly Tinged Purple

The stars are threshed, and the souls are threshed from their husks.

Then you'll see the world as it is: infinite.

~ William Blake

Pour water on thyself: thus shalt thou be a Fountain to the Universe.
Find thou thyself in every star! Achieve thou every possibility!

~ Aleister Crowley

Just as when Dante emerged from Hell and the first thing he saw was the starry sky, so the Star follows the Tower.

We see an unimaginably beautiful blue goddess, clad in starlight, or starlight personified. The Star card never fails to bring these words from *The Book of the Law* to mind: "Sing the rapturous love-song unto me! Burn to me perfumes! Wear to me jewels! Drink to me, for I love you! I love you! I am the blue-lidded daughter of Sunset; I am the naked brilliance of the voluptuous night-sky. To me! To me!" This passage always arouses a feeling of longing, and hope, just as the sight of the night sky fills one with the perfection of the moment and the awareness of eternity. The Star is Nuit, who gives "unimaginable joys on earth: certainty, not faith, while in life, upon death; peace unutterable, rest, ecstasy; nor do I demand aught in sacrifice."

The Star is the Zodiacal trump of Aquarius, and like the water bearer, she is depicted pouring ethereal waters from a vessel. Most representations of the Star have our lady of the Stars bearing two cups, one of gold and one of silver. Tabula Mundi's Star has shown Nuit with a solar cup and a lunar cup, washing in the milk of the stars. The silver cup and the golden cup have morphed into the moon and the sun, pouring out the stars of the night and the sunset. Behind her is the starry sky; in fact she is the personification of the sky itself. A large seven pointed star is in the background, surrounded by seven more for the seven planets. From this central star, an infinite spiral of stars unfurls against a geometric sky; the unfolding of a set of infinite universes. The seven pointed star is the star of Venus, and the Star of Babalon. The waters are the Sea of Binah. The Star goddess is an aspect of Babalon, the Scarlet Woman; the sacred Harlot of Lust and the Great Mother of the Empress. This is the manifestation of Nuit as Star. Her letter is Hé, meaning window, the view of the infinite canopy of the night sky. This is the primal Hé, the Great Mother or first Hé of YHVH. Her nature is Love.

The Star goddess calls to mind the Babylonian Ishtar, the Mesopotamian Astarte, and the Sumerian Inanna, all names of the same goddess of love. She is also parallel to Aphrodite, and Isis, mother of Horus. Interestingly, both Ishtar and Astarte contain the word "star," and Inanna's name is derived from the Sumerian *nin-an-ak* meaning "Lady of Heaven." The "House of Heaven" was her temple, a site of sacred prostitution where the high priestess would choose a young man to represent Dumuzi, her consort, in the *hieros gamos*, or sacred marriage. Astarte was the deified evening star, usually shown naked alongside a star within a circle, a symbol of Venus. Ishtar also was a personification of Venus, and the courtesan of the gods. Her most famous myth describes her descent into the underworld, where in what may be the earliest striptease, she had to remove an article of clothing at each of the seven gates, until she stood naked. This gradual revealing of herself was the unveiling of truth.

In the Epic of Gilgamesh however, Ishtar sent the Bull of Heaven after Gilgamesh when he spurned her advances. (While the Star card is the aspect of the goddess in her nature as Love, these goddesses all are many-faceted and have multiple and varied natures, and are also goddesses of War. "Many-throned, many-minded, many-wiled, daughter of Zeus."[10]) The Star maiden, dweller between the waters, on the boundary between earth and water, also brings to mind Siduri, the holy barmaid who keeps a tavern by the edge of

10   *The Book of Thoth* pg 75

the sea at the ends of the earth, or the underworld, in the Epic of Gilgamesh. The bar at the edge of Hell, one could call it. The Star card follows the Tower. Gilgamesh is on a quest for immortality and arrives battered, apparently looking more disreputable than other patrons of the bar at the edge of Hell, and so at first her door is barred. But when he explains his quest and travails as the reason for his appearance she invites him in and gives him food and drink and a place to rest. Her advice to him is that his quest is unnecessary and to enjoy and delight in life. This is a card of renewal, devotion, clear sight and infinite vision.

The Oracle

Hope, joy, and truth shine like a beacon. Seek your dreams with devotion. The view is clear and unclouded if one is free from illusion. Achieve thou every possibility!

XVIII – THE MOON

THE MOON

Ruler of Flux and Reflux; Child of the Sons of the Mighty

Zodiacal Trump of Pisces; Jupiter (also Neptune) rules, Venus exalted

Hebrew letter: Qoph (back of head)

Tree of Life: Path 29 from [7] Netzach (Victory) to [10] Malkuth (Kingdom)

Color Scales: Crimson, Buff Flecked Silver-White, Light Translucent Pinkish Brown, Stone

Stranger, dreams verily are baffling and unclear of meaning, and in no wise do they find fulfillment in all things for men. For two are the gates of shadowy dreams, and one is fashioned of horn and one of ivory. Those dreams that pass through the gate of sawn ivory deceive men, bringing words that find no fulfillment. But those that come forth through the gate of polished horn bring true issues to pass, when any mortal sees them. But in my case it was not from thence, methinks, that my strange dream came.

~ The Odyssey

The gates of horn and ivory are a literary device about distinguishing between true and false dreams, inspired by a play on the Greek words for horn and ivory, which were similar to words that meant to fulfill and to deceive. Here the gates of horn and ivory are depicted as pillars shaped like models of a hand and a head. The hand is marked with symbols of palmistry showing the lines of Neptune and the Moon. It is shown giving the horned hand of witchcraft, said to be a mudra to expel demons and ward off the evil eye. The head has the markings of phrenology.

Passing between the gates is a ship with a figurehead of a female Oneroi. The Oneroi were black winged demons who lived near the gates. They were the relations of Nyx, the personification of Night, and Hypnos, the god of sleep in Greek mythology, and sent you dreams either prophetic or false from one of the two gates. The figurehead of this Oneroi was modeled on a siren on a column in St. Petersburg. It also was inspired by the story of what might be the most famous ship's figurehead, that of the ship Cutty-Sark, named for the witch Nannie Dee who is nick-named "Cutty-Sark" in Robert Burns' poem Tam O'Shanter. In the poem she wore a *sark*, Scots for petticoat, that she had been given as a child, so it was far too short, or *cutty*. The figurehead on the ship is the witch with long black hair clutching a tail of grey horse hair. In the poem, a farmer gets habitually drunk and one night stumbles upon a sabbat scene of witches dancing with the devil in a haunted church. He loses his reason at the erotic sight, interrupting them by leering at the young witch in a short petticoat and crying out "Weel done, cutty-sark!" They then give chase and he barely escapes over the water, Nannie Dee catching hold of his horse's tail. The poem concludes, "Now, wha this tale o' truth shall read, Ilk man and mother's son, take heed; Whene'er to Drink you are inclin'd, Or Cutty-sarks rin in your mind, Think ye may buy the joys o'er dear; Remember Tam o' Shanter's mare."

The Moon is the Zodiacal trump of Pisces, and the Hebrew letter for the card is Qoph, meaning the back of the head. From the back of the phrenology head, a door opens and a lunar moth emerges. Pisces as the last of the signs is most mutable, like the flux and reflux of the Moon. The Moon card is often shown with a crawfish, lobster, or crab climbing from the waters, and sometimes a scarab beetle as on the Thoth card. This beetle is Khepra, carrying the Solar Disk through the dark night. We see here the figurehead is a hybrid creature with one arm a crawfish claw, clutching the pod of an opium poppy. Climbing one of the gates, a mechanical scarab clutches an eerily lit pearl, the midnight sun, or a crystal showing dreams. The Book of Thoth says of this path, "Here is a weird, deceptive life. The fiery sense is baulked. The moon has no air. The knight upon this quest has to rely on the three lower senses: touch, taste and smell. Such light as there may be is deadlier than darkness, and the silence is wounded by the howling of wild beasts." It is a moment of the mystic Dark Night of the Soul, the madness of intoxication of the senses and the dark moon of poisoned witchcraft. Yet in madness there is grandeur, inspiration, and adventure. *Let the illusion of the World pass over thee, unheeded, as thou goest from the Midnight to the Morning*[11]. *Roll up the Excrement of the Earth, to create a Star!*

The Oracle

You are passing through the gates of dreams; take heed to tell the true dreams from illusions. This is the passage through darkness, the darkest hour before the dawn. Stray not from the path of True Will.

11   *Book of Thoth* pg 259

THE SUN

XIX – THE SUN

Lord of the Fire of the World

Planetary Trump of the Sun

Hebrew letter: Resh (head)

Tree of Life: Path 30 from [8] Hod (Splendor) to [9] Yesod (Foundation)

Color Scales: Orange, Gold Yellow, Rich Amber, Amber Rayed Red

IT IS ENDED NOW, WHAT I HAVE SAID CONCERNING THE
EFFECTS OF THE SUN. FINISH OF THE TABULA SMARAGDINA.

What I have said or taught of the Solar Work, is now finished.

The perfect Seed, fit for multiplication.

~ Dr. Sigismund Bacstrom's translations and notes on the *Emerald Tablet*

While the previous card, the Moon, has the letter for "back of the head," the Sun has the letter Resh, meaning "head." But this is not the back of the head or the door to the subconscious, but rather the front and central head, in this case the pineal grand. The pineal gland is said to be named thus because it is the shape of a pine cone, a symbol of growth in the Fibonacci sequence and the gland said to be the seat of consciousness. Its relationship with light gives it the function of the third eye. Buddha's head is also depicted as shaped like a pine cone. In Michelangelo's depiction of God's creation of Adam, God's background imagery is distinctly in the shape of the human brain, suggesting God is either created by the brain or accessed by it. In Lon Milo DuQuette's book about Crowley's Thoth tarot, he refers to Thelema as a form of Sun worship, and adds "And when I use the word Sun, I am also referring to myself." The Sun is but another star, and in Crowley's Book of the Law, "every man and every woman is a star." We have the eye, the head, and the heart, all connected in the symbolism of the Sun.

The Thoth tarot and others often show twins on the Sun card. The Rosetta tarot shows a detail from the Sistine Chapel, God's finger putting the spark of life into Adam, the twin created in his image. Tabula Mundi shows the twins as the crowned snakes of the caduceus. The heart vessel marked with the all-seeing eye and topped with the pineal cone is the orb between them, topping the caduceus. This is how the staff of Osiris is often shown, as a pine cone topped staff twined with twinned snakes. This is a visual representation of the force of kundalini summoned from the base of the spine to the third eye in the forehead, with the twin snakes being the channels of the Sanskrit *ida* and *pingala* spiraling up the central pole of *sushumna*. As the force rises, it expands and awakens the third eye. The pine cone opens and releases its seeds.

The twins call to mind the sign of Gemini which is ruled by Mercury. Ever there is a connection between the Sun and Mercury. They travel closely together, and the number of the Sun's trump reduces to that of the Magus. Mercury is a form of Hermes, and proto-Hermes was a Babylonian god of spring and fertilization, an agent of the Great Mother associated with the spring sun. This proto-Hermes was a snake god, but he was not a single snake like the great Earth goddess, but the double snake both male and female, whose emblem was the Kerykeion or caduceus, said to be the god himself and a predecessor of the Priapic herm-god.

The theme of twins also calls up the mythology of twinned Suns, or sons. Here, two six pointed stars or solar symbols have been twinned to make the geometric form of a twelve pointed star, to span the signs of the Zodiac. The crescent refers to the connection with Yesod, as the card is on the path between Yesod, sphere of the Moon, and Hod, sphere of Mercury. The signs of the Sun's journey are shown on the Mobius strip of the lemniscate or solar analemma. This figure eight shape is formed when the apparent position of the Sun is recorded every day at the same time throughout the solar year, and thus functions as a glyph of eternity. This glyph is also present on the Magus, card of Mercury, and Lust, trump of Leo, the sign which the Sun rules.

The card also has multiple triangles and hexagrams embedded as reference to the Supernals and Tiphareth. The Sun card is the *Lord of the Fire of the World.* The tongues of the snakes form the glyphs of Aries and Sagittarius, completing the fire sign trinity along with Leo, the sign the Sun rules. Alternately the tongues are Aries and Mars, as a subtle reference to the Sun's exaltation in Aries, and the "double Mars" at the start of solar spring in the zodiacal decan map. The Sun is shown as a winged disk with wings in a folded position and the flying disk of the Sun is marked with the decanates of the Zodiac, so that the card can serve as a map of the memory palace of the court cards and the related minor arcana.

The Sun glyph is an expansion of the Rose and the Cross. While the points are twelve symbolizing the Zodiac, they also should be considered infinite. The four arms of the cross have multiplied and are the rays of the Sun expanding in every direction, piercing the body of Nuit. According to Crowley the Sun card is thus Heru-ra-ha, the Lord of the New Aeon. This is the Aeon of new freedom for mankind as we look to Light, Life, Liberty and Love.

The Oracle

The light of health and glory shines upon you. Connect the head with the heart, and be free. Realize the source of all life. Avoid delusions of grandeur and the best life has to offer will be yours.

XX – THE AEON

THE AEON

The Spirit of the Primal Fire

Elemental Trump of Fire and of Spirit

Hebrew letter: Shin (tooth)

Tree of Life: Path 31 from [8] Hod (Splendor) to [10] Malkuth (Kingdom)

Color Scales (Fire): Glowing Orange Scarlet, Vermillion, Scarlet Flecked Gold, Vermillion Flecked Crimson

Color Scales: (Spirit): Prismatic Colors, White, White fading to Grey, Dark Purple Nearly Black, Red, Yellow, Blue, Black outside

Azoth is poured on once more, and the intensity of the fire is raised, for the soul must be "sweated out." The lapis must be burned strongly and for a long time.
~ J.C. Barchusen, *Elementa chemicae*

Concerning the Aeon, o my Son, learn that the Sun and His Vicegerent are in all Aeons, of Necessity, Father, Centre, Creator, each in His Sphere of Operation. But the Formula of the past Aeon was of the Dying god, and was based upon Ignorance. For Men thought that the Sun died and was reborn alike in the Day and in the Year; and so also was the Mystery of Man. Now already are we well assured by Science how the Death of the Sun is in Truth but the Shifting of a Shadow; and in this Aeon (o my son, I lift up my Voice and I make Prophecy!) so shall it be proven as to Death. For the Body of Man is but his Shadow, it cometh and goeth even as the tides of Ocean; and he only is in Darkness who is hidden by that Shadow from the Light of his true Self. Now therefore understand thou the Formula of Horus, the Lion God, the Child crowned and conquering that cometh forth in Force and Fire! For thy Changes are not Phases of thee, but of the Phantoms which thou mistakest for thy Self.
~ *Liber Aleph vel CXI*, Verse 99

In the old packs this was the card of the last Judgment, representing the destruction of the world by fire in the Aeon of Osiris. The Thoth deck reinvented the card as the Aeon, showing the figures from the Stele of Revealing heralding the birth of the Aeon of Horus. The fiery god Horus takes the seat of the Hierophant in the East, replacing airy Osiris. This is the same story being depicted here, but in a different way. The Aeon is the elemental trump of both Fire and Spirit. Here is all perception of the great correlations; the bigger picture revealed. Nut, the circumference ever eternal, is here as the personification of the starry heavens, shown combing stars from her hair with the letter Shin. Hadit, the central point, is shown as the winged disk above. The union of the goddess of unlimited possibility with the god of the secret central seed produces Horus the child, Heru-ra-ha.

Horus the child is depicted as the Ouroboros dragon in the alchemical retort which is being heated in a tomb shaped like a keyhole filled with fiery lava. The keyhole is a subtle tie with the Hierophant, the priest-initiator welcoming the New Aeon and the mythologies of the Legend of Pasiphae, the woman and the beast as moon and sun. For the Book of the Law proclaims "For he is ever a sun, and she a moon. But to him is the winged secret flame, and to her the stooping starlight." The three Aeons embedded in the memory of mankind are that of Isis, Osiris, and now Horus. The one to follow is said to be that of Maat, another even subtler connection with the Hierophant.

The beginning of the solar cycle is the Aries point, and in the foreground are two plinths. The left represents the tail end of Pisces and has the Omphalos while the right has the start of Aries with a sprouting seed. The perspective of the card is intended to put the viewer in the picture, as if standing before the vessel at the edge of the keyhole. Just outside of the frame on the border of the card, is a small circle. This is the sign of spirit, this is Hadit, this is you. This is the point in the center of the circle, the "flame that burns in every heart of man, and in the core of every star."[12]

In the background, the morning sun rises on a solstice through the monument of Stonehenge, lighting the crucible. This is a representation of Horus at dawn. Stonehenge, an ancient monument of the Osirian age, has been considered a solar clock determining the Saros cycle of eclipses, measured by the phases of the moon marked out by 56 Aubrey holes. These lunar phases are shown superimposed on the sky as a comet streaks by, on its own cycle of passage.

The numeral of the card is twenty, a number associated with the generational cycles of man, and when multiplied a hundredfold, a number associated with world ages. In the Aeon of Horus we are Suns, never dying and self-illuminated.

12   *Book of the Law*, Chapter II

The Aeon follows the Sun, where we see both Hadit and Heru-ra-ha, or Horus the Child. It precedes the Universe which comes at the end of all. It is fitting then that it represents a destruction of the old world by fire, when the fiery god Horus took the place of Osiris as Hierophant in the East. Heru-ra-ha, like the Sun, manifests as a dual god. His active form is Ra-hoor-khuit and his passive form is Hoor-pa-kraat, and he is said also to be Hru, the angel of tarot invoked at the start of the journey. Presumably in another two thousand years or so, the double-wanded one will again "have crushed an Universe; & nought remains."

The Oracle

The bigger picture is revealed and a new age is upon you. Take the first step of initiation, the old ways are gone. Awaken, purified and renewed by fire, reborn.

XXI – THE UNIVERSE

The Great One of the Night of Time

Planetary Trump of Saturn and Elemental Trump of Earth

Hebrew letter: Tau (cross)

Tree of Life: Path 32 from [9] Yesod (Foundation) to [10] Malkuth (Kingdom)

Color Scales: Indigo, Black, Blue Black, Black Rayed Blue

THE UNIVERSE

ת ▽ ち

All journeys have secret destinations of which the traveler is unaware.

~ Martin Buber

We are come unto a palace of which every stone is a separate jewel, and is set with millions of moons. And this palace is nothing but the body of a woman, proud and delicate, and beyond imagination fair. She is like a child of twelve years old. She has very deep eyelids, and long lashes. Her eyes are closed, or nearly closed. It is impossible to say anything about her. She is naked; her whole body is covered with fine gold hairs, that are the electric flames which are the spears of mighty and terrible Angels whose breastplates are the scales of her skin.

~ *The Vision and the Voice*, 9th Aethyr

The Fool, having entered the wormhole, exits the tube torus as a being transformed into the Bride, Malkuth. The Ouroboros portal is still there, but this is the other side. The circle has been squared, and Kether is in Malkuth. The essence of the Great Work has been accomplished, and is ready to return.

There are infinite ways to say the same thing. The Fool and the Universe. The beginning, and the end. The Eye of Shiva. The Alpha and the Omega. Kether and Malkuth. The infinitely contracted point, and the ever expanding cross and circle. Life and death. The ouroboros. As above, so below. The highest, and the lowest. The portal, the vesica piscis, the Shemhamphorash. The final Hé. The spiral forces.

The maiden emerges from the ouroboros portal as the center of four, the ever expanded point. Her eyes are closed, and she dances with the spiral forces dextro and lævo-rotary. Her dancing partner is Heru-Ra-Ha of the Sun card. We see in the four corners the creatures of the fixed signs, the "Holy Living Creatures" of the Merkabah chariot throne. These are an order of angels associated with Kether, yet here they are on the final path to Malkuth. These signs contain the four Royal Stars of the Heavens. Regulus is the heart of the Lion (Leo, *Lust*), Watcher of the North. Antares is the heart of the Scorpion (Scorpio, *Death*) and Watcher of the West. Fomalhaut is the mouth of the fish (Aquarius, *Star*, pours into the mouth of the Southern Fish), and is the Watcher of the South. Aldebaran is the eye of the Bull (Taurus, *The Hierophant*) and Watcher of the East. These four signs are the infinite arms of the Tau cross. Each is associated with one of the Princes of the courts. These watchers are also each associated with one of the four archangels, Michael in the East, Oriel in the West, Raphael in the North, and Gabriel in the South. The path of the Universe is where the adept first begins to develop the four virtues: *To Will, To Dare, To Know,* and *To Keep Silent.*

Above is the Tetractys of the Pythagoreans, a form of the Tetragrammaton and the Tree of Life in a pyramidal shape of ten points aligned in four rows with four points on each side. The Monad (unity), The Dyad (polarity), The Triad (trinity), The Tetrad (cosmos). The Decans, the Elements, the Dimensions. A Pythagorean prayer to the Tetractys reads "Bless us, divine number, thou who generated gods and men! O holy, holy Tetractys, thou that containest the root and source of the eternally flowing creation! For the divine number begins with the profound, pure unity until it comes to the holy four; then it begets the mother of all, the all-comprising, all-bounding, the first-born, the never-swerving, the never-tiring holy ten, the keyholder of all." Dion Fortune in Mystical Qabalah states "The point is assigned to Kether; the line to Chokmah; the two-dimensional plane to Binah; consequently the three-dimensional solid naturally falls to Chesed." The first three-dimensional solid is the tetrahedron, a form of the Tetractys.

The Universe is the planetary trump of Saturn, Binah, the Great Mother. But she is also Malkuth, the Daughter, and the element of Earth. This is appropriate as the Daughter "sits upon the throne of the Mother." The idea of form originating in Binah has now been developed and made manifest. Below is a gear, symbolizing the rings of Saturn, and the element of Earth. Positioned as it is, it is also the eye of Shiva, the all-devourer and all-begetter.

Shiva's eye is the gear that turns the Universe, and "the Aeons are but the pulsings of thy blood." [13]

The Oracle

The other end of the portal is reached, and thus, the crystallization and fulfillment of the whole matter involved. Complete expansion has been achieved. This is completion, the Great Work accomplished, and the wholeness inherent within. The seed has sprouted and grown to maturity, bearing fruit.

13   *Book of Thoth* pg 143, from the Vision and the Voice, 9th Aethyr

Random Artist Notes on the Major Arcana

The Fool: The figure was modeled on a posable anatomical model showing muscular structure. I guess this is appropriate for the Fool in a way for its generic and blank aspect, from which anything can be formed. It also helped me to get the odd perspective. The idea of the Fool passing through a wormhole in the fabric of space-time was divinely inspired. The hard part was deciding what a wormhole in said fabric looked like in a way that could be drawn with marker, magic or otherwise.

The Magus: The idea for the Magus as a DJ was downloaded from the ethers one night while half awake and half asleep. It was the night of a full moon and an eclipse, and that night the ideas and images for four cards (Magus, Priestess, Empress, and Emperor) downloaded into my conscious mind simultaneously while I was lying in bed awake, thinking about the cards. I wish it was always that easy.

The Priestess: The Priestess was inspired by a painting of a woman at twilight by William Bouguereau, which showed an archetypal Sophia dipping her toes in water, with a lunar crescent in the sky. Something about it is so evocative of the Priestess. The idea for the pomegranate hearts comes from a painting I did years ago as an allegory of alchemical ash, or what is left after all has been transformed. This was one of the ideas that came with the Magus, as in, the idea to combine all these elements in this card came together in the vision of this card that night.

The Empress: I wanted this Empress to have a fierce and protective demeanor and not be the traditional heavily pregnant woman. The heart hive image came to me years ago before creating this deck, in a dream, and became part of an earlier painting of a winged heart full of honeycomb and surrounded by bees. Finding a way to show the heart both within her body and as an image large enough to see what was illustrated was challenging. This was another one of the cards that came with the Magus, as in, the ideas came together in the vision of this card that night.

The Emperor: The faces on the buskins of the figure are somewhat of a personal joke. I was reading Graham Hancock's book *The Mars Mystery* at the time, and was thinking about the face on Mars, and happened to find a picture on the web that compared the face on Mars to the image of Crowley's face in headdress—they look remarkably similar! The Devil made me do it.

The Hierophant: The card was modeled on a traditional Tibetan Rinpoche. It is not an obvious Thelemic depiction of the Hierophant as initiator, but sometimes the Buddhist doctrines especially of Tibetan tantra overlap those of Thelema.

The Lovers: There were some astro-synchronicities in play when this card was drawn. The new moon was in Gemini and eclipses on the Gemini/Sagittarius axis were happening. Also we had a Venus/Sun conjunction. The female character in the Lovers is the Empress—the card of Venus. The male character is the Emperor—the card of Aries, which is a sign of dignity for the Sun. When I drew the background of this card I understandably had Led Zeppelin's "Black Dog" stuck in my head. This means nothing in terms of the cards meaning, only that I am a fan of Led Zeppelin. (Incidentally, my favorite Zeppelin song is "Kashmir" and I want Jimmy Page's dragon embroidered suit. I'd totally wear it, after a good steam cleaning. Yes, I could pull it off.)

The Chariot: Thinking about the Hebrew letter Cheth, and its meaning of enclosure, combined with the cardinal waters on the path, I could not help but see it as a great pipeline for the Charioteer to surf. The hippocampi were inspired by an ancient artwork showing the sea god and his consort pulled by horses, which were actually hippocampi. It displayed the god's triumph after obtaining his bride's consent, with the help of the persuasion of dolphins.

Adjustment: I come from an area with long winters, so I used to go ice skating as a kid. If you have ever skated, you know that it requires constant minute adjustments to balance, but once you master that, there is beautiful flow. It just seems very Venus/Saturn to me: the balance, the correction, the cold beauty! Also in case you were wondering, both the musical notes and the patterns of dots and dashes on the ice are random and not Morse code. Though maybe it is like when people used to play a record backwards, and there is something there I don't know about.

The Hermit: This Hermit was modeled on an illustration of Merlin by HJ Ford in one of the old King Arthur books. The idea came to me during the new moon when it was in the sign of Virgo. When I saw him entering into the underground chamber it struck me as the perfect visual representation of the Hermit's path and role as guardian and guide of the lower regions, and the descent into matter.

Fortune: There was no real model for this card. Like the Magus, this is another image that came to me in a state between sleep and waking. I have no idea why Hermanubis appeared as a ring tailed lemur, and as a matter of fact, when I saw it I thought it was a sloth until I looked it up and realized it was a lemur; shows how much I know! Same with the other creatures, the three eyed owl and the hand serpent showed up fully formed. Appropriately enough, this is the trump of Jupiter and the card showed up just as Jupiter stationed direct, after a long retrograde period transiting my fifth house of creativity.

Lust: This card got done just as we were entering the Year of the Snake. Lust was inspired by seeing a statue of Durga, while pondering the Virgo Lucifera of the Chemical Marriage and the concept of the woman straddling the lion just as fall (Virgo) overtakes summer (Leo). Someday I may do an alternate version with nudity and more enflamed and ecstatic abandon as in the Thoth card.

The Hanged Man: Would you believe "Tied to the Whipping Post" (Allman Brothers) started playing when I started to paint this? "Good Lord, I feel like I'm dyin.'" Also years ago before I did either of the decks I did a mixed media painting that was a clear forerunner of the Hanged Man in both the Rosetta and Tabula Mundi. It showed a man within a tree, and a heart-shaped swarm hanging from the right branch. Another astrological synchronicity was present. When I drew the artwork for this card the Sun, Mercury, Venus, Mars, Neptune and Chiron were all in Pisces, which is mutable water and thus the wateriest of water signs, and the new moon directly after it was created joined them! Add in Saturn in Scorpio and most of the zodiac then was in a water sign. "So long and thanks for all the Fish!"[14]

Death: At the time of creating this card I mentioned to someone that I wondered if it was a faux pas to put a salmon in the Nile. Around here they spawn in rivers, but they are not likely there. Or maybe they are, I don't know. Anyway he said he thought it was funny that I was concerned about the authenticity of the salmon's habitat when it was being clutched by a mythological creature ridden by a skeleton in a hat. To which I replied that actually, it is an Atef Crown. The art for this card got done when the moon was just past full and waning into the sign of Scorpio.

---

14   In *The Hitchhiker's Guide to the Galaxy*, this is the message left by dolphins for
       Earthlings when they left Earth for hyperspace.

Art: I wanted to draw the Green Lion as a winged Diana personified, as if the two beings from the Lovers card were merged and transformed. The figure needed to be aiming the arrow upward and seen from behind. The inspiration was loosely from a sculpture of Artemis but she wasn't depicted as a lion, winged and tailed, so that was imaginary. Interestingly, when I drew this card the moon was waning in the sign of Sagittarius, and it was over an Easter weekend which I found amusing because the card depicts the Orphic egg and esoteric womb symbolism.

The Devil: *Chase the Devil* by Max Romeo, with lyrics addressed to "Lucifer Son of the Morning" was on the radio when I started the artwork for The Devil, and in a special case of coincidence, it came on just as I started to write the chapter on the card, very many months later! I suppose it may be also interesting to note, that like the Fool, the Devil was modeled using a generic posable form and imagination.

The Tower: The inspiration for the Tower card came after a long period of being blocked and stuck. Then I was obsessed with other things, like going "nutting" (collecting hickory nuts), of course on the Devil's Nutting Day. Finally, the lightning flashes. Of course, the breakthrough came on the day of the October full moon lunar eclipse in Aries right before Hallows Eve. Since the Tower is the trump of Mars (which rules Aries) and a full moon eclipse is also a culmination or ending, it felt right. One door closes and another opens and all that. I always marvel that there seems to be an astrological event that brings the cards through, especially when I get stuck for a while. So finally this image of the Tower comes through and I get the sketch fully drawn in pencil. At first my vision was just of looking up "worm's eye view" at a blasted and falling Tower whose entrance is the gaping mouth of a Caledonian boar with flames shooting out of it. At some point strange hybrid flying creatures (chimaera, giant hawk, dragon and gryphon-like lion serpent) appear out of nowhere in place of the usual human falling figures. Like the Hermit, the main figure of the bird inverted was inspired by an illustration by HJ Ford. They have the Yod in common I guess. Funny story: Once I told someone who asked if I had received a birthday present, that I had gotten a big head of Shiva. (I'd received a large heavy sculpture of the head of Shiva.) She looked puzzled and then asked if that meant that I got stoned. I only mention this because Shiva the Destroyer is a large part of the symbolism of this card. And because it is funny.

The Star: This card came to me during the night, moments before a new moon solar eclipse, when the Sun and Moon conjoin. The silver cup and the golden cup have morphed into a lunar and a solar cup, pouring out the stars of the night and the sunset. The exquisite posture of the figure was inspired by a statue of the femme fatale Salome. While the story of Salome and her mother's request for the head of John the Baptist is rather brutal and has naught to do with this card, there is an interesting parallel in that Oscar Wilde, in his play called *Salome* refers to her erotic dance as the "dance of the seven veils" calling to mind Ishtar and her removal of clothing at the seven gates. Perhaps the request for the head by the mother was a Queen of Swords moment; there is a connection to Aquarius through the Princess of Swords.

The Moon: The idea for the drawing of this Moon card came during the dark of the moon (sometime during the darkest period of the lunar cycle, the three days preceding the new moon). I painted the colors during the full moon, and finished it while the Moon was waning again. The model for the gate of horn is my pepper grinder. It sounds strange but so is the Moon card.

The Sun: The largest statue of a pine cone in the world is in Rome, called the Pigna, which is Italian for pine cone, of course. It is a first century Roman statue in a courtyard of the Vatican called, no surprise, the Courtyard of the Pinecone. It is a 13 foot tall bronze pine cone flanked by twinned peacocks, originally part of a Roman fountain near the Pantheon. This pine cone is just one of the many wonders that came up in the wormhole for the card. Also, yes, in order to draw the solar lemniscate marked with the zodiacal signs, I had to make a paper Mobius strip as a model to see how the glyphs would twist. (Otherwise I might have written them backwards or upside down.) Also long after drawing this card, I found a drawing of Robert Fludd's Memory Theatre[15] that he used in his personal memory system. It looks very much like the Sun in this card, four rotated triangles within a hexagram. It is speculated to be a plan of Shakespeare's long lost Globe Theatre. It was interesting to see, as I designed this card to create a visual mnemonic of the decanates.

---

15   See the Appendix for a diagram.

The Aeon: This is such an important card in the Thoth deck. I wanted to be very careful when attempting to portray anything showing the characters of the Stele of Revealing in any other way. I hope I did it justice as it was very important to me as well. It should be mentioned also that some say Heru-ra-ha, seen in both the Sun and the Aeon card, is also Hru, the angel set over the dominion of the Tarot invoked at the start of the chapters on the cards.

The Universe: "She is naked; her whole body is covered with fine gold hairs, that are the electric flames which are the spears of mighty and terrible Angels whose breastplates are the scales of her skin." Someday, I will paint a gigantic painting of the visualization of that sentence, and then I can die happy. For now, this was the best I could do. I wanted to show the maiden of the Universe exiting the other side of the wormhole that the Fool entered, and I pictured it as having the form of the tube torus. The perfect inspiration for how to do this came from a wood engraving by M. C. Escher, one of my favorite artists.

The Point and Circle: A Ride on the Wheel

The Minor Arcana

WHEEL AND — WOA!
The Great Wheel of Samsara.
The Wheel of the Law [Dhamma].
The Wheel of the Taro.
The Wheel of the Heavens.
The Wheel of Life.
All these Wheels be one; yet of all these the Wheel
of the TARO alone avails thee consciously.
Meditate long and broad and deep,
O man, upon this Wheel, revolving it in thy mind!
Be this thy task, to see how each card springs necessarily from
each other card, even in due order from The Fool unto The Ten of Coins.
Then, when thou know'st the Wheel of Destiny complete, mayst thou perceive
THAT Will which moved it first. [There is no first or last.]
And lo! thou art past through the Abyss.
~ *The Book of Lies KE Φ*. OH

If the Taro(t) is a wheel, then the cards are the ride or the journey;
motion and rest. In Chapter 78 of *The Book of Lies*, Frater Perdurabo
describes the Tarot as being not only the universe as it is, but also
the Magical Path. He instructs his followers to treat the sequence
of the cards as cause and effect, and thus one discovers the "cause
behind all causes." He reminds us that the universe is not to be
contemplated as a phenomenon in time but is ever revolving.

The world is like a ride in an amusement park, and when you choose to go on it you think it's real because that's how powerful our minds are. The ride goes up and down, around and around, it has thrills and chills, and it's very brightly colored, and it's very loud, and it's fun for a while. Many people have been on the ride a long time, and they begin to wonder, "Hey, is this real, or is this just a ride?"

~ Bill Hicks

What is a wheel, but a point within a circle? The point as the central hub (Kether) evolves into the axle of a line, around which revolves the wheel. This is the structure of the Tarot, a vehicle with the four wheels of the suits.

The Point refers to the Aces and the Circle to the 36 decanic cards. The Zodiac, or the circle of thirty six decans, is the circle within the point expanded. The point within the circle is also the glyph of the Sun, of the element hydrogen, the fertilized egg, the secret seed, and of alchemical gold. In the Book of the Law Hadit identifies himself as the point in the center of the circle, the axle of the wheel, the cube in the circle. It is one, and none, the union of opposites. Once again, it all boils down to sun worship.

Just as the trumps issue from the Fool, the minor arcana issue from the Aces. The Aces stand alone and are given their own chapter. The thirty six other minor arcana have been grouped by suit element, but could also have been grouped according to astrological quadruplicity. There are three astrological quadruplicities or modalities; that of the cardinal, the fixed and the mutable, each of which has four signs, one for each element.

In the Tarot, the Cardinal signs correspond to the Twos, Threes, and Fours. The Fixed signs are assigned the Fives, Sixes, and Sevens. The Mutable signs are the Eights, Nines, and Tens. So as not to be confusing, note that this method of grouping the numbers in sets of three differs from the grouping by triplicity or the three sets of three sephiroth of the Tree of Life. In that methodology, the groups of three sephiroth begins with the Supernals Kether, Chokmah and Binah or Ace, Two, Three. This is mirrored by the groupings of Chesed, Geburah and Tiphareth (4,5,6) and then Netzach, Hod and Yesod (7,8,9) with Malkuth (10) as a pendant. Interestingly, if we were to flip the Tree of Life putting Kether in Malkuth, the Ace would then be the stand-alone sephira and the groupings would be arranged aligning with the quadruplicities of the cardinal, fixed, and mutable signs.

The Minors follow the traditional Golden Dawn assignments as follows:

Wands Yod, Father, Fire and Atziluth, the Archetypal World (Godhead)
Cups primal Heh, Mother, Water, Briah, the Creative World (Spiritual)
Swords Vav, Son, Air, Yetzirah, the Formative World (Astral–Psychological)
Disks final Heh, Daughter, Earth, Assiah, the World of Action (Physical–Material)

What Crowley refers to as the Naples Arrangement describes the evolution of the Sephiroth, or Numbers, in a summarized sequence as follows:

ooo Nothing
oo Nothing Without Limit
o Limitless Light
1 The Point
2 The Line
3 The Plane
4 The Solid
5 Time/Change/Motion
6 Consciousness
7 Essence of Being
8 Thought
9 Bliss
10 Reality

As far as translating this into the small cards of the Tarot, it suffices to say that the Aces begin the cycle at number 1, the Point, as the first positive manifestation of the *idea* of the element. Each successive numerical progression moves away from the ideal and towards the actual, in progressive degradation and unfolding. At the center of the system at the sixes, the elemental force has become manifold yet is balanced. From there the element begins to dissipate or spiritualize itself. At the nine it reaches its penultimate state and the peak of its fixity of force. At the ten the element is materialized and pushed to its consummate state. Expiration is imminent as it readies to transmute to the Ace of the following suit.

How the Tabula Mundi Minors Were Created

Liber Theta directly describes the process used for the creation of the small cards of Tabula Mundi, in a reverse engineering of the meditation described in the section of *Liber Theta* called "Meditation on the Minor Arcana." It begins by saying that meditation on the Minor Arcana should follow meditation on the Major Arcana, because the Trumps are the basis for the composition of the smaller cards. After some description of the meditation itself, it continues to say that your understanding of the Minor Arcana cards will be the basis of your understanding of the Court cards that follow.

For each of the minors, in the case of the 36 small cards the meditation pattern entails placing the minor card between its two related trumps; in the case of the courts, placing them above the three associated small cards.

This is essentially how the Minor Arcana of Tabula Mundi were created, though the meditation pattern was done on the non-physical level and the minors themselves did not yet exist. To come up with the design of each small card, I visualized in my mind's eye the related trumps. This was usually done in a somewhat meditative or altered mind state, most often during the wee hours of night when in a hypnagogic state of consciousness but sometimes while day dreaming as well. While building the visualization of the trumps in all detail in the mind's eye, I would simultaneously hold in mind the images and symbols of the two related trumps, the element, the influence of the sephira of the tree of life, the card's formal name, and its meaning until the idea or design of the small card presented itself as a combination of these factors. A similar process was done for each of the courts but beginning with its three related decanic cards as progenitors.

The Aces, standing alone and of Kether, and being the Point created from the nothingness of Ain, Ain Soph and Ain Soph Aur, were a different process of pure meditation on the seed of the element as the point of Kether. In addition when creating the Aces, each was considered as a letter of the divine name YHVH. The Ace of Wands thus corresponds to Yod, the Ace of Cups to primal Hé, the Ace of Swords to Vau, and the Ace of Disks to final Hé.

It is suggested that when studying the small cards of Tabula Mundi, that they are placed between their associated trumps for meditation in order to see how the trumps were deconstructed and reassembled to create them, and similarly, to do so with the Courts and their related small cards. To obtain the color scales for the Minor cards, see the color scales listed under each of their associated Majors.

When creating the Minor Arcana two through ten, I wanted to not only incorporate the decanates, but also the elemental descriptions as they manifest for each zodiacal sign. For each sign, I've made sure that at least one of the decans contained the appropriate manifestation of the elements as follows, chosen for which one or ones of the sign's decans seemed most appropriate. The following list is the best comprehensive grouping of information on this topic I've found. This is from Mary K. Greer's website, reprinted with permission. It is not her own material but was copied from an unpublished manuscript by *Frater Sub Spe* [John Brodie Innes] which according to Mary was owned at one time by the Theosophical Library in NY but has since been sold to an unknown person. John Brodie Innes was a leading member of the Hermetic Golden Dawn's Amen-Ra temple in Edinburg, and was believed to have been a teacher to Dion Fortune. I like this list because as a reader of diverse esoteric texts I often discover descriptions of things like salient or waving flames, certain kinds of clouds or earth or conditions of sea, associated with specific cards. This rather sums them up:

Aries: Ascending Flames. A Great and Ruling Force.

Leo: Rushing Flames. A Force Wise.

Sagittarius: Darting Flames. A Force Great and Potent.

Taurus: Fertile land in a valley. A Force Exalted.

Virgo: Undulating land and low hill. A Force Just.

Capricorn: Precipitous, rocky and barren land. A Force Strong and Mighty.

Gemini: Cirrhous and flecked cloud. A Powerful Force.

Libra: Cumulo-stratous clouds. A Force Illustrious.

Aquarius: Rain descending from clouds. A Force Manifesting and
    Manifested.

Cancer: Eddies of swirling water. A Force that renders Powerful.

Scorpio: Undulating surface of water. A Wisely Dispensing Force.

Pisces: Breaking waves of the sea. A Force Avenging.

Now, while it is not always easy to comprehend the difference between these various descriptions of forces, you can absorb them as you would a line of poetry. And the emotional impact of the descriptions of the various aspects of the manifestations of the elements is as undeniable as the weather.

A final thing to note about the decanic minor cards is that the three decan cards of each sign were designed so that they fit together as one zodiacal image of all three decans. This is a secret of the cards that will be revealed in a future edition.

The Point at the Center

The Aces

Some of the symbols for Kether are the Point and the Crown, and in Tabula Mundi, the point and crown symbolism is shown in the Aces both literally and also as a consequence of the geometric design they are all based on. This design involves a series of Golden Ratio related circles, decreasing in size from bottom to top for the feminine aces (cups and disks) and increasing in size from bottom to top for the masculine aces (wands and swords). The resulting triangle formed from the apex (point and crown) to the base is used to form the elemental symbol.

The Aces are singular, and stand alone. But they can be said to contain the germ of the rest of the cards of the suit. The Aces are not the element itself; they are titled as the "root" or seed of their respective element. In plants, a root is defined as the underground support of a plant that conveys nourishment. As a noun, another definition is the basic cause, source or origin of something. *Liber Theta* describes the Aces as the tendency to step away from unity in one of the four directions of the elements, or one could also say in one of the four letters of the divine name YHVH, each bearing the *potential* for manifestation of the element. Thus the Aces are the secret seed, the sperm at the center of the egg, the point in the circle.

The Aces are assigned to Kether on the tree of life. Like the Fool, Kether has a nascent quality. They are embryonic and incipient rather than born. They also have a connection with the Princesses, who are said to be the "throne of" the Ace, or the final recipient of that which is inherent within it. If the uppermost tip of the Yod in YHVH is Kether or the Ace, the Princess is the container below that holds it all as the final Hé and Malkuth.

ACE OF WANDS
ROOT OF THE POWERS OF FIRE

YOD
THE ACE OF WANDS

Root of the Powers of Fire

With the Princess of Wands as its throne, rules the quadrant of space for Cancer-Leo-Virgo, and the area of Asia

Color: Brilliance

The Aces are filed under Kether, and one could say that the Ace of Wands is the most Kether-like of all, as it is the first of the minors. All of the small cards, not just the Wands, are contained therein, as each of the small cards flows down the tree of life in progression, and the four trees (one for each suit) are connected from Malkuth of one to the Kether of the next. So the Ace of Wands is the categorical initiator and signifies the immanent inception of the fiery creative force. Crowley calls it a "solar-phallic outburst" (of course he does). It is also said that Spirit rules the four elements, and as in the Tarot, Fire does double duty for Spirit, Fire begins as overseer of the progression through the suits. Yet the Aces are not Kether itself, and are not spiritual entities, but more an elemental "Blind Force" of the Tetragrammaton.

The Ace of Wands of Tabula Mundi shows a worm's eye view of a towering and monumental wand in the form of a venerable tree. At the crown of the tree is an ancient bearded face both hidden and revealed in the swirling forms of the bark. Below in the trunk of the tree or body of the wand, vague and amorphous forms are visible but as yet undefined. These are the "First Swirlings" of manifestation and indicate the remainder of the small cards concealed within the first Ace that have yet to take shape. Thus the Tree of Life itself is a glyph of the unfolding of fire. The Wand has flames in the positions of the ten sephiroth to represent the primordial outpouring of fiery energy.

Some of the titles of Kether are evocative of this imagery: *Concealed of the Concealed. Ancient of Ancients. Ancient of Days. The Most High. The Vast Countenance. The Head which is not. The One in All, and All in One. The*

Inscrutable Height. I Am. (Et al.) These are Qabalistic koans, for Kether is essentially unknowable.

The Ace of Wands is mapped to the Yod or Supernal Father of YHVH, and so is of both Kether and Chokmah, the first Force, or the positive potency. It is said to symbolize natural force, as opposed to invoked force. It is the very beginning stage of the process of the godhead manifesting in matter. This is the force of initiation, one step before manifested will. This is the spark that ignites the will. It is potency and creative energy, the birth of all things from the divine One. It is the first tendency or initiative of the world of spirit to head towards matter.

The Seed

The seed grows the root of the element of Fire. This is the initial spark of divine will, which becomes things of Force: creativity, energy, potency, and passion. The goal is the power to Will.

Hè primal
THE ACE OF CUPS

ACE OF CUPS
ROOT OF THE POWERS OF WATER

Root of the Powers of Water

With the Princess of Cups as its throne, rules the quadrant of space for Libra-Scorpio-Sagittarius, and the area of the Pacific

Color: White Brilliance

The Ace of Cups is the Root of the Powers of Water. This card is mapped to the primal Hé or Supernal Mother of YHVH. Like all Aces, it is of Kether, but where the Ace of Wands was Force or the first motion, the Ace of Cups is the first Form so also Binah, the "Bright Fertile Mother" receiving the Yod and bringing forth fruitfulness. The Ace of Cups is the feminine counterpart to the Ace of Wands; the yoni to complement the phallus. You can see they are pairs if you compare them, as the Ace of Cups was built on the same sacred geometry structure as the Ace of Wands (a series of Golden Ratio circles), only inverted.

Here we have Kether acting upon Binah; ripples form in the great dark ocean of matter. The point and the crown are emblems of Kether, and we see a point or droplet fall creating a splash in the form of a crown. The Cup is formed from a great shell encrusted with pearls and a glowing emerald or ruby crystal. It is meant to suggest the Grail (the hidden emerald), and the Cup of Babalon (the visible ruby). It is in the form of the Cup of the Stolistes[16], an illustrative cup form which encapsulates the nine sephiroth exclusive of Kether.

In the illustration of this Ace of Cups, the middle pillar is hinted at, with Malkuth and Yesod as the base and the apex of the cup's lower triangle formed by the roots, and the eye in the tree hollow is in the position of Tiphareth. (This is the same eye as seen in the Hanged Man; Mem, the card of elemental water.) The dark space in the hollow is Daath, where Binah and Chokmah are united. Per Book T, the falling water on either side of the cup is meant to in essence suggest the shape of the letter of the Supernal Mother, Hé primal. As

16   See Appendix for diagram

the card of Hé primal, and the original root of Water, this Ace is the seed of fertility and conception, love and joy. It is the productiveness of First Form.

This card took a lot longer than I expected to form. This is interesting, because Briah or Water is the world of creation. Not conscious thought (Yetzirah), not physical creation (Assiah), but the first creation of the prerequisites or pre-conditions needed in order to create. And that is exactly the part that took so long, waiting for the conditions to arise, and the idea of the card to gestate.

The Seed

The seed grows the root of the element of Water. This is the receptiveness that becomes things of Form. Here are the beginning stirrings of love, conception, beauty and devotion. The goal is love, the power to Dare.

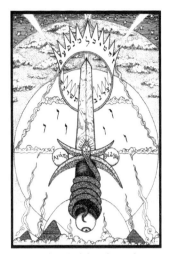

Vau
THE ACE OF SWORDS

Root of the Powers of Air

With the Princess of Swords as its throne, rules the quadrant of space for Capricorn-Aquarius-Pisces, and the area of the Americas

Color: White Brilliance

ACE OF SWORDS
ROOT OF THE POWERS OF AIR

The Ace of Swords is the Root of the Powers of Air, and mapped to the Vau or Son of YHVH. Thus in one sense it also reminds us of Tiphareth, the Son or Lesser Countenance, a product of the union of the Supernal parents. The following quotes of Crowley's are instrumental in understanding the illustration of this card:

"The pommel of the Sword is in Daath, the guard extends to Chesed and Geburah; the point is in Malkuth . . ."

"He shall await the sword of the beloved and bare his throat for the stroke." In the throat is Daath—the throne of Ruach. Daath is knowledge. **This final destruction opens the gate of the City of the Pyramids."** ~ *Book 4, Chapter VIII*

"Finally, from Kether, the supreme, descends directly upon him, though the Path of Gimel, the High Priestess, the triune light of Initiation. The Three-in-One, the Secret Mother in her polymorphous plenitude; these, these alone, hail him thrice blessed of the Supernals! The card represents the Sword of the Magus crowned with the twenty-two rayed diadem of pure Light. The number refers to the Atu; also 22=2 X II, the Magical manifestation of Chokmah, Wisdom, the Logos. Upon the blade, accordingly, is inscribed the Word of the Law, This Word sends forth a blaze of Light, dispersing the dark clouds of the Mind." ~ *Book of Thoth*

"In consecrating a weapon, Aleph is the whirling force of the thunderbolt, the lightning which flameth out of the East even into the West. This is the gift of the wielding of the thunderbolt of Zeus or Indra, the God of Air. Lamed is the Ox-Goad, the driving force; and it is also the Balance, representing the truth and love of the Magician. It is the loving care which he bestows upon perfecting his instruments, and the equilibration of that fierce force which initiates the ceremony." ~ *Magick in Theory and Practice*

The Ace of Swords is the Root of the Powers of Air. Will and Love combine to wield the sword of Reason. The sword is marked with 93/93, and the Greek words for Love and Will, "Agape" and "Thelema." This card is mapped to Vau, the Son, third letter of the divine name YHVH and the combination of the fire of the Father and the water of the Mother. Here is the invoked force of the Son as opposed to the natural force of the Ace of Wands and the Father. This is the mighty sword of the intellect, the weapon that pure thought can wield, and the seed of the classical element of Air. It is a card of prescience. Raised upward it invokes the spiritual crown, and points at Lamed as the arbitrator of divine authority. Aleph, its counterpart is hidden behind the blade. These are Justice, or Adjustment, and the Fool in partnership. Pointed downward it evokes evil, and thus the intellect is a potent weapon that needs to be rightly wielded. If so rightly held, it brings clarity, and cuts away darkness.

The Seed

The seed grows the root of the element of Air, invoking the powers of reason. This is intellect, as a tool of justice. The goal is the power to Know.

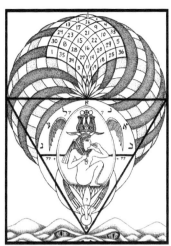

Hè Final
The Ace of Disks

Root of the Powers of Earth

With the Princess of Disks as its throne, rules the quadrant of space for Aries-Taurus-Gemini, and the area of Europe and Africa

Color: White, flecked gold

ACE OF DISKS
ROOT OF THE POWERS OF EARTH

This is Hè final of the Tetragrammaton; the Daughter and the Root of the Powers of Earth. The Daughter resides in Malkuth, the Gate, and the sphere of the sum total of creation. This Ace of the final letter of YHVH corresponds to the final of the four powers of the Sphinx: To know, to will, to dare . . . and, to keep silence. The following quote from Tao Te Ching will help demonstrate the illustration of this card:

Those who know do not talk. Those who talk do not know. Keep your mouth closed. Guard your senses. Temper your sharpness. Simplify your problems. Mask your brightness. Be at one with the dust of the Earth. This is primal union. He who has achieved this state Is unconcerned with friends and enemies, With good and harm, with honor and disgrace. This therefore is the highest state of man. ~ *Tao Te Ching 56*

The card shows Babalon and the beast conjoined: 666 as the magic square of the sun combined with 156 (77+ (7+7)/7 +77). The card shows a whirling solar disk, illustrating the combination of Sun and Earth. The card is materiality in all senses.

The Earth Ace card shows the babe in the egg of blue.[17] Harpocrates of Hoor-Paar-Kraat, Heka; the god of silence and the passive twin of Horus. This god is associated with Kether or the Fool, and the egg of blue with the Mother

---

17   The Ace of Disks is often used as the signature card of the creator. In place of a signature, this card has visual ties to the Sabian symbol for the degree of my ascendant, Aquarius 7 "A child is born of an eggshell." Thus the babe in the egg of blue does double duty here. It was conceived and sketched on my solar return.

and Daughter formula of the Earth Ace. Harpocrates is also the mystical absorption of the work of creation, the Hè final of the Tetragrammaton.[18]

Earth's child has not yet been born. The egg sits upon a lotus of the Nile. The Nile, according to Crowley, symbolizes the Father, fertilizing Egypt, the lotus and Yoni. The Nile is also the home of Sebek the crocodile who follows and threatens Harpocrates. Sebek can be seen hidden in the hills of Malkuth; the perils of incarnation. Yet Harpocrates is considered to be the symbol of Dawn breaking upon the Nile, or the psychological process of wakening. Sebek the Devourer is also the creator. As part of the Hé final process of the magical formula of the Tetragrammaton, Sebek transmutes Hé final to the Yod of YHVH. Crowley says of the crocodile in the Fool card "to initiates, this crocodile helps to determine the spiritual meaning of the card as the return to the original Qabalistic zero; it is the "Hé final" process in the magical formula of the Tetragrammaton. By a flick of the wrist, she can be transmuted to reappear as the original Yod, and repeat the whole process from the beginning."[19] Reflect on this in conjunction with the understanding of the connection of this Ace with the Princess of Disks as the throne of the Ace of Disks. Both are marked with the name of Babalon.

The Seed
The seed grows the root of the element of Earth, the birth of action in the world of matter and materiality. This is wealth, and incarnation. Yet remember the connection of matter with Spirit, for here it begins. The goal is the power to Keep Silent and to take action with discernment.

18   Book of Thoth pg 62
19   Book of Thoth pg 63

The Circle

The Decans

The thirty six small cards each represent one spoke or ten degrees of the 360 degree circle of the zodiac. This is the universe bounded and defined, though it in truth is infinite, as Nuit "she, the circumference, is nowhere found." These thirty six cards are also the seventy-two names of God; a day and a night angel are assigned to each one.

The small cards of the tarot are defined by a complex interaction between the sephira as expressed through the four elements and the four worlds, combined with the decan of the zodiac and its planetary ruler. Liber Theta describes the four elemental associations of fire, water, air and earth as being expressed on the same horizontal plane, while the four worlds they correspond to of Atziluth, Briah, Yetzirah, Assiah as being stacked worlds of the vertical plane.

The Two through the Ten of the four suits comprise thirty six cards that correlate to the thirty six decans of the zodiac. The decans are the division of the 360 degrees of the zodiac into ten degree segments, with each astrological sign having 30 degrees or three sections of ten degrees. The first or ascending decan, or from 0–10 degrees of a sign, represents the inrush or inception of the sign's energy. The middle or succedent decan, from 11–20 degrees, has the sign most firmly established in its identity, while the final or cadent decan from 21–30 degrees shows the sign's fullness heading for dissipation. Each decan is assigned a planetary ruler. Each of the signs and each of the planets has a corresponding trump. These trumps were deconstructed and combined reconstructed together with the sephira, element, card title, and meaning to form the small card.

The tarot Twos, Threes, and Fours are the first, second, and third decans of the Cardinal signs. The Fives, Sixes and Sevens are the first, second and third decans of the Fixed Signs, and the Eights, Nines and Tens are the first, second and third decans of the Mutable signs. In the following sections more will be explained about what Cardinal, Fixed and Mutable might mean, but it basically mirrors the descriptions of the decanic sections, with Cardinal being a force of inception, Fixed being an established force, and Mutable a culminating and dissolving force. Cardinal signs initiate, Fixed signs maintain, and Mutable signs change. We could simplify this as the cycle of begin, continue and end.

Each decanic segment of the sign is said to be ruled by, or influenced by, a planet. While there is more than one system for assigning the planets, for this purpose the planets are assigned according to an ancient astrological system of Chaldean order, or order of the planets based on relative orbital speed of motion. Thus the order is Saturn, Jupiter, Mars, Sun, Venus, Mercury, Moon and repeats. Putting the Sun at the center, the order also shows the distance of the planets from the Sun, and the Moon from the Earth (The Sun switches place with Earth in the sequence.) If an earth centered perspective is taken this shows the arrangement of the planetary spheres.

There are also other nifty tricks like connecting the circular ordered planets with a septagram to derive the order of the related days of the week, or assigning all of the planets that orbit the sun to the number of their associated sephira, to see that when totaled, they come to 36, the number of small cards. But these mathematical wonders are a digression. For the purposes of a discussion on the small cards, it suffices to know that each decan is assigned a planetary ruler. When we say that the first decan of Taurus is ruled by Mercury, we do not mean that Taurus is ruled by Mercury. Taurus is ruled by Venus in general. But to that specific decan is given the overlay of the planet Mercury.

To begin with the Two of Wands as an example, this card is a Two and thus a cardinal sign. It is a Wand, and thus the cardinal sign of the element fire, or Aries. Note that as the Twos, Threes and Fours represent the 3 decans of each of the cardinal signs, the Two of Wands is the first decan of Aries, with the Three of Wands being the middle decan and the Four of Wands the last decan. The Two of Wands, or the first decan of Aries, is said to be "ruled by" the planet Mars. If we were then to follow the Chaldean order of the planets as listed above, this would make the Three of Wands or the middle decan of Aries ruled by the Sun, and the final decan, the Four of Wands, ruled by Venus.

Note that many tarot texts when referring to the planetary rulerships of the decans, will erroneously refer to them as a "planet-in-sign," which is not exactly correct. The Two of Wands is not "Mars in Aries"; rather it is the "first decan of Aries, ruled by Mars." While to some extent this is semantics, it is an important distinction to avoid thinking of the tarot attributions as functioning identical to the way a planet in a sign would function in the birth chart. The tarot cards are more complex than that, each being a combination of influences of the number and its related Sephira on the Tree of Life, the specific decan or position within the astrological sign, and the ruler of said decan, and what happens when they intersect. To go back to the example of the Two of Wands, it can be broken into its parts. It is a Two, so like all Twos, Threes and Fours it is a cardinal or initiating sign. As a Two, it is the first decan of a cardinal sign, so one might say it has an additional quality of initiating. As a Two it is also assigned to the sephira of Chokmah on the Tree of Life, a fiery and male influence, and also an initiator of sorts, being the first spark below Kether, again an initiating quality of force. As a Wand, it is the fire sign of Aries, and as the first decan of Aries it is ruled by the planet of Mars, which also rules the sign of Aries itself and is again a fiery male force. Deconstructed like this, one can see that the individual parts that make up this card share a similarity and have an affinity for each other. With all of these qualities of a fiery, initiating, male force, is it any wonder the card is called "Dominion" in the positive sense of the word as sovereignty? It is a combination of Aries (The Emperor) with Mars (The Tower) in the sephira of Chokmah.

FIRST DECAN OF ARIES: RULED BY MARS

THE EMPEROR

THE TOWER

TWO OF WANDS
DOMINION

THE TWO OF WANDS: DOMINION

One will see though as we journey through the descriptions of the small cards that the parts deconstructed are sometimes more disparate and less compatible. This is the reason why certain cards with seemingly favorable planet and sign compositions can be so negative, as they may not function well where they have been placed on the Tree of Life according to the energies of the sephira.

In Tabula Mundi, we shall see how the small cards take this process of deconstruction to a visible degree. The designs thus serve as a mnemonic for the related trumps and their energies. But in addition to the related trumps, there is an influence from the sephira or number of the card. For this I did not use imagery for the trump of the planet a sephira was associated with. I kept it pure to the two trumps of the decan. But the way the images were interpreted into the meanings of the card was most definitely influenced by the planetary "flavor" of the sephira, as all except Chokmah have a planet assigned. (Chokmah as the sephira of first force is assigned the entire zodiac.) So for example, all of the tarot Threes have the additional influence of Saturn, for the sephira of Binah, regardless of what sign and decan ruler is assigned. But the tarot Threes won't draw images directly from the Universe card, unless they also happen to have the rulership of Saturn over the decan as in the Three of Swords.

To use the Ten of Disks for another example, which is the last decan of Virgo ruled by Mercury, I've drawn from the imagery of the trumps the Hermit (Virgo) and the Magus (Mercury). As a Ten though the meaning of the card also has the character of Malkuth, which gives the influence of Earth. This plays out with its mythology around the Hermit as psychopomp, and Persephone and the descent below as well as the warning to take care not to cling to wealth, but the card does not directly draw from the imagery of Earth's card, which is also the Universe, as the Universe does double duty as the trump of both Saturn and Earth.

When exploring the Minor Arcana of Tabula Mundi, be sure to compare each card to the two related Major Arcana, as finding and pondering the shared images and similarities, and considering the Minors as the combined energies of the two Majors, will yield much as to their meanings. It may also be an interesting exercise to compare all of the cards of a sign, or all of the cards of a certain planet. For example, you could compare all of the cards of the sign of Aries, and see how the planetary rulerships affect the decans. In this case, that would be the trump of the Emperor placed above the Two, Three, and Four of Wands, with the trumps that rule the decans (Tower, Sun, Empress) beneath each Minor. Then you could add the court cards of the decans, which in this example would be the Queen of Wands as the main court of the sign

THE HERMIT ℞

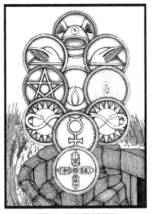

TEN OF DISKS
WEALTH

THE MAGUS ☿

THE TEN OF DISCS: WEALTH

who takes the first two decans and the Two and Three of Wands. The court card for the Four of Wands would be the Prince of Disks, who is mainly of the following sign, Taurus, but picks up the stitch as his shadow card. In this way, your knowledge of tarot will teach you astrology, and vice versa.

Alternatively, you could explore all of the cards of any planet. Using Mars as an example, you would place the Tower, with its related cards beneath it. Mars actually has six related Minor Arcana, while the other planetary trumps have five, since Mars gets repeated at the start of the vernal equinox and end of the winter in the Chaldean planetary order. So the cards of Mars you would place beneath the Tower are the Two of Wands, the Nine of Swords, the Seven of Wands, the Five of Cups, the Three of Disks, and the Ten of Cups. Note that like the Tower, the cards all have the glyph of Mars on them, making them easy to find. It is that pointy rather phallic erect looking glyph, perfectly appropriate for Mars and cards of the Tower.

As a reference for the decans and their rulerships, the Sun card in Tabula Mundi actually shows the Chaldean order of the planets assigned to the signs and their thirty six decans in a ring surrounding the Sun. This not only fits with the meaning of the Sun card but also serves as a visual reference illustrating how the astrological signs, the planets, and the four suits interact.

♈	**Cards of Aries:** The Emperor – Zodiacal Trump of Aries Two of Wands – Dominion – Aries decan 1 ruled by Mars Three of Wands – Virtue – Aries decan 2 ruled by Sun Four of Wands – Completion – Aries decan 3 ruled by Venus Queen of Wands (decans 1 and 2) Prince of Disks (shadow only, decan 3)
♉	**Cards of Taurus:** The Hierophant – Zodiacal Trump of Taurus Five of Disks – Worry – Taurus decan 1 ruled by Mercury Six of Disks – Success – Taurus decan 2 ruled by the Moon Seven of Disks – Failure – Taurus decan 3 ruled by Saturn Prince of Disks (decans 1 and 2) Knight of Swords (shadow only, decan 3)
♊	**Cards of Gemini:** The Lovers – Zodiacal Trump of Gemini Eight of Swords – Interference – Gemini decan 1 ruled by Jupiter Nine of Swords – Cruelty – Gemini decan 2 ruled by Mars Ten of Swords – Ruin – Gemini decan 3 ruled by the Sun Knight of Swords (decans 1 and 2) Queen of Cups (shadow only, decan 3)
♋	**Cards of Cancer:** The Chariot – Zodiacal Trump of Cancer Two of Cups – Love – Cancer decan 1 ruled by Venus Three of Cups – Abundance – Cancer decan 2 ruled by Mercury Four of Cups – Luxury – Cancer decan 3 ruled by the Moon Queen of Cups (decans 1 and 2) Prince of Wands (shadow only, decan 3)
♌	**Cards of Leo:** Lust (Strength) – Zodiacal Trump of Leo Five of Wands – Strife – Leo decan 1 ruled by Saturn Six of Wands – Victory – Leo decan 2 ruled by Jupiter Seven of Wands – Valour – Leo decan 3 ruled by Mars Prince of Wands (decans 1 and 2) Knight of Disks (shadow only, decan 3)

♍	### Cards of Virgo: The Hermit – Zodiacal Trump of Virgo Eight of Disks – Prudence – Virgo decan 1 ruled by the Sun Nine of Disks – Gain – Virgo decan 2 ruled by Venus Ten of Disks – Wealth – Virgo decan 3 ruled by Mercury Knight of Disks (decans 1 and 2) Queen of Swords (shadow only, decan 3)
♎	### Cards of Libra: Adjustment (Justice) – Zodiacal Trump of Libra Two of Swords – Peace – Libra decan 1 ruled by the Moon Three of Swords – Sorrow – Libra decan 2 ruled by Saturn Four of Swords – Truce – Libra decan 3 ruled by Jupiter Queen of Swords (decans 1 and 2) Prince of Cups (shadow only, decan 3)
♏	### Cards of Scorpio: Death – Zodiacal Trump of Scorpio Five of Cups – Disappointment – Scorpio decan 1 ruled by Mars Six of Cups – Pleasure – Scorpio decan 2 ruled by the Sun Seven of Cups – Debauch – Scorpio decan 3 ruled by Venus Prince of Cups (decans 1 and 2) Knight of Wands (shadow only, decan 3)
♐	### Cards of Sagittarius: Art (Temperance) – Zodiacal Trump of Sagittarius Eight of Wands – Swiftness – Sagittarius decan 1 ruled by Mercury Nine of Wands – Strength – Sagittarius decan 2 ruled by the Moon Ten of Wands – Oppression – Sagittarius decan 3 ruled by Saturn Knight of Wands (decans 1 and 2) Queen of Disks (shadow only, decan 3)
♑	### Cards of Capricorn: The Devil – Zodiacal Trump of Capricorn Two of Disks – Change – Capricorn decan 1 ruled by Jupiter Three of Disks – Work – Capricorn decan 2 ruled by Mars Four of Disks – Power – Capricorn decan 3 ruled by the Sun Queen of Disks (decans 1 and 2) Prince of Swords (shadow only, decan 3)

≈	**Cards of Aquarius:** The Star – Zodiacal Trump of Aquarius Five of Swords – Defeat – Aquarius decan 1 ruled by Venus Six of Swords – Science – Aquarius decan 2 ruled by Mercury Seven of Swords – Futility – Aquarius decan 3 ruled by the Moon Prince of Swords (decans 1 and 2) Knight of Cups (shadow only, decan 3)
)(	**Cards of Pisces:** The Moon – Zodiacal Trump of Pisces Eight of Cups – Indolence – Pisces decan 1 ruled by Saturn Nine of Cups – Happiness – Pisces decan 2 ruled by Jupiter Ten of Cups – Satiety – Pisces decan 3 ruled by Mars Knight of Cups (decans 1 and 2) Queen of Wands (shadow only, decan 3)
♄	**Cards of Saturn:** The Universe – Planetary Trump of Saturn Seven of Disks – Failure – Taurus decan 3 ruled by Saturn Five of Wands – Strife – Leo decan 1 ruled by Saturn Three of Swords – Sorrow – Libra decan 2 ruled by Saturn Ten of Wands – Oppression – Sagittarius decan 3 ruled by Saturn Eight of Cups – Indolence – Pisces decan 1 ruled by Saturn
♃	**Cards of Jupiter:** Fortune – Planetary Trump of Jupiter Eight of Swords – Interference – Gemini decan 1 ruled by Jupiter Six of Wands – Victory – Leo decan 2 ruled by Jupiter Four of Swords – Truce – Libra decan 3 ruled by Jupiter Two of Disks – Change – Capricorn decan 1 ruled by Jupiter Nine of Cups – Happiness – Pisces decan 2 ruled by Jupiter
♂	**Cards of Mars:** The Tower – Planetary Trump of Mars Two of Wands – Dominion – Aries decan 1 ruled by Mars Nine of Swords – Cruelty – Gemini decan 2 ruled by Mars Seven of Wands – Valour – Leo decan 3 ruled by Mars Five of Cups – Disappointment – Scorpio decan 1 ruled by Mars Three of Disks – Work – Capricorn decan 2 ruled by Mars Ten of Cups – Satiety – Pisces decan 3 ruled by Mars

Cards of the Sun:

The Sun – Planetary Trump of the Sun

Three of Wands – Virtue – Aries decan 2 ruled by Sun

Ten of Swords – Ruin – Gemini decan 3 ruled by the Sun

Eight of Disks – Prudence – Virgo decan 1 ruled by the Sun

Six of Cups – Pleasure – Scorpio decan 2 ruled by the Sun

Four of Disks – Power – Capricorn decan 3 ruled by the Sun

Cards of Venus:

The Empress – Planetary Trump of Venus

Four of Wands – Completion – Aries decan 3 ruled by Venus

Two of Cups – Love – Cancer decan 1 ruled by Venus

Nine of Disks – Gain – Virgo decan 2 ruled by Venus

Seven of Cups – Debauch – Scorpio decan 3 ruled by Venus

Five of Swords – Defeat – Aquarius decan 1 ruled by Venus

Cards of Mercury:

The Magus – Planetary Trump of Mercury

Five of Disks – Worry – Taurus decan 1 ruled by Mercury

Three of Cups – Abundance – Cancer decan 2 ruled by Mercury

Ten of Disks – Wealth – Virgo decan 3 ruled by Mercury

Eight of Wands – Swiftness – Sagittarius decan 1 ruled by Mercury

Six of Swords – Science – Aquarius decan 2 ruled by Mercury

Cards of the Moon:

The Priestess – Planetary Trump of the Moon

Six of Disks – Success – Taurus decan 2 ruled by the Moon

Four of Cups – Luxury – Cancer decan 3 ruled by the Moon

Two of Swords – Peace – Libra decan 1 ruled by the Moon

Nine of Wands – Strength – Sagittarius decan 2 ruled by the Moon

Seven of Swords – Futility – Aquarius decan 3 ruled by the Moon

The following diagram of the Tree of Life gives the planetary correspondences:

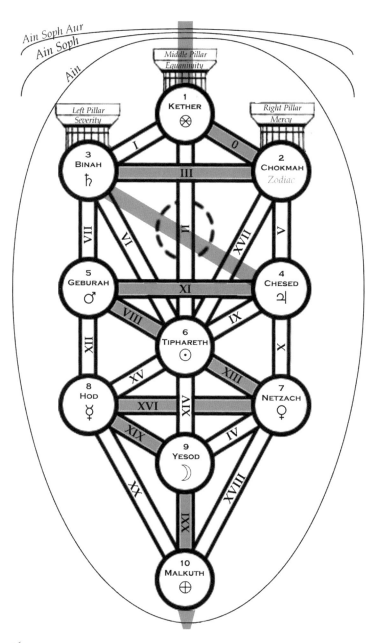

The Cardinal Spokes of the Wheel

The tarot Twos, Threes and Fours represent the first, second and third decans of the cardinal signs, and the stations of Chokmah, Binah, and Chesed.

The Cardinal signs (Aries, Cancer, Libra and Capricorn) are also often called the angular signs. If the zodiac was placed on the wheel of a horoscope chart starting with the first degree of Aries on the rising point of the horizon, these signs would be on the angles of the chart, the cross quarters or cardinal directions of the compass show the ascendant or rising at Aries, the descendant or setting at its opposite sign Libra, Capricorn at the midheaven or zenith, and its opposite sign Cancer at the imum coeli or nadir.

The Cardinal signs initiate the seasons. The word *cardinal* is based on the Latin word for hinge, as they indicate the turning point of the season. Around March 20th, the first day of spring in the northern hemisphere, is also zero degrees of Aries. These signs are thus sometimes referred to as the equinox signs (Aries/Libra) or Solstice signs (Capricorn/Cancer).[20] Cardinal signs have the energy of inauguration. That is to say, they are initiators and start things. They are quick and vigorous, aggressive and can be domineering, controlling or manipulating. They don't like to take second place—it is foreign to them!

Within the Twos, Threes and Fours, the Twos are the first decan and so can be considered the most cardinal of the cardinal cards as they are the initiation of the initiators. Their essence is pure and swift. With the Threes, the Cardinal force is established in the middle decan of the sign. The Fours are the culmination of the cardinal signs. While fully expressed and seemingly stable, the force is dissipating as the disruption of the Fives is on the horizon.

On the Tree of Life, the Twos correspond to Chokmah, the sephira of *Wisdom*, or the first force and the Father or King. As Chokmah is assigned to the Zodiac itself rather than a particular planet, it is a pure force and

20   With apologies to those in the southern hemisphere, if a mention of any seasonal
      designation is indicated, the northern hemisphere orientation will be the default
      due the orientation of the author.

thus the Twos represent the element first appearing in an uninfluenced and uncontaminated condition. With the Two, the element makes its first real appearance from the possibility contained in the Ace. Each Two manifests with simplicity; expressing a duality; either partnership or polarity.

The Threes correspond to Binah and the Queen, and are of the sephira called *Understanding*, or the first form, and have the flavor of Saturn. Things have triangulated and here the element goes beyond its first appearance, and has a will towards form. Binah accepts what Chokmah offers and gestates it. The initial appearance expressed in the Two has been fertilized; a potential has now been set into motion.

The Fours correspond to Chesed, called *Mercy*, and have the additional influence of Jupiter or law. The Fours are a unique case. As the last of the cardinal trinity they are the culmination and dissipation of the cardinal energies. But they are cardinal and also the first sephira below the supernal trinity of Kether, Binah, and Chokmah, and thus function almost with the energy of Aces; the Aces of the more mundane world. They show the element fully formed in realization, a matter settled, and they often come with a blessing of sorts. I like to think of them as a plateau. While a solid manifestation and seemingly stable, nothing stands still and so while the established thing is in a state of completion it should not necessarily be considered enduring as there is also the possibility of future disruption by the Five.

The Fixed Spokes of the Wheel

The tarot Fives, Sixes, and Sevens represent the first, second and third decans of the Fixed signs, and the sephiroth of Geburah, Tiphareth, and Netzach.

The fixed signs of Leo, Scorpio, Aquarius, and Taurus, are known as the Kerubic signs that are central to their seasons and hold down the universe. You may recognize these as the foundational corners of the Universe card, and the Royal Stars of the Watchers. Being in the middle of the triplicity of the Cardinal, Fixed, Mutable trio, they contain the point of the fulcrum and thus great power in that they are central, and firmly established in their signs.

At this point in the year, the seasons that began with the equinox or solstice are now well on their way. Fixed signs are determined and potent. They carry on the energies of the onrush started with the cardinal. At this point in the zodiacal cycle, the signs have great strength.

The Fives, of Geburah, off the middle pillar and below the Supernals, have the influence of the planet Mars. Mars being a warlike planet combined with Geburah's position on the Tree of Life has a disruptive effect on the previous mundane manifestation of the Four, which can be necessary though disruption is often unpleasant. Geburah is the sephira of *Severity*, and conflict. It is severity requiring strength. *Fiat justitia ruat caelum is* a Latin legal term meaning "Let justice be done though the heavens fall." This sums up the energy of this sphere.

Tiphareth has the influence of the Sun and the Sixes of Tiphareth express the best possible configuration of the suit. It is the Son, so both the child and the future King. Here the element has unfolded into a complex expression while still remaining balanced. Tiphareth is central to its grouping by zodiacal sign, at the heart of the Tree of Life as well as drawing from the Supernals. Tiphareth also gets more paths fed into it than any other sephira, making it incredibly rich for study. It has a direct connection to every sephira except Malkuth, the Son's exiled bride. Within the numbered sephira, Tiphareth corresponds to the center and point of balance and is the sephira of *Beauty* and harmony. It is the point of connection between the ideal or higher self aspects of the upper sephiroth, and the lower sephiroth of personality.

The Sevens of Netzach are on the other side of the middle pillar from Geburah and are associated with Venus, Mars' natural pair. Thus they function as a pair with and a remedy for the Fives and seek to balance each other. They form another natural pairing with the Eights at the foot of the other pillar of the Tree; where the Sevens are instinctual the Eights are logical. The Sevens are hard to grasp mentally, as they function on another level far from the mental. It is a level that artists tap into; one that is visceral and non verbal. This is the fiery sephira of *Victory* and what is required to attain it in each suit. One can expect though that as they are off the middle pillar and even lower on the tree that they are imbalanced, and the degenerate tendencies of the Sevens are usually due to personal weakness. The Sevens are "purification by fire" and require an action to transform them into Victory.

The grouping of the decanates of the fixed signs mapped with the sephira illustrates how pivotal this section of the Tree is. I was reminded of that constantly while doing the artwork for the decans of the fixed signs, and noticed how the cards of Tiphareth were affected by their surrounding cards and vice versa. When contemplating the Fives, Sixes and Sevens it is useful to see them in context with each other, and to see the Sixes as the fulcrum of balance between the others.

The Mutable Spokes of the Wheel

The tarot Eights, Nines, and Tens represent the first, second and third decans of the Mutable signs, and the sephiroth of Hod, Yesod, and Malkuth.

The mutable signs are Sagittarius, Pisces, Gemini, and Virgo. These come along last in the solar cycle of their respective seasons, and show the force that first began in the cardinal and then strengthened in the fixed now mutating as the force prepares for entry to a new season. As the final mode, Mutable signs morph and transmute things in order for new beginnings to occur. The sephira of these decans are the lowest of the Tree of Life. Thus the pure element that was embryonic in the Ace, first manifest in the Twos, Threes and Fours, and challenged and strengthened in the Fives, Sixes, and Sevens, is now in its most dilute form.

The Eights correspond to Hod, the sephira of *Glory* with the influence of Mercury. They are opposite the Sevens on the Tree, and equally imbalanced, but where the Sevens are non verbal, the Eights have the mental qualities of Mercury. Because with the Eights, the element is starting to dissipate on the pillar of Form, the Eights can either support and direct the element or burden it, depending on their associated zodiacal and planetary attributions.

Yesod, called *Foundation*, is the home of the four Nines, and has the influence of the Moon. The element is at its penultimate expression or crystallization of idea and expression. The lunar magnetism here shows emotional or psychological patterns that have reached a state of development that is now fixed for either beneficial or detrimental purposes. Though they are low on the Tree, they are the *Foundation* for the entire Tree in the middle pillar and thus for the most part are stable, with the exception being the Nine of the suit of Swords. In Yesod, the suit of mind and reason is taken over by the lunar primitive instincts.

The four Tens correspond to the sephira Malkuth, the *Kingdom*, the ultimate expression and culmination of the suit. This is where the adept learns discernment and wise discrimination. It is associated with Earth or the entire material plane of the elements. At this point the element is ready to transmute to the next world or elemental Ace below (yet another illustration of the maxim Kether is in Malkuth). Here is the complete unfolding of the suit. At the stage of the Tens, the elemental force is so dissipated and ready for mutation, that each is about to pass into a lower form. The exception is the final card of the lesser arcana, the Ten of Disks, which as the last card can only begin again at the top of the cycle.

Velle, To Will

The Wands

ר

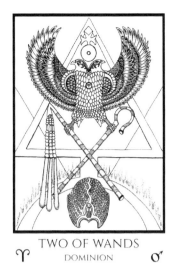

TWO OF WANDS

Lord of Dominion

First decan of Aries, ruled by Mars

Chokmah of Atziluth/Fire

Trumps: Emperor, Tower

Knight Scale for Chokmah: Pure Soft Blue, plus the colors scales of the related trumps

TWO OF WANDS
♈ DOMINION ♂

The Lord of Dominion combines energies of the Emperor, card of the cardinal sign Aries, and the Tower, card of Mars which is also the traditional ruler of Aries. It is in Chokmah of Atziluth, the sephira of the first force and of Kings of the element of fire and the archetypal world of the godhead. The force of fire has been seeded. It is clearly a very male card of rulership and as such is replete with symbols of its namesake, Dominion. Here falls the very first spontaneous beginning of fire and the spring equinox in the northern hemisphere.

Tabula Mundi's Two of Wands shows the double headed eagle, done in an Egyptian falcon motif as a suggestion of Horus. The double headed red eagle is a symbol of the Emperor and is often shown as the emblem on his shield as in the Thoth deck, and on the Tabula Mundi Emperor with a single head making up part of the compass of the 'compass and square' on the card. In alchemy, the red eagle represents the red tincture, fiery and with the solar nature of gold. In heraldry, the double eagle looks East and West, representing rule in all directions, and authority in both secular and religious matters.

Above is shown the orb surmounted by a cross, another typical symbol of the Emperor's dominion over the earth, the four directions, and the quadrants of heaven. The crossed Wands clutched by the Eagle are shown as an Egyptian crook and flail, symbols of kingship, the pharaoh's authority, and the functions of a king, to both shepherd and punish; to rule. In the masculine Twos, the wands and swords, they are almost universally portrayed in the Saltire, or crossed X position, a posture signifying resolution and resolve.

This card also draws from the energy of the Tower. Many Tower cards show the top of the tower as a crown. Below, as a reminder that War and the martial qualities of the Tower are present, is the Blue War Crown or Khepresh of Egypt, a military helmet worn both in battle and ceremonially, to celebrate the God King and his victories. It is blue and decorated with golden solar disks or "storms on the surface of Mars," and topped with the uraeus cobra, yet another symbol of divinity, authority, sovereignty and claim over the land. This crown was often worn in military representations but also was said to be an evocation of the pharaoh's divine power or godlike stature on earth. Interestingly, this crown is sometimes called the Blue Crown of Mars, as its phallic shape is said to be a symbolic representation of Mars with a flared debris ring around its girth distorted by close proximity to Earth. The crowns of Egypt are said to be depictions of, or worn by, the god-forms often represented by planets. Behind the design, a flaming symbol of Mars reinforces the symbolism.

The Augur: The crook & flail; the double eagle, the Blue War Crown of Mars. *Affirmative will makes a conquest.*

Deck Comparisons

In the Rider Waite Smith deck, the Two of Wands shows a man with two wands, looking out over his kingdom and holding the orb surmounted by a cross. The Thoth card shows two fiery crossed Tibetan ceremonial daggers. Similarly, the Rosetta Two of Wands shows two daggers in the form of a *was*-sceptre and vajra, suggesting the crook and flail and in shapes symbolic of the Ram and the glyph of Mars. Tabula Mundi shares the orb surmounted with a cross with the RWS, and the crossed wands of the Thoth and Rosetta in Tabula Mundi take the shape of the crook and flail. To these are added the double headed eagle, the Blue War crown of Mars, and the glyph of Mars with ascending flames. All of these cards of the first decan of Aries share the nature of Chokmah of Fire, the first force demonstrating the will towards conquest.

THree of wands

THREE OF WANDS
VIRTUE

Lord of Virtue (Established Strength)

Middle decan of Aries, ruled by the Sun

Binah of Atziluth/Fire

Trumps: Emperor, Sun

Knight Scale for Binah: Crimson, plus the colors scales of the related trumps

The Lord of Virtue is the middle decan of the cardinal sign Aries, and combines the energies of the Emperor with the Sun, in Binah, the sephira of first form and of Queens, with the element of Fire. The seed of fire shot forth by the Two has quickened in the womb and there is new growth. The seeds have sprouted and symbolic spring is established. The male essences of the Emperor and the Sun have been contained within the feminine sephira and proved fruitful. Binah, being Saturnine, gives form to the element. As the central decan of the sign, strength or virtue has been fully established. Virtue here is in the sense of righteousness, honor, dignity and purity; from the Latin *virtus* meaning "valor, merit, moral perfection." *Vir* as the root of words like virility have a masculine connotation, as do the Sun and the Emperor. These masculine forces have found the perfect container in the sphere of feminine Binah.

The Tabula Mundi three wands are done in a Greco-Roman style. The central wand is the caduceus of the Sun topped by the ram horns of the Emperor. The caduceus is a wand said to have the power to wake the sleeping, and is symbolic of health as evidenced by its adoption as a symbol of the medical profession. The two flanking wands are topped by the pine cone symbol from the Sun card symbolic of the pineal gland of the brain.

The ram horn is often used as a symbol of strength and fertility. In Egypt, ram gods were associated with virility, war and the soul of the sun. Amun-Ra, a solar creator god and king of the gods, was often depicted with the head of a ram. Pharaohs' called themselves "beloved of Amun," referring to the blessings of their fertility. In West Africa, the Dwennimen, a symbol made from stylized ram horns, signifies the combination of humility with strength, a virtuous stance.

The pine cone is symbolic of human enlightenment. The pineal gland referred to by the pine cone symbolism, is a photoreceptive gland of the brain that regulates our seasonal rhythms and is associated with the third eye, said by Descartes to be the "principal seat of the soul."

The three wands are connected together by the solar analemma, the infinity symbol created by the plotting of the position of the sun in the sky at a certain time of day (as noon) at one locale measured throughout the year. This creates the shape of a figure eight and indicates the infinite strength of the undying Sun and its ever repeating and undeviating path. Behind the wands is a geometric design suggesting solar flares.

The Augur: The Thrysus wand, the caduceus, the ram horns. *The strength inherent in virtue has been fully established and a new cycle of creativity ensues.*

Deck Comparisons

The RWS Three of Wands shows a robed man holding one wand, with two wands planted behind him, as he gazes toward the distant horizon. The Thoth card shows three Lotus wands against a stylized backdrop of radiating solar flames, and glyphs of the Sun and Aries. The Rosetta card has a central wand with an opened lotus on the top surmounted by a rising sun and a solar symbol on the bottom, surrounded by two wands with lotus buds on the top and ram horns on the bottom, joined by the analemma. Similarly it is backed by the outwardly radiating symbolic solar flames. Tabula Mundi's card has a central lotus wand as caduceus, topped by ram horns and flanked by Thrysus wands, with the solar disk and analemma. All show the themes of the middle decan of Aries, Binah of Fire demonstrating the established solar forces in gestation.

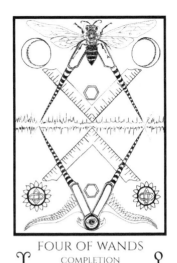

Four of Wands

Lord of Completion (Perfected Work)

Last decan of Aries, ruled by Venus

Chesed of Atziluth/Fire

Trumps: Emperor, Empress

Knight Scale for Chesed: Deep Violet, plus the colors scales of the related trumps

FOUR OF WANDS
♈   COMPLETION   ♀

The Lord of Completion is the final decan of the cardinal sign Aries. It combines the energies of the Emperor with the Empress, a perfect pairing, in Chesed, the sephira of manifestation and realization; thus, the work is perfected and brought to completion. The element of fire seeded in the two, gestated and quickened in the three, is now born fully in the four. The Will is manifest. As a four, it is complete and solid, and stable for the time being, though as the final decan of Aries the Aries energy is in its final stage.

In the Tabula Mundi Four of Wands, the four wands are formed of two compasses and two squares. The eagle-headed compass and square from the Emperor card has been complimented by its perfect reflection in the form of a compass and square topped by the Empress' bee symbolism. This association of the compass and square with the male and the female or the square and the circle, is quite ancient. In Chinese mythology, the first sovereigns were called Fu Xi and Nuwa, the only survivors of a great flood. They are depicted entwined, with Fu Xi, the male, holding the carpenter's square and Nuwa holding the compass, taking the measure of the universe at the founding of the new world and the dawning of a new age. In the bible, these would be Joseph and Mary. They symbolize a perfect pairing and the duality of the universe; alpha and omega and the interaction between yang and yin that underlies cosmic unity. The square represents earth and the compass heaven. This mythology is a precursor to the Masonic depiction of the compass and square. Duncan's Masonic Monitor of 1866 explains them as: "The Square, to square our actions; the compasses, to circumscribe and keep us within bounds with all mankind."

The eagle and the bee are often paired symbolically, as on the coat of arms of Napoleon I. The eagle, emblem of the Emperor, signifies military victory while the bee, symbol of the Empress, signifies the Empire. The eagle, as Jupiter's bird, is fitting in the sephira of Chesed. The day after his coronation was completed Napoleon had an eagle placed at the top of the shaft of every flagpole. The bee was chosen as the oldest symbol of the sovereigns of France. Only Napoleon, his Empress, his hand-picked high officers, and recipients of the Legion of Honor, were allowed to wear the bee.

Both the eagle and the bee are symbols used in freemasonry. The great seal of the United States has on one side, the eagle, with the pyramid on the other. The mottos "out of many, one" and "Providence favors our undertakings" and "A new order of the ages" seem to compliment the mythology of the symbols and stories of this card. In heraldry, the eagle is for courage, strength perspicacity and immortality; the king of the skies. The bee in heraldry signifies diligence, indefatigable effort, creativity and well-governed industry. In Tabula Mundi the eagle and the bee perform similar functions symbolically to the ram and the dove, for Martial and Venusian qualities.

The Augur: Fu Xi and Nuwa, square and compass, bee and eagle. *The Will is manifest in the perfect pairing of force and form bringing order and fulfillment.*

Deck comparison:

The RWS Four of Wands shows what appears to be a wedding, with a couple carrying bouquets and wreaths under a garlanded archway. The Thoth Four of Wands has the four wands arranged in a circular design, each with one end having the head of a ram for Aries, and the other end the dove of Venus. The Rosetta has the four wands made up from the glyphs of Aries and Venus and arranged in a mandala, with the ram and dove flanking. Tabula Mundi's card shows Fu Xi and Nuwa as the bee and eagle of the reflected square and compass. The last decan of Aries shows Chesed of Fire, where the will born in the Two and gestated in the Three is now manifest in the marriage of the perfect pairing of solar and lunar forces.

five of wands

FIVE OF WANDS
♌   STRIFE   ♄

Lord of Strife

First decan of Leo, ruled by Saturn

Geburah of Atziluth/Fire

Trumps: Lust, Universe

Knight Scale for Geburah: Orange, plus the colors scales of the related trumps

The Five of Wands, Lord of Strife, is the first decan of the fixed sign of Leo, ruled by Saturn, in the sephira of Geburah of Atziluth, the station of Severity and the element of Fire. Geburah is fiery and Leo is fiery, but Saturn is restrictive. Here the heaviness of Saturn and the Earth (Universe) combined with the fire element of Leo (Lust) creates a situation like magma; a volcano under pressure.

In this card's background we see the black mountain from the card of Lust bursting forth as a volcano. Volcanoes are symbols of fire and earth, with great and severe strength. Volcano fire lurks beneath the surface of the earth, continually building up pressure until it explodes into manifestation. Holding fire and passion too tightly eventually leads to cataclysmic explosion; there is a need to let off steam.

Also for Lust and the Universe, or Leo and Saturn, we have a portrayal of Zurvān, a Mesopotamian demonic god of growth, maturity, and decay dating to around the 13th century BCE. Zurvān was the chief Persian deity before the emergence of Zoroastrianism. The name derives from the Persian word *zruvan*, meaning time, and is without gender. Zurvān was associated with the *axis mundi* or the centre of the world and appeared under two aspects: Limitless Time and Time of Long Dominion. The latter emerges from Infinite Time, lasts for 12,000 years, and returns to it. This resonates with Saturn as Chronos, and the formal title of the Universe card, *The Great One of the Night of Time*. Zurvān was originally associated with three other deities: Vayu (wind), Thvarshtar (space), and Ātar (fire); an appropriate description of volcanic energy.

Zurvān is usually depicted as a winged, leontocephaline deity, naked and encircled by a serpent representing the motion of the Sun, ruler of Leo.

Yet here the serpent is also a fitting representative of the Universe card. The Lust card also combines the Lion and Serpent, for Teth. Zurvān is often shown holding a staff and keys and standing on a globe. His open mouth is said to breathe fire, and an inscription found on one of his statues refers to "lions who burn incense . . . through whom we are consumed ourselves."

In this card Zurvān is portrayed as a composite figure combining the four Royal Watchers of the Universe card (the Lion, the Bull, The Eagle, and the Man). Behind him two of the wands are scythes of Saturn. He is shown with clenched fists, denoting pressure. He holds a Tau cross, Tau being the letter associated with the Universe card and the Tau cross being associated with crucifixion. This is a force under tension seeking release, the conflict that results from the upheaval of Geburah, and Leo being restricted by Saturn.

The Augur: Zurvān, the volcano, the Tau cross and sickle. *Pressure builds and seeks release.*

Deck Comparisons
The RWS Five of Wands shows five men battling with staves. The Thoth Five of Wands shows the wand of the Chief Adept central, flanked by phoenix and lotus wands, for purification and resurrection by fire. The Rosetta Five of Wands has a central basalt wand in the shape of the goddess Pasht or Sekhmet, inscribed with the zodiacal glyphs and flanked by a phoenix wand, a scythe, and two lotus wands. Tabula Mundi shows Zurvān perched on his orb in a sea of volcanic lava, flanked by Saturnine sickles and gripping the Tau cross. The first decan of Leo, Geburah of Fire, shows the pressure of necessary but destructive forces mounting.

SIX OF WanDS

Lord of Victory

Middle decan of Leo, ruled by Jupiter

Tiphareth of Atziluth/Fire

Trumps: Lust, Fortune

Knight Scale for Tiphareth: Clear Pink Rose, plus the colors scales of the related trumps

SIX OF WANDS

♌   VICTORY   ♃

The Lord of Victory is the second decan of Leo, ruled by Jupiter, in Tiphareth of Atziluth, the sephira of Beauty, with the element of Fire. For Leo, we have the Lust card and for Jupiter, Fortune, paired in the station of the Sun. There is harmony of element and planets, in the center of the Tree of Life. Jupiter says "go big or go home" and Leo just has to shine. Nothing less than Victory is due.

On the card we have the lion from the Lust card posed with the crowned owl from the Fortune card, in a heraldic display. A lion, creature of the Sun, sits poised in perfect balance with the owl, a creature with a more lunar nature. Though the owl is from the trump Fortune of the planet Jupiter, Jupiter is exalted in Cancer, thus a lunar influence. Yet here they stand side by side sharing the honors.

In heraldry, the lion stands for deathless and dauntless courage and the lion shown here would be said to be in the position of a "lion sejant" which means sitting on his haunches, with both forepaws on the ground. As the king of beasts it historically symbolizes bravery, strength, and royalty. In *sejant* position, the lion is paused in the moment of victorious celebration, firm in his majesty of pose, calmly looking before him.

He is crowned with the wreath of victory. In Rome the wreath was made of laurel and symbolized Victory itself. Heraldry gives "peace and triumph" as the meaning of laurel. In ancient Greece, the wreath was made of olive and was known as *kotinos*. It was given as a prize for winners of the Olympic Games. The wild olive trees it was made from grew near the temple of Zeus (Jupiter) and could only be cut with golden scissors by a a "pais amfithalis" (a boy whose parents were both alive). The boy would place them on a gold-ivory table for the Hellanodikai, the judges of the games who would make the wreaths and crown the winners.

The lion here is shown paired with the owl. The owl in heraldry means "one who is vigilant and of acute wit" and here the owl in shown standing in the position called "in its vigilance" with one leg raised. The owl wears a crown with the heraldic meaning of royalty.

Above the heraldic animals are six sprouting wands in the shape of an upright triangle for fire. Behind them, the Sun sits in the position of Tiphareth, the Moon at Yesod, and the Rose at Malkuth. The Rose is from the Lust card as is the solar lemniscate of balance. The rose in heraldry signifies hope and joy, and here the rose is golden as the specific message of a yellow or gold rose is "worthy of trust or treasure."

The Augur: Lion sejant, heraldic owl, the laurel and kotinos. *Beauty and harmony of the force of Will leads to a climactic triumph.*

Deck Comparisons

The Rider Waite Smith Six of Wands shows a man riding a white horse, in what looks like a victory parade. His horse has rich trappings and he is crowned with a laurel wreath and bears a wand also topped with a laurel wreath. The crowd raises the other wands in salute. The Thoth Six of Wands has the adept wands in perfect balance; a pair of wands with serpents and winged disks, a pair of phoenix wands, and a pair of lotus wands, crossed in a diamond grid with flames at the junctures. The Rosetta Six of Wands has the wands in a similar diamond grid with flames at the junctures, but the central wands with the winged disks are topped with Olympic torches and have the body of a lion goddess with her hands folded at rest. They are flanked by wands topped with Vajra and lotuses. Tabula Mundi shows the lion and owl in heraldic display, wearing the crown and the laurel. All of the cards for this middle decan of Leo, Tiphareth of Fire, show that the solar forces in balance create an Olympic victory.

seven of wands

SEVEN OF WANDS
♌   VALOUR   ♂

Lord of Valour

Last decan of Leo, ruled by Mars

Netzach of Atziluth/Fire

Trumps: Lust, Tower

Knight Scale for Netzach: Amber, plus the colors scales of the related trumps

The Lord of Valour is the last decan of Leo, ruled by Mars in Netzach of Atziluth, the sephira of Victory with the element of Fire. As the final decan of fire sign Leo, it is given the Lust card, combined with the rulership of the Tower for Mars. A whole lot of fire and masculinity here, battling it out in the sephira of Netzach, the domain of feminine Venus. It is going to take Valour to prevail or the soldiers will burn the fields.

From the Lust card, here in the last decan of Leo the lion has morphed into another large cat, the tiger. From the Tower card we have the dragon. The card portrays the classic battle of Tiger versus Dragon according to Shaolin martial arts and in Feng Shui. Tiger versus Dragon is a story of balance between male and female energies. In Feng Shui the dragon is male and the tiger female. The dragon rises as the celestial guardian of the east and the tiger sets as the guardian of the west. The dragon represents blood and the yin within the yang, while the tiger represents chi, the yang within the yin. They must balance.

"Tiger versus lion" in Shaolin martial arts is used to symbolize the line overcoming the circle and vice versa. The tiger fights in a straightforward attack bulldozing its opponent. The dragon fights using circular flexible attacks. Both the tiger and dragon are Buddhist symbols known as oppositional symbols—one reflecting a 'hard' style or an attacking and unrelenting form of martial arts on the offensive; this is symbolized by the Tiger. The 'soft' style is represented by the Dragon and is a form that embodies a defensive and more fluid 'circular-attack'. Like the yin-yang symbol, tiger and dragon have come to be interpreted to represent duality and balance of opposing forces. Here in the card we see them reversed, with the dragon attacking hard style and the tiger performing a circular move of defense. The tiger's goal is to take away part of the dragon's power and force the order of the world back into a perfect balance of yin and yang energies. At the battle rages, fire chases them uphill and a flaming Tower burns in the background. A lit torch leads the way with a grid of six crossed wands opposing the bearer on the quest towards the burning tower.

Sevens show the difficulty to be overcome in order to achieve Victory. In the suit of fire, what is needed is courage and passion with which to meet opposition. The imbalance has created a melee, a disordered battle and it will take a feat of individual valour as well as strength, force and an unrelenting thrust.

The Augur: Tiger vs. Dragon, blood and chi, defense and offense. *Take courage amidst opposition.*

Deck Comparisons

The Rider Waite Smith Seven of Wands shows a man with a stave on the defensive against six other staves. The Thoth Seven of Wands shows the same adept wands, phoenix wands, and lotus wands from the six opposed by a large menacing club, with flames at the junctures. The Rosetta Seven of Wands shows two large wands shaped like the glyph of Mars with the body of a lion, flanked by phoenix and lotus wands and opposed by a heavy wooden stave, also with flames at the junctures. Tabula Mundi's version shows the epic battle of Tiger versus Dragon, where blood and chi circle in the dance of defense and offense. The last decan of Leo is Netzach of Fire and the cards share a theme of valiant defense.

EIGHT OF WaNDS

Lord of Swiftness

First decan of Sagittarius, ruled by Mercury

Hod of Atziluth/Fire

Trumps: Art, Magus

Knight Scale for Hod: Violet, plus the colors scales of the related trumps

EIGHT OF WANDS
SWIFTNESS

The Lord of Swiftness is the first decan of mutable fire sign Sagittarius, with the decan of the sign being ruled by Mercury. It is in the sephira Hod, called *Glory*, which also gives the influence of Mercury. This double Mercurial flavor combined with a mutable sign gives swiftness, the ennobled and etherealized fire.

The related trumps are Art, for the sign of Sagittarius and the Magus for the decan ruler Mercury. The card portrays the caduceus wand from the Magus card and the winged sandals of Mercury. The caduceus is topped with a quartz crystal. It is shown with eight rays of light being broken up into prismatic colors, adding a contribution of the rainbow from the Art card. Admittedly, this card draws on the idea of the wands as rays as in the Thoth deck, but in this deck it is shown in a way to illustrate how it is derived from the two related trump cards.

The caduceus wand was carried by the Greek god Hermes, also known as Roman Mercury. It was often carried by messengers of the gods. Interestingly, it is also said to have been carried by Iris, goddess of the rainbow, in her role as a divine Olympian messenger. This brings it full circle with the rainbow symbolism of Sagittarius. Iris was the daughter of a cloud nymph who traveled with the speed of the winds. She was married to Zephyrus, the god of the West wind, the gentlest of the four winds. Iris had many titles and poetic monikers including *Chrysopteron* meaning Golden Winged, *Podas ôkea* meaning swift footed or *Podênemos ôkea* meaning wind-swift footed, and *Aellopus* meaning swift-footed like a storm-wind. She is usually shown either as a winged maiden or as a rainbow, and is associated with messages and the onset of new endeavors. The rainbow itself is a symbol of divine communications, and a path or bridge to heaven. Another association with Sagittarius can be found as far back as ancient Sumer, as the Sumerian farmer god Ninurta has as his weapon a bow and arrow, and wore a crown described as a rainbow.

The caduceus wand and winged sandals are of course also the tools of Hermes, and said to be the origin of the design of the glyph of Mercury. By association the caduceus is symbolic of trade, commerce and communication. The winged sandals are called *taleria* the neuter plural of the Latin *talaris*, "of the ankle." They were said to be made of imperishable gold and to give the ability to fly swift as a bird.

The dendrites are firing. The card's association with vibrating light and electricity hints also at the swiftness of brilliant ideas, the unexpected "light bulb" moments that one needs to pay attention to before they swiftly pass away. Speak them out; or send yourself a message and write them down.

The Augur: The Caduceus, the Taleria, Iris. *Brilliance is fleeting; catch the rainbow if you can.*

Deck Comparisons

The Rider Waite Smith Eight of Wands shows eight wands flying though the air. The Thoth Eight of Wands shows a geometric form with red electrical rays pulsing outward and a rainbow above. The Rosetta Eight of Wands shows light waves passing through a geometric crystal and becoming rainbows. Tabula Mundi 's card shows eight prismatic rays extending from a crystal topped caduceus and flanked by the Taleria sandals. This card is the first decan of Sagittarius, Hod of Fire, and all share an association with the speed of light and thought.

nine of wands

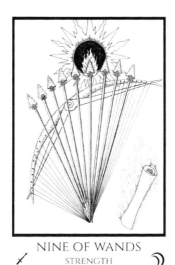

NINE OF WANDS
STRENGTH

Lord of Strength

Middle decan of Sagittarius, ruled by the Moon

Yesod of Atziluth/Fire

Trumps: Art, Priestess

Knight Scale for Yesod: Indigo, plus the colors scales of the related trumps

The Lord of Strength is the middle decan of Sagittarius[21]. This decan is ruled by the Moon, and is in Yesod, the sephira of the Moon. The dual lunar influence combined with the central decan of the sign in the middle pillar at the sephira called *Foundation*, gives the type of strength that gains its potency from change and flexibility, from the fluctuations of the Moon. Everything in Nature changes and vibrates, from the smallest parts of the atom to the largest organisms and systems. Crowley makes mention of how speed affects balance and equilibrium, and uses the example that one cannot draw a straight line if the hand is not steady and shakes. This is something I was reminded of constantly while drawing the Art for this deck in permanent marker; all those straight arrows. Though the fire of Sagittarius is sublimating and dissipating, the card is called the Lord of Strength. This is the strength inherent in mobility. Sagittarius is always looking forward and always in motion. The Moon's fluctuations are welcome here.

The related trumps are Art for the sign Sagittarius and the Priestess for the Moon, the decan's ruler. The Wands here are nine flaming arrows. The Bow is a thematic similarity between the two trumps of this card. The Nine of Wands shows the lunar bow, a symbol that is both the Priestess' bow and lyre of Artemis and the moon bow from the green winged hermaphrodite of the Art card. Artemis is the Greek goddess of wildness and the hunt. She was the daughter of Zeus who is the Roman equivalent for Jupiter, ruler of Sagittarius, and the sister of Apollo, god of the Sun. In the Homeric Hymn to Artemis, her

---

21   This is the minor card associated with the Sun sign of the author of *Book M*.

epithet was *Khryselakatos*, "of the Golden Shaft," and *Iokheira* (Showered by Arrows). The name Artemis itself has several speculations as to its etymology. It may come from the Persian root *arte* meaning great and holy mother of nature, or it may come from a Greek root word meaning "to shake" referring to her as the shooter of darts, which highlights the meaning of strength with motion and mobility.

Also from the Art card we see the solar disk at the point of eclipse totality. This is a reference to Art's placement on the Tree of Life between the sephira of the Sun (Tiphareth) and the sephira of the Moon, (Yesod). Here it illustrates how the motion of the Moon in its cycles can even overpower the Sun at conjunction, if only for a moment. As it says in *The Vision and the Voice*," The moon waneth. The moon waneth. The moon waneth. For in that arrow is the Light of Truth that overmastereth the light of the sun, whereby she shines." The forces of the feminine Moon are in perfect conjunction and balance with the masculine Sun. The solar influence also confers an aspect of vitality and the strength of health.

The Augur: The lunar Bow, the flaming Arrow, eclipse totality. *Flexibility gives strength; continue to look forward and remain adaptable and you will achieve harmony through balance of conscious and unconscious forces.*

Deck Comparisons

The Rider Waite Smith Nine of Wands shows a man whose head appears to be bandaged, holding a Wand with eight more Wands in the ground behind him. The Thoth Nine of Wands shows eight red arrows whose arrowheads are lunar crescents, with a central wand with one solar head and one lunar head. The Rosetta Nine of Wands shows eight green arrows whose arrowheads are the eight phases of the Moon, with a central wand that is a spiral horn with one solar head and one head showing the solar eclipse at totality. Tabula Mundi's Nine shows the lunar bow and flaming arrow, the scroll and the moment of lunar eclipse. The middle decan of Sagittarius is Yesod of Fire, and the cards share a theme of lunar flexibility being the key to strength.

ten of wands

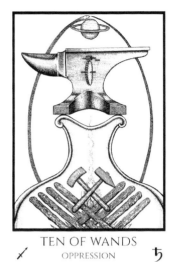

TEN OF WANDS
OPPRESSION

♐   ♄

Lord of Oppression

Last decan of Sagittarius, ruled
by Saturn

Malkuth of Atziluth/Fire

Trumps: Art, Universe

Knight Scale for Malkuth: Yellow, plus
the colors scales of the related trumps

The Lord of Oppression is the final decan of the mutable fire sign Sagittarius. The decan is ruled by Saturn, and it is in the sephira of material and earthy Malkuth. The spiritual fire of Sagittarius is smothered by the weight of Saturn and Earth, giving an atmosphere of overbearing repression.

The related trumps of the card are the Sagittarian trump, Art, and the Universe card for Saturn (as well as Malkuth). The beautiful and ethereal rainbows cannot withstand the weight of the entire Universe; this is Oppression.

From the Art card we have the alchemical vessel, weighted down with a huge and heavy anvil, representing leaden Saturn for the Universe card. The Anvil is marked with the gear from the Universe card, here as a force of power that grinds one down. It is the feeling of being just another cog in the machine and a symbol of industrial society.

Within the blocked alchemical vessel, there is barely any oxygen for the fires of Sagittarius to burn, especially considering the weakened state of the last decan. The vessel is nearly stoppered by the force and weight of the anvil. Yet the anvil is a symbol of the smith Hephaestus, the ugly and lame son of Zeus, king of the gods and the Greek form of Jupiter, ruler of Sagittarius. To be a smith one must have the strength. The burden is heavy and requires self sacrifice.

Enclosed inside the vessel are eight crossed wands surmounted by two wands in the form of a hammer and pick, or hammer and chisel. In mundane and heraldic usage the hammer and pick simply referred to mines, miners, and mining, or extracting ore from the earth. But it has been adopted as a symbol of the oppressed working classes of the industrial revolution. Alternately, the card could have used the similar hammer and sickle symbolism, the sickle being appropriately Saturn related. The hammer and sickle has a similar association with proletarian struggle.

Crowley says of this card "The Wand has conquered; it has done its work; it has done its work too well; it did not know when to stop; Government has become Tyranny." This is a card of material selfishness and callous cruelty. No empathy or concern for humanity, or for oneself, is shown here. It is a card of crushing burden. As a Ten card, it is of Malkuth, the sephira that hangs detached from the other nine on the Tree. This indicates its detachment from the spiritual fire, and its readiness to proceed to the next element.

The Augur: The Anvil, the Hammer and Pick, the industrial gear. *Inertia impedes progress, and it takes great effort to shoulder a burden and resist that which grinds you down.*

Deck Comparisons

The Rider Waite Smith Ten of Wands shows a man bent by the awkward weight as he tries to carry ten wands over his back and shoulders. The Thoth Ten of Wands shows eight cold looking crossed wands with claws, surmounted by two iron bars with fierce heads on one end and sharp points on the other. These bars are reminiscent of Tibetan dorjes. The Rosetta Ten of Wands is similar to the Thoth but has the scythes of Saturn and the large central iron bars have horse heads and sharp hooves. Tabula Mundi's card depicts the anvil, industrial gear, and Hammer and Pick symbolism. The last decan of Sagittarius, Malkuth of Fire, shows the fire force's last gasp at control.

Audere, To Dare

The Cups

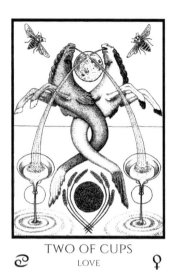

TWO OF CUPS
LOVE

TWO OF CUPS

Lord of Love

First decan of Cancer, ruled by Venus

Chokmah of Briah/Water

Trumps: Chariot, Empress

Queen Scale for Chokmah: Grey, plus the colors scales of the related trumps

T he Lord of Love pairs the Chariot, trump of cardinal sign Cancer, with the Empress, trump of Venus, in Chokmah of Briah, the sephira of force combined with the element of Water and the creative world of the spirit. As a Two, it is the first decan of its sign, Cancer, and thus the inrush of the energy of the sign, in a sign itself which is cardinal water and thus inflowing inaugural water energy.

The Chariot is the bearer of the Grail, Cancer is the sign of motherhood, and the Empress is the Door of Heaven and the salt water of the womb. The Empress on the Tree of Life by path position bridges Chokmah and Binah, the supernal parents, and the Chariot bears the grail, vessel of our lady of Babalon, containing the red blood and white gluten. Is it any wonder that combined they make the Lord of Love? What else but a merging of masculine and feminine polarities in an act of Love, the Will-to-Love, and water in its purest and highest form, has the power of creation?

In the Tabula Mundi Two of Cups the hippocampi of the Chariot are entwined; the white horse and the black, the light and the dark forming a perfect polarity. In mythology, hippocampi from the Greek for horse-monster are horses on the top and dolphins on the bottom, and are associated with Poseidon whose chariot was drawn over the surface of the sea waters. In alchemy the dolphin, from the Greek root *delphys*, has the dual meaning of womb and both dolphins and fish are associated with the mysteries of procreation due mans' origination in the waters of the womb. A section of the brain has also been named the hippocampus after this mythological creature. Humans have two sections of the brain called hippocampi, one on each side, related to memory and navigation.

To echo the light/dark polarity, and emphasize the Moon's connection with the sign of Cancer, the card has the two opposing phases of the moon that are light and dark, namely the full and the new. Opposing phases of the moon also occur on the card of the Empress, and on the bits of the horses on the Chariot.

Above the joyfully entwined hippocampi are two bees from the Empress card. Bees here are for the creative impulse and the building of sweetness. Bees are often used as feminine symbols of the harmony that results in creativity. Their collection of nectar is made into honey, honey is made into mead, and the word "honeymoon" comes from the ancient custom of gifting newlyweds with a month's worth, or "moon's" worth, of mead in order to encourage fertility. In practice this card sometimes indicates the possibility of pre-pregnancy, or at the very least of a honeymoon period.

The Augur: The hippocampi, new & full moon, honeymoon of mead. *A harmonious pairing triggers the beginnings of love and gestation.*

Deck Comparisons

The RWS Two of Cups contains a man and a woman seemingly pledging their love over a symbolic toast (perhaps with mead), while above them is a winged lion atop a caduceus, whose snakes' twining shape echo the entwining of the animals of the other cards. It seems all feminine tarot Twos have this sinuous, S like shape much like the male Twos have the saltire. In most Golden Dawn decks the Two of Cups contains lotuses and entwined dolphins in the colors of argent and or (silver and gold), and they are shown in the Thoth deck as well, though they look more like koi fish than dolphins and are a rosy tint for the Venusian influence. The Rosetta also contains the lotuses and two dolphins, but less fish-like and in the traditional colors of silver and gold. Tabula Mundi pairs the new and full moon with twined light and dark hippocampi, and wheat shafts and bees. The first decan of Cancer is Chokmah of Water, and the cards share imagery of the beginning force of love and fertility from a matched pair.

THREE OF CUPS
ABUNDANCE ☿ ♋

THree OF Cups

Lord of Abundance

Middle decan of Cancer, ruled by Mercury

Binah of Briah/Water

Trumps: Chariot, Magus

Queen Scale for Binah: Black, plus the colors scales of the related trumps

The Lord of Abundance is the middle decan of Cancer, combining the essences of the Chariot, trump of Cancer with the Magus, trump of Mercury, in Binah of Briah, the feminine sephira of the great Mother's oceanic waters combined with the element of Water and the creative world of spirit. The result is the Lord of Abundance. It was amusing to me to lay out the three trumps that rule the three decans of Cancer side by side: the Empress, the Magus, the Priestess. The Magus, in the middle, as a three in the sephira of Binah, is completely surrounded by goddesses. The Lord of Abundance indeed. This middle decan also contains the exaltation of Jupiter (15 degrees Cancer) and this enhances the fortunate aspect.

The card has three cups, and rising from the waters of each cup is a hand, just as in the Magus card a hand rises from the cup on the table, bearing a sword. But these hands hold symbols of abundance and of the surrounding goddesses; wheat for the Empress on one side, a pomegranate for the Priestess on the other. The central hand holds a golden apple.

The golden apple is a prize featured throughout history in many tales of mythology. Most often they are associated with a heroic quest and themes of beauty, wealth, and immortality, sometimes being stolen away from the garden of a king, or from a fearsome guardian. The lesson in some of these myths echoes what Crowley says about this card. Mercury in his role of psychopompus calls to mind the story of Persephone also symbolized by the pomegranate on the card which is both a symbol of abundance and a temptation. While this is a beautiful card of plentitude and profusion, this is just a subtle suggestion that it is best not to cling tightly but to enjoy it while it lasts. Perhaps this is the practical element introduced by Saturn's association with Binah.

The moon rules the sign of Cancer in whole and just as the Two of Cups showed the two faces of the Moon's polarities, the Three of Cups has three phases: that of the fullness of the moon, between the waxing and waning quarters. Of the four major phases of the moon, the three are shown that hold the abundance of light. Only the empty or dark phase is omitted.

Where the dark phase would be located, is a representation of the canopy of the Chariot, beneath which is a shield with the Hindu lingam and yoni. The starry canopy represents manifestation and the lingam and yoni is symbolic of the union of male and female forces which combine to create the birth of a third thing. In this case what has been manifested is emotional abundance and the joy of union.

The Augur: The Golden Apple, wheat & pomegranate, the lunar phases of light. *The prize is joy and pleasure in love, plentitude and fertility.*

Deck Comparisons

The RWS Three of Cups shows three beautiful maidens reminiscent of the goddesses of the Three Graces in a garden with fruits and flowers, joyously raising a toast. The Thoth card shows three beautiful voluptuous cups made of pomegranate seeds being filled as water pours from golden lotuses. The Rosetta Three of Cups is similar but the cups have golden wheat shafts and pomegranates. Tabula Mundi's card shows hands rising from the cups bearing gifts: a golden apple, a pomegranate and wheat shafts. The three lunar phases of light flank them. This card is the middle decan of Cancer, Binah of Water, and the cards share a theme of emotional abundance as the first stirrings of the prior card are quickened and gestated to give form to love and fertility.

four of cups

FOUR OF CUPS
LUXURY

Lord of Luxury (Blended Pleasure)

Last decan of Cancer, ruled by the Moon

Chesed of Briah/Water

Trumps: Chariot, Priestess

Queen Scale for Chesed: Blue, plus the colors scales of the related trumps

The Lord of Luxury is the final decan of Cancer, ruled by the Moon which is the planet of Cancer, in Chesed of Briah, the sephira of manifestation associated with the abundance of Jupiter. One would think perfection had been attained with such a seemingly perfect combination. While that is true in a sense, the pleasure is blended, and the luxury it speaks of can after a time be a little stifling. Much like a womb, it is certainly pleasant but one must outgrow it. The Four, being below the Abyss, cannot be considered completely stable, though there can be a pause here to enjoy the luxury while it lasts. While Chesed is fiery the fire is here combined with an excess of water: Briah, Cancer, and the Moon. One can only indulge for so long, and warm waters cool in time.

The trumps associated with this card are the Chariot for Cancer and the Priestess for the Moon. The great wave is cresting; it is overflowing at its peak of power but about to make a descent. The four cups are symbolically represented by the four major phases of the Moon. In the preceding two cards, we had the polarity of the new and full moon for the Two of Cups, Love, followed by the Three of Cups, Abundance, showing all of the three lit phases of the Moon. Here in the Four, the cycle is completed with all four quarters of the Moon phase present in a diamond shape. At their center is a scallop shell open to show a large pearl.

The pearl, an object of beauty and luxury, is one of the stones associated with the sign of Cancer. The oldest gemstone, pearls are often a symbol of perfection. Hindu mythology claims that Krishna discovered the first pearl and presented it to his daughter on her wedding day, and indeed, the pearl is associated with the luxury of weddings and coronations, which mark a high point and subsequently a new phase approaching.

It was once believed that the growth of pearls was influenced by the Moon. Pearls are created as the culmination of a process within the body of the mollusk when a central seed such as a sand grain is covered layer by layer with nacre to soften and sooth the irritation the object would otherwise cause. Symbolically, they often represent emotional wisdom acquired with experience. As the pearl grows it becomes larger and more luxurious. At some point the pearl grows too large for the body of the shell. Many types of pearls can be harvested without harm to the creature itself, which then can generate a new pearl. Thus when you reach the point of luxury in your journey through Briah, realize that it is a cyclical emotional high point that will need to be reseeded to provide for new highs of the future.

The Augur: The great wave, all four moon phases, the pearl. *The completion of an emotional cycle is comfortable for a time.*

Deck Comparisons

The RWS image shows a person sitting under a tree, being offered a fourth cup from a cloud as he contemplates three cups before him with his arms crossed as if he has had enough. The Thoth Four of Cups shows four golden cups, the top two overflowing with water into two below, balanced on their roots upon a wind tossed sea with a grey foreboding sky behind. The Rosetta has almost the same configuration except the cups have lunar handles waxing and waning. Tabula Mundi's card shows the four phases of the moon in completion, and a pearl born along on a great cresting wave. This card is the final decan of Cancer, Chesed of Water, and things of the emotional realm are peaking.

FIVE OF CUPS

FIVE OF CUPS
DISAPPOINTMENT

♏ ♂

Lord of Disappointment (Loss in Pleasure)

First decan of Scorpio, ruled by Mars

Geburah of Briah/Water

Trumps: Death, Tower

Queen Scale for Geburah: Scarlet Red, plus the colors scales of the related trumps

The Five of Cups, Lord of Disappointment is the first decan of the fixed sign of Scorpio, ruled by Mars, in the sephira of Geburah of Briah, the station of Severity and the element of Water. What could have happened? The disturbance of luxury is deeply disappointing. Just when you least expect it, the abundant fullness of the great wave of water in the Four of Cups has dried up completely leaving cracked earth and empty cups. The waters of Scorpio have evaporated due the magnified Mars influence of the combination of the flaming Tower and fiery Geburah. Double Mars just got too hot and the waters stagnated, putrefied and burned up. There is too much heat, too much fire, and not enough water to go around. Luxury doesn't last forever; the pendulum swings to disappointment.

From the trump of Scorpio, Death, we have the pyramids as monuments in place of a Tower, and the seas of Scorpio have dried. Instead of shining towers in the distance we have the tombs of long dead dynasties. Crowley says of the card that "the sea is arid and stagnant, a dead sea, like a "chott" in North Africa." A chott is defined as a shallow lake or marsh with brackish or saline water, especially in northern Africa. Chotts are dry during the summer, at which time they are also characterized by salt deposits and a lack of vegetation. This must be summer, because the lakebed is bone dry and salty. Matter has triumphed over spirit, and the waters have putrefied.

The fish from the Death card is a desiccated carcass. The Chinese character for fish, yu, looks a bit like fish bones depending on the script and is pronounced the same as the Chinese character for "abundance" or "surplus." The fish symbol is therefore used to symbolize the wish for "more" as in more good fortune. But it looks like luck and pleasures have run out here, and the fish is naught but a skeleton of bones.

The severity of Geburah here plays out in the emotional realm. The lap of luxury is no more; here we have the death of pleasure. The desert is the realm of Set, the usurper who was envious of, and then killed, his own brother Osiris. The desert is the home of draught and hunger and is a hard place to survive in, and symbolizes the hardships that stand between people and their dreams. What is needed is the end of drought and the ability to reconnect with and revitalize the emotional waters in order to renew the parched earth.

The Augur: Empty cups, fish bones, the Chott. *The triumph of matter over spirit is emotional severity and leads to letdown.*

Deck Comparisons
The RWS Five of Cups shows a man in a black cloak, gazing at three spilled and empty cups, with two cups remaining upright, though they appear empty. There is a river with a bridge in the background. The Thoth Five of Cups shows five empty cups in the shape of an inverted pentagram, with the requisite Golden Dawn drooping lotuses. The Rosetta Five of Cups has five cups of cracked glass in a geometric arrangement. Their centers form a star pentagram while their bodies form an inverted pentagram. The lotus plants have no blossoms but they have roots shaped in the glyphs of Mars and Scorpio sinking into fissured earth seeking moisture. Tabula Mundi's broken and spilled cups rest on cracked earth with a pile of fish bones. The first decan of Scorpio, Geburah of Water, is a place where the Martial influence has caused emotional disruption.

SIX OF CUPS

Lord of Pleasure

Middle decan of Scorpio, ruled by the Sun

Tiphareth of Briah/Water

Trumps: Death, Sun

Queen Scale for Tiphareth: Yellow (gold), plus the colors scales of the related trumps

SIX OF CUPS
♏ PLEASURE ☉

The Six of Cups, Lord of Pleasure is the middle decan of the fixed sign of Scorpio, ruled by the Sun. It is in the sephira of Tiphareth of Briah, the station of Beauty and harmony, with the element of Water. Six cups are arranged in a downward triangle formation for the element of Water. An eagle soars high above the landscape as the sunlight sparkles on the waters. We have a double dose of the Sun here, with the Sun's rulership of the decan and the placement of the Sun in Tiphareth. Crowley calls this card the influence of the Sun on water, and speaks of pleasure in its highest sense of effortless well being, satisfaction of desire and the fulfillment of sexual will.

For this middle decan of Scorpio we look to the Death card for the eagle, the highest aspect of the sign of Scorpio. For the decanate rulership, we have the Sun card and thus the rising sun and the twelve pointed star made up of the four triangles of the zodiac. Tiphareth of Water is about harmony of matters of the heart. The four triangles that form the twelve pointed star call to mind the anahata or heart chakra, with its lotus of twelve petals. The triangle times four is the combination of heaven (three) and earth (four). The three is the result from the combination of male and female to create a third thing, while the four is manifestation. This resonates with the card's additional meaning of fertility, from the Sun's light upon the deep waters of Scorpio.

The eagle has been associated with the Sun throughout history. The Abenaki solar deity Kisosen, meaning "sun bringer," was an eagle who opened its wings to create the day and closed them at night. In Babel, the eagle was the symbol of the noon sun, as also in Egypt was the falcon-eagle. The Pueblo Indians associated eagles with the physical and spiritual energies of the sun as well as symbols of greater sight and perception. The Pertho rune takes the shape of the flight of an eagle, and signifies mysterious luck, enjoyment of sexuality, being free from entanglements and being lifted above the ordinary cares of life to obtain far seeing vision.

The other well known symbol that combines the eagle with the sun is the winged disk with stylized eagle wings, and sometimes twinned uraeus serpents like in the Sun trump. The winged solar disk has been found in ancient Egyptian culture associated with both Horus and Ra-Horahti, gods of the Sun. As a form of Horus, the winged solar disk is a symbol of Hadit. In Sumerian, Assyrian and Mesopotamian culture the winged sun was associated with Shamash, Ashur and Enlil. It also is found in many variations in Hittite, Anatolian, Persian (Zoroastrian), South American, Australian and Christian symbolism. It has been speculated that one origination of this motif is the display of the solar corona at the time of an eclipse, which sometimes fans out at the moment of totality to create two wings and sometimes also a tail of light around the central darkened disk. In other Middle Eastern mythology, the disk depicts a mythical celestial body called Nibiru. In most cases, the combination of eagle wings with the sun disk symbolizes the gods, the sun, rising above and renewal of life or divinity, as well as majesty, power and eternity of the spirit.

In ancient Persia, a symbol of Zoroastrianism was a winged sun called a *fravahar*, which comes from an Iranian word that means "I choose" and implied that the choice was of goodness and justice. Others say it comes from the words *far* and *khvar* meaning "shining" with divine grace, as if soaring on wings of light, or from *fravati* meaning "divine protection." Another translation of *fravati* is "move forward power" or movement in the direction of divine truth. The meaning of the fravahar is symbolic of the happiness of man based on good thoughts and deeds, the flight of the soul towards progress and bliss.

The Augur: The eagle, the *fravahar*, the Pertho rune. *Harmony of the heart gives the ability to soar.*

Deck Comparisons

The Rider Waite Smith Six of Cups shows a village scene, and a young boy handing a cup of flowers to a girl. The other cups all contain flowers. The Thoth Six of Cups shows six golden cups being filled by six golden lotuses over a sunlit sea. The Rosetta also has the sunlit sea, the golden cups and lotuses, but has the lotus roots in the shape of the glyph of Scorpio and a Sri Yantra design behind, that has the male and female triangles united symbolic of the womb of creation and the harmony of earth, sky and heaven. Tabula Mundi's eagle and winged sun echo the themes of the middle decan of Scorpio, Tiphareth of Water, where balanced solar forces are a pleasurable emotional influence.

seven of cups

SEVEN OF CUPS
DEBAUCH

♏ ♀

Lord of Debauch (Illusionary Success)

Last decan of Scorpio, ruled by Venus

Netzach of Briah/Water

Trumps: Death, Empress

Queen Scale for Netzach: Emerald, plus
the colors scales of the related trumps

The Seven of Cups, Lord of Debauch, is the final decan of the fixed sign of Scorpio, ruled by Venus. It is in the sephira of Netzach of Briah, the station of Victory, with the element of Water. It is a card of weakness and delusion; Venus does not like the fading decan of Scorpio. What is needed for Victory is the ability to see through illusion.

It is the sephira of Venus, and the decan is ruled by Venus; one would think it was no problem. But Venus is unhappy paired with Scorpio, and so she drinks. Though it is double Venus, all that deigned to appear from the Empress card was the pair of moons from the background, inconstantly waning and waxing. Venus is having a pout.

What we see in the card is the landscape of Scorpio from the Death card, but now there is a dual image. From the desert comes the mirage. The mirage is an optical phenomenon in which light rays are bent to produce a distortion of a distant image. But that is in the desert. This card is also a swamp.

From the swamp gas, come the will-o-the-wisps. And from the cups, rise ephemeral embryonic forms. The will-o-the wisp is an atmospheric ghost light seen over bogs and swamps. It comes from the Latin name *ignis fatuus* meaning "foolish fire." Paranormal enthusiasts call them "orbs" or ghost lights. The size of the orbs can range from that of a candle flame to the size of a man's head. The orbs on this card mirror in size and order those on the Death card.

The American anthropologist John G. Owens says of the will-o-the-wisp: "It is generally observed in damp, marshy places, moving to and fro; but it has been known to stand perfectly still and send off scintillations. As you approach it, it will move on, keeping just beyond your reach; if you retire, it will follow you. That these fireballs do occur, and that they will repeat your motion seems to be established, but no satisfactory explanation has yet been offered that I have heard. Those who are less superstitious say that it is the ignition of the gases rising from the marsh. But how a light produced from burning gas could have the form described and move as described, advancing as you advance, receding as you recede, and at other times remaining stationary, without having any visible connection with the earth, is not clear to me."

Folklore has is that they are spirits or fairies that attempt to lead travelers to their demise. In Northern Europe they were thought to mark the spot of treasure but only if taken when the light was there. In Book IX of Milton's *Paradise Lost*, Satan is described as a will-o-the-wisp in tempting Eve to partake of the fruit of the Tree of Knowledge, and of good and evil. The will-o-the-wisp also makes an appearance in *The Lord of the Rings* in the Dead Marshes outside of Mordor. This is from Sam's point of view: *He first saw one with the corner of his left eye, a wisp of pale sheen that faded away; but others appeared soon after: some like dimly shining smoke, some like misty flames flickering slowly above unseen candles; here and there they twisted like ghostly sheets unfurled by hidden hands.*

The Augur: The mirage, swamp gas, the will-o-the-wisp. *Here is the illusion of intoxication; false lights that lead astray.*

Deck Comparisons

The Rider Waite Smith Seven of Cups has a person contemplating seven floating cups, each with a different enigmatic specter rising from it. The Thoth Seven of Cups has seven cups floating in a snotty looking sea. Weak looking lotus flowers drip slime into the cups. The Rosetta Seven of Cups has similar snotty cups but in this case the lotuses are obscene looking corpse lilies. Tabula Mundi's card has mirages and will-o-the-wisps rising from swamp gas. The last decan of Scorpio is Netzach of Water, and the cards share a common theme of spectral delusion and degeneration.

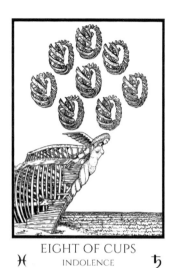

EIGHT OF CUPS
ℋ   INDOLENCE   ♄

EIGHT OF CUPS

Lord of Indolence (Abandoned Success)

First decan of Pisces, ruled by Saturn

Hod of Briah/Water

Trumps: Moon, Universe

Queen Scale for Hod: Orange, plus the colors scales of the related trumps

The Lord of Indolence is the card of the first decan of Pisces. This decan is ruled by Saturn. The sephira is Hod of Briah, the sephira called *Glory* which is the foot of the Pillar of Severity, with the element of Water. Hod's reason is burdened by the heaviness of Saturn and the illusion of Pisces.

The related trumps are the Moon for the sign of Pisces, and the Universe for Saturn, which rules the first decan. Eight cups are fashioned from bleached and cracked boards in the shape of the tube torus portal from the Universe card. Surely these cups won't hold water. From the Moon card we have the ghostly waters of sleep. The barge of the Moon has become a ghost ship and run aground. The ship has been abandoned.

The waters of Pisces influenced by Saturn are calm but stagnant. Time, melancholy and regret have spoiled pleasure. Here the water is portrayed as shown in the Moon card; as patterns of the brain waves of sleep. These are the poisoned waters of enchantment and stagnation. Washed up on shore is a shipwreck. The figure head has been worn away by time. The ribs of the ship are bleached and rotten. The crew has been dispatched to Davy Jones' Locker, a sort of purgatory for drowned sailors. Davy Jones is the equivalent of the sailors' Devil, for the association with Saturn and thus Capricorn. The origin of the name is unclear but is thought to reference an incompetent sailor who turned into a mythological fiend.

The Rime of the Ancient Mariner is a lengthy poem by Samuel Taylor Coleridge about supernatural dangers and punishments. The mariner and his crew anger the spirits by killing an albatross that had led them away from peril. They are sent into uncharted and overly calm waters. "Day after day, day after day, We stuck, or breath nor motion; As idle as a painted ship Upon a painted ocean. Water, water, everywhere, And all the boards did shrink; Water, water, everywhere, Nor any drop to drink." The poem goes on to describe their encounter with a ghost ship, where with a roll of the dice the crew loses their souls to a skeleton named Death, and the mariner to a supernaturally pale woman of nightmare called "Life-in-Death."

Crowley calls this card the "apex of unpleasantness" and suggests that the ill luck that comes from indolence is somehow one's own fault. Sloth, inertia and torpor are to blame. The cups can't hold water, representing the lack of emotional maturity and the loss of fluidity. What should be flowing is rigid. Renunciation has become self-sacrifice. One loses heart and soul and becomes depressed and idle. Success has been abandoned and relinquished through dearth of discipline and lack of interest.

The Augur: *Rime of the Ancient Mariner*, the ghost ship, the waters of sleep. *The ship runs aground through the lack of emotional maturity, and something is abandoned.*

Deck Comparisons

The Rider Waite Smith Eight of Cups shows a man heading for the hills in the moonlight, abandoning eight stacked cups. The Thoth deck shows eight broken and dented cups stacked over a swampy looking sea with drooping pale lotuses and a dark sky. The Rosetta Eight of Cups is much like the Thoth, but the cups are rusted and have the planet Saturn and the glyph for Pisces built into their stems. Tabula Mundi shows a ghost ship grounded on the shores of sleep and cups that won't hold water. The Eight of Cups is the first decan of Pisces, Hod of Water, where Saturn's restricting force in the sphere of mind brings emotional disillusionment, disinterest, and abandoned dreams.

NINE OF CUPS

NINE OF CUPS
HAPPINESS
♓   4

Lord of Happiness

Middle decan of Pisces, ruled by Jupiter

Yesod of Briah/Water

Trumps: Moon, Fortune

Queen Scale for Yesod: Violet, plus the colors scales of the related trumps

The Lord of Happiness is the middle decan of Pisces in Yesod, the sephira of Foundation on the middle pillar in the watery world of Briah. This sephira has the influence of the Moon, further enhancing the water element. The decan is ruled by benevolent and expansive Jupiter, the ancient ruler of sign Pisces. Every element is harmonious and in balance and the end result is happiness. This is one of the most fortunate cards in the pack. This penultimate cups card is the water force perfected.

The related trumps are the Moon for Pisces and Fortune for Jupiter. We have a return of the creatures or Gunas of Fortune: the ring-tailed lemur wearing the lunar crescent, the three eyed owl wearing a crown, and the hand-serpent which here is presenting the viewer with the larger half of the wishbone. This is in reference to the folklore of the Nine of Cups being the "wish card" and indicating the fulfillment and granting of the querent's fondest wish. The custom of saving the wishbone of a fowl as a means of wish fulfillment is said to date from Roman times. In the British Isles this bone was called the "merrythought." Once dry, two people each make a wish and pull an end of the merrythought; the one whose half is larger is said to get their wish.

The creatures are making merry around nine cups. The two cups in the foreground are spiraling drinking horns. In ancient times these ceremonial drinking vessels were known as *rhytons*, from the Greek words meaning "from the flowing." These were often used for ritual libations and offerings to the gods. In the background, seven drinking bowls are arranged above and spill flowing water to the rhytons below. These shallow bowls were known as *mazers* to the northern Europeans and as the quaich in Scotland. Mazers were generally wooden and ornamented with precious metals, sometimes

136

having metal straps between rim and foot like the ones shown here. The lip edge often had a bacchanalian inscription. These were for celebratory use and sometimes given as commemorative prizes. The bowls were known in Greece as *kylix* and often had scenes of festivity etched inside the bowl. These were often Dionysian scenes of a humorous or sexual nature that would only become visible once the bowl was drained. Kylix bowls were primarily used at the symposium, a social drinking party of festivity and discourse.

From the Moon card the koi fish have been brought forth and multiplied. There are nine fish, one for each cup. The ones in the background peep and leap joyfully from the mazers, while two fish in the foreground form the glyph of Pisces. In Feng Shui, nine is the luckiest number of fish to keep in a pond or fishbowl. Nine fish are said to bring prosperity, energy and good fortune. At the bottom of the card, waves dance in merriment.

The Augur: Rytons, mazers, the "merrythought." *Raise a toast to the pleasure of creativity, prosperity, sensual satisfaction and wish fulfillment.*

Deck Comparisons

The Rider Waite Smith deck shows a successful merchant seated, with a curved array of nine chalices behind him. The Thoth Nine of Cups shows nine purple cups arranged in the geomantic figure Laetitia, with golden lotuses pouring water into the cups. The Rosetta Nine of Cups is arranged and colored like the Thoth, but the cups have twisting fish and the glyphs of Jupiter. Tabula Mundi's card shows the creatures of Fortune in celebration, where fish leap from mazers and the big half of the wishbone is offered. The middle decan of Pisces, Yesod of Water, brings a jovial influence that is cause for happiness.

Ten of Cups

Lord of Satiety (Perfected Success)

Last decan of Pisces, ruled by Mars

Malkuth of Briah/Water

Trumps: Moon, Tower

Queen Scale for Malkuth: Citrine (N), Olive (E), Russet (W) and Black(S); Saltire, plus the colors scales of the related trumps

TEN OF CUPS
♓ SATIETY ♂

The Lord of Satiety is the final decan of Pisces, the zodiac's endpoint. This decan is ruled by Mars. The dates of the decan span the very last days of winter preceding the first day of spring, and thus this is the "double Mars" in the Chaldean planet sequence that begins again with Mars at the vernal equinox. As a Ten, the card is associated with Malkuth, in the creative spiritual world of Briah and elemental water.

The related trumps are the Moon for Pisces and the Tower for Mars as ruler of the decan. The cups in this card are shaped like opium poppy pods, from the Moon card, and are stacked in a tetractys pyramid of ten. Water gushes and spills, overflowing the unstable cups. The ocean is patterned like in the Moon card, in the manner suggestive of the brain waves of sleep. Behind the stack of cups, one of the griffins from the Tower card is seen perched on the top step of a step pyramid of ten steps like the Egyptian pyramid of Zoser or Djoser. In Mesopotamia, these pyramids were religious monuments called ziggurats. They often featured a shrine or temple at the summit and were called the "Hill of Heaven" or "Mountain of the Gods."

Griffins are a martial symbol in antiquity and often guarded treasure. In Dante's *Divine Comedy*, Beatrice rides away through paradise on a griffin that commentators sometimes refer to as symbolically representing either Christ or the Pope. In Milton's *Paradise Lost*, a gold-guarding griffin is referred to in describing Satan.

The griffin holds a poppy pod in his beak, as he guards the stack of ten opium poppy pod cups. The opium poppy is a symbol of Morpheus, god of sleep and dreaming. In Victorian flower language, poppies can indicate oblivion, and the eternal sleep of death. Poppies are also sacred to Demeter, who used them in a brew in order to sleep through the long and seemingly endless winter while her daughter Persephone was imprisoned in the Underworld. In China, the poppy is a symbol of beauty, rest and success. But poppies by the association with opiate induced stupor also can indicate sloth, addiction and overindulgence. Opiates work by fooling the brain into mimicking endorphins, which makes them highly addictive. It is easy to go from perfection to too much. Crowley says of this card, "As it is written: "Until a dart strike through his liver." The pursuit of pleasure has been crowned with perfect success; and constantly it is discovered that, having got everything that one wanted, one did not want it after all; now one must pay." There is a seeming contradiction here with the card's former title of Lord of Perfected Success. A footnote to this card in Liber Theta cautions that it is not such as good card as stated, and represents "boredom, and quarreling arising therefrom; disgust springing from too great luxury. In particular it represents drug-habits, the sottish excess of pleasure, and the revenge of nature."

The element of water has reached its pinnacle and can go no further, and thus is due for disruption. Mars is a jarring force when combined with the ethereal and spiritual nature of Pisces, a sign given to dreaming and escapism. Mars here is the Tower's strike against seeming perfection. It is all very dreamy and pleasant for a time, as a definite ultimate success has been reached, but it isn't stable.

The Augur: Zoser's step pyramid, the opium poppy, the griffon. *There is pleasure, but it is easy to go from perfection to over satiation.*

Deck Comparisons
The Rider Waite Smith Ten of Cups seems to ignore any possibility of excess and only shows the perfection; a tableau of a happy family. Two children dance while the parents arm in arm survey ten cups in a rainbow. The Thoth Ten of Cups shows ten overflowing golden cups perched a little tilted in a Tree of Life formation. The Rosetta Ten of Cups has the golden cups in the shape of ram's heads, each with a golden fish stuffed in its mouth. The cups are in the Tree of Life formation superimposed over the glyphs of Mars and Pisces. Tabula Mundi's card shows poppy pods stacked and in the mouth of griffon, with Zoser's pyramid upon the sea of sleep. The Ten of Cups is the last decan of Pisces, Malkuth of Water. Emotional pleasure, while a state of perfection walks a fine line between satiation and excess, as the Martial forces prepare to jumpstart a cycle.

Scire, To Know

The Swords

ו

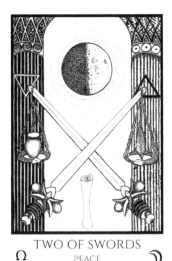

TWO OF SWOrDS

Lord of Peace (Peace Restored)

First decan of Libra, ruled by the Moon

Chokmah of Yetzirah/Air

Trumps: Adjustment, Priestess

**Prince Scale for Chokmah: Blue pearl
grey, like mother-of-pearl, plus the
colors scales of the related trumps**

TWO OF SWORDS
PEACE
♎   ☽

The Lord of Peace is the first decan of the cardinal sign Libra, which is ruled by the Moon. It is in Chokmah of Yetzirah, the sephira of wisdom in the formative or astral-psychological world of mind. Crowley's naming of the cards has removed the word "restored" from the name as his argument is that as a Two, no disruption has previously happened. The Two of Swords is the first manifestation of the element of Air, and as such is in perfect balance.

The related trumps are Adjustment and the Priestess. Two swords resembling the sword of the Ace are crossed in perfect symmetry in a saltire arrangement, the saltire in heraldry having the meaning *resolution*. From the Adjustment card, to emphasize the theme of balance and for the sign of Libra, the swords serve as a fulcrum balancing the scales. These are the scales of Truth, of the goddess Ma'at. Ma'at was the ancient Egyptian goddess of the balance who stood for truth, justice, morality, law and order. She maintained and regulated all things in the universe and all actions of beings, to prevent degeneration into chaos. Her laws kept the peace by adhering to divine order.

The card shows the two pillars from the Priestess card, also called Boaz and Jachin of Solomon's temple and positioned at the entrance of Masonic temples. Boaz, meaning *strength*, is the black pillar, and Jachin, meaning *he establishes*, is the white pillar. Boaz faces north while Jachin faces south. These pillars, dark and light, yin and yang, represent the forces of polarity or the negative and positive in equilibrium. They also stand in for the two sides of the Tree of Life, the Pillar of Severity and the Pillar of Mercy. The Moon in the background reminds us that the mind, like the moon, is subject to fluctuations, and that mental flexibility results in intellectual harmony.

From the Priestess card is a representation of the scroll she carries, a symbol of knowledge and wisdom conscious and unconscious. Here it can be symbolic of a treaty, but in general it is said to be the Torah, the written law of the five books of Moses. Torah means instruction or guidance and offers both commentary on the stories of creation and religious teachings for an ideal way of life for those who follow it. Alternatively the scroll represents the volume of sacred law on the Masonic altar, containing the Bible, the Veda, the Koran, and other holy writings so as to be inclusive of all the books of all the faiths of its members. This acceptance of all doctrines as one faith under which each candidate is obligated according to his or her own moral compass is part of the path of peace. Even with divisions and polarities there can be balance and compromise. This spirit of creative resolution however does not preclude tension, as effort is required to remain in harmony with swords crossed.

The Augur: The scale of Ma'at's balance, the pillars Boaz and Jachin, the scroll of sacred law. *Division is resolved with effort and mental equanimity is the result.*

Deck Comparisons

The RWS deck shows a blindfolded woman on a rocky shore, holding two swords crossed aloft in balance with the moon behind her. The Thoth deck shows the two swords crossed piercing a rose, a traditional Golden Dawn depiction of the card. Behind are stylized pin wheeling forms. The Rosetta deck has the crossed swords and rose, with the sword hilts of the zodiacal glyphs and the rose winged and emitting rays of light. In the background are bursts of light representing the dendrites and synapses of the mind. Tabula Mundi's card has the crossed swords as the fulcrum of a scale, weighing the heart against truth with the scroll positioned centrally between the dark and light pillars. The first decan of Libra is Chokmah of Air, where the flexibility of the Moon's rulership gives mental balance to the first emanation of thought.

THree of swords

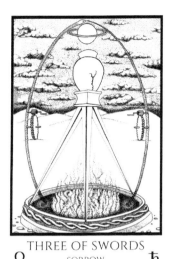

THREE OF SWORDS

Ω   SORROW   ♄

Lord of Sorrow

Middle decan of Libra, ruled by Saturn

Binah of Yetzirah/Air

Trumps: Adjustment, Universe

Prince Scale for Binah: Dark Brown, plus the colors scales of the related trumps

The Three of Swords, Lord of Sorrow, is the second and middle decan of Libra, which is ruled by Saturn. It is in Binah of Yetzirah, the sephira of the Great Mother in the formative world of Air and the mind. The great ocean of Binah here is the Abysmal Womb of memory and rebirth; the waters of the collective unconscious. This is the darkness of Binah, the mourning of Isis; the pierced rose, the mind forcing open the mysteries of nature. This is the sorrow of the Buddha, the melancholy probing that leads to enlightenment. To understand joy and rapture one must also experience sorrow. Did you ever know something you fear might happen, even though you told yourself it wouldn't really? And then, it did.

The trumps associated with this card are Adjustment, and the Universe. From the Adjustment card, at the pinnacle of the tripod of swords the heart-jar of the soul from the balance of Ma'at perches in the place of the Oracle of Delphi. The pervasive pierced heart symbolism of most Three of Sword depictions is replaced by the heart jar, cracked open. The motto inscribed at the shrine of the Oracle is said to be "Know Thyself."

In the Book of Thoth Crowley makes reference to the 14th Aethyr in association with Binah of Air. An excerpt from the Vision and the Voice on this Aethyr states: "There is a veil of such darkness before the Aethyr that it seems impossible to pierce it. But there is a voice saying: Behold, the Great One of the Night of Time stirreth, and with his tail he churneth up the slime, and of the foam thereof shall he make stars. And in the battle of the Python and the Sphinx shall the glory be to the Sphinx, but the victory to the Python. Now the veil of darkness is formed of a very great number of exceedingly fine black veils, and one tears them off one at a time. And the voice says, There is no light or knowledge or beauty or stability in the Kingdom of the Grave, whither thou goest. And the worm is crowned. All that thou wast hath he eaten up, and all that thou art is his pasture until to-morrow. And all that thou shalt be is nothing. Thou who wouldst enter the domain of the Great One of the Night of Time, this burden must thou take up."

The depiction in this card is of the tripod of the Oracle of Delphi, who is also known as the Pythia. The mythology describes the Pythia as delivering oracles while in a frenzy induced by vapors rising from a chasm in the earth. The name "Pythia" comes from the original name of Delphi, Pytho, which was derived from the Greek verb *pythein*, meaning "to rot." This makes allusion to the decomposition of Python, the monstrous earth dragon of Delphi depicted as a great serpent. Python had been sent by Hera to pursue Leta when she was pregnant by Zeus with Apollo and Artemis, so that she could not deliver anywhere the sun shone. Later Apollo avenges his mother by killing Python near the rock cleft of the Oracle.

The reference to the oracle is apt for the dark chasm in the earth, the rising steam of the dark waters from the womb of chaos, and the sorrow that can result from the forcing of mysteries in pursuit of occult knowledge. Saturn above from the Universe card bears witness to the darkness, and the quality of form inherent in Binah. Also from the Universe card is the Ouroboros for Python and the gears which grind on, the inevitability that sorrow comes to us all. It all takes place within the Ouroboros. The sky behind is dark with rain clouds.

The Augur: The Oracle of Delphi, the Pythia, the cracked heart-jar. *Know thyself, and the sorrow that leads to enlightenment.*

Deck Comparisons

The Rider Waite Smith Three of Swords has the omnipresent heart pierced by three swords against a stormy sky, imagery which Smith borrowed from the Sola Busca deck. The Thoth deck shows the traditional Golden Dawn depiction of a rose pierced by swords against a background of black chaos, with the central sword that of the Magus. The Rosetta deck also has the pierced rose, but the rose is winged and the wings form the shape of a heart and have hidden glyphs of Saturn. The central sword is that of the Ace and the two flanking swords have the zodiacal glyphs on the hilts, while the background has grey and dismal dendrites of the mind against a black background. Tabula Mundi shows the heart-jar in the position of the Pythia on the tripod, the Oracle of Delphi. The middle decan of Libra is ruled by Saturn, and is Binah of Air, where black sorrow leads to insight.

four of swords

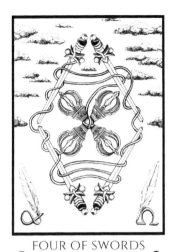

FOUR OF SWORDS
Ω   TRUCE   ♃

Lord of Truce (Rest from Strife)

Last decan of Libra, ruled by Jupiter

Chesed of Yetzirah/Air

Trumps: Adjustment, Fortune

Prince Scale for Chesed: Deep Purple, plus the colors scales of the related trumps

The Four of Swords, Lord of Truce, is the last decan of Libra, which is ruled by Jupiter. It is in Chesed of Yetzirah, the sephira of *Mercy* in the formative world of Air and the mind. Here we have a double influence of Jupiter, as the planet that rules the decan and as Chesed is the sephira of Jupiter. Jupiter is associated with law and dogma, as is Libra, and swords with the intellect. Here the application of law allows for rest from strife. The Fours suggest structure and sometimes rigidity; as do laws. Sometimes this structure, though inflexible, can be a refuge.

The four swords are arranged in a diamond shape. The diamond shape is known as a symbol of ascension, clarity and wisdom. Native Americans associate the diamond with the butterfly, a symbol of air, and the immortality that results from leaving a legacy. The diamond is the shape of the rune *Ingwaz*, meaning harmony, unity and agreement.

From the Fortune card we have the loom's shuttle, shaped like a Vajra, weaving the swords together in common cause with the blue thread of truce. The weaver's shuttle is also symbolic of the Fates, three crones also known as the Moirai, who watched that the fate assigned to every being by eternal laws might take its course without obstruction. Some say Zeus, also known as Jupiter, is the only being who could command them; others claim that even he was subject to their law. The crones were considered the daughters of Zeus and Themis, who was the embodiment of divine order and law.

The four-arms of the Vajra symbolize many things that come in fours, among which are the four immeasurables (compassion, love, sympathetic joy and equanimity). This can also be considered "rest from strife." In the background, the cloudy sky of the previous card is clearing. In the foreground are feather quills writing, as a contribution from both the feather of truth from Adjustment and the feathered pen of Fortune. Here they write the Alpha and Omega from the Adjustment card, together and in tandem. The truce is written and covers all things beginning and ending, from alpha to omega. The alpha and omega are referred to in the Book of Thoth as the "two witnesses in whom shall every word be established." Crowley calls these the "Judex and Testes of Final Judgment; the testes, in particular, are symbolic of the secret course of judgment whereby all current experience is absorbed, transmuted, and ultimately passed on. This all takes place within the diamond formed by the figure which is the concealed *Vesica Piscis* through which this sublimated and adjusted experience passes to its next manifestation."

The Augur: The Vajra, the rune *Ingwaz*, the Treaty of Alpha and Omega. *Take refuge in stabilization.*

Deck Comparisons

The RWS Four of Swords shows a figure with palms together, lain upon a slab decorated with a carved sword in a chapel with a stained glass window and three hanging swords. The Thoth Four of Swords has four swords points together to form a St. Andrew's cross; behind this is the rose of 49 petals and a background reminiscent of lightning. The Rosetta Four of Swords has four swords that extend from the corners of the card to the center, meeting at the rose which has four wings to form a diamond shape and a background of light rays and dendrites. Tabula Mundi shows the four swords in diamond formation, joined in truce with the winding threads of the Vajra-shuttle, and the feather pens in the foreground signing the treaty of the two witnesses' Alpha and Omega. The Four of Swords is the last decan of Libra, Chesed of Air, where Jupiter as the ruler of the decan gives law structure, which creates a mental refuge from stress.

FIVE OF SWORDS

♒ DEFEAT ♀

FIVE OF SWORDS

Lord of Defeat

First decan of Aquarius, ruled by Venus

Geburah of Yetzirah/Air

Trumps: Star, Empress

Prince Scale for Geburah: Bright Scarlet, plus the colors scales of the related trumps

The Five of Swords, Lord of Defeat, is the first decan of the fixed sign of Aquarius,[22] ruled by Venus. Here it is placed in the sephira of Geburah of Yetzirah, the station of Severity in the astral world of Air. The trump of Aquarius, the Star, here combines with the trump of Venus, the Empress. We have two feminine energies in the sephira of fiery Mars.

The card shows the white dove of Venus under attack by a dark bird of prey for Aquarius, resembling a raven or crow. The dove was carrying a message of peace in the form of a rose; the rose has been utterly destroyed or "torn asunder and falling" as in the traditional Golden Dawn description. The dove had built its nest in what it thought was a secure square form. But it had lowered its defenses and built from four broken swords. In peace time, the swords had been broken up, but now the nest comes under sinister attack. It presented an easy target for the raven or raptor, as shown by the large dark and disruptive fifth sword which totally overpowers the four and breaks into the nest. The humanitarian sign of Aquarius ruled by peace loving Venus is no match for the fiery sephira of Severity. Here in the element of Air is shown mental weakness that leads to defeat. Sentimental thinking can make one lose a competitive edge. Crowley calls it intellect enfeebled by pacifism, and says the card can also imply betrayal and treachery.

---

22   The author's ascendant sign degree falls in this decan, unfortunately. Like Crowley, I've put some personal touches to some of the cards that mark certain astrological elements of my chart. Thus incorporated into the design is a subtle reference to the Sabian symbols both for Aquarius 7, the author's rising degree and Aquarius 20, the degree of a first house planet (Moon) in the author's chart. The Sabian symbols are "A child born of an eggshell" and "A large white dove bearing a message."

Pope John Paul II began an annual tradition of releasing white peace doves on the last Sunday in January to symbolize the need to pray and work for world peace. Interestingly the date of the last Sunday in January falls in the first decan of Aquarius symbolized by this card. Unfortunately the tradition had to be discontinued when crows and seagulls immediately and violently attacked the white doves. Just moments after they were released from the hands of the participating children, the doves were dismembered, triggering all sorts of end times speculation.

Because doves mate for life and work together to build nests and raise young, they have been revered as symbols of friendship by diverse cultures. White doves are a traditional symbol of peace and pacifism in Christian, Judaic, and Pagan iconography. The goddesses associated with Venus are typically portrayed with doves: Aphrodite, Ishtar, Inanna and Astarte. In the epic of Gilgamesh a white dove was released after the deluge. This story is echoed by the biblical tale of Noah first releasing a raven and then releasing a dove after the flood. The raven was apparently too smart to return to the stifling ark.

The word raven in addition to the name of the bird can also mean rapine, rapacity, violent plundering and theft. They have a reputation for cunning and malignity, which goes well with the card's meaning of potential treachery. The message here is to take a more active stance to protect what you hold dear, and that passivity is not always the wisest course of action.

The Augur: The Raven, the Dove, the broken swords. *Intellect weakened by passivity and sentiment causes the loss of the competitive edge.*

Deck Comparisons

The Rider Waite Smith Five of Swords shows a smirking man picking up swords abandoned by dejected and disinterested rivals. The Thoth Five of Swords shows five beat up and unmatched swords arranged in an inverse pentagram of rose petals on a field of asymmetrical stylized wings and swastikas. The Rosetta Five of Swords a central cracked sword with a hilt shaped like a monkish figure. The sword destroys a rose of five petals superimposed on an inverse pentagram, and is flanked by bent swords with the appropriate zodiacal glyphs. The background dendrites of the mind are tangled. In the Tabula Mundi card, four broken swords form a dove's nest. The nest and the dove's Venusian rose are destroyed by the powerful fifth sword of a raven. This card is Geburah of Air, the first decan of Aquarius ruled by Venus, and the cards share a theme of forces disrupting and conquering, to eliminate mental weakness caused by sentiment.

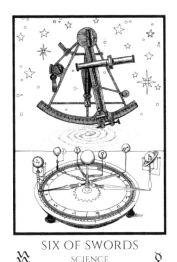

SIX OF SWOrDS

Lord of Science (Earned Success)

Middle decan of Aquarius, ruled by Mercury

Tiphareth of Yetzirah/Air

Trumps: Star, Magus

Prince Scale for Tiphareth: Rich Salmon, plus the colors scales of the related trumps

SIX OF SWORDS
SCIENCE

♒︎   ☿

The Six of Swords, Lord of Science, is the middle decan of the fixed sign of Aquarius, ruled by Mercury. It is here placed in the sephira of Tiphareth of Yetzirah, the station of Beauty in the Astral World with the element of Air. Everyone is happy here in solar central Tiphareth, and Mercury is well matched with the air sign Aquarius. The balance of this harmonious sephira combines well with the sign Aquarius' detached mental processes, and the mental strength and flexibility of Mercury.

The trump of Aquarius is the Star, and the trump of Mercury is the Magus. From the Star card, we have the stars themselves, and from the Magus card the swirling galaxy from his hand and some new implements. Both cards share the symbolism of the spiral galaxy. Here we have instruments of celestial navigation. Above we have the sextant, from the Latin word *sextus*, meaning six, or *sextāns*, meaning one-sixth. This refers to the frame of the sextant which is in the shape of a sector which is approximately ⅙ of a circle (60°).

Sextants are used both for navigation and astronomy. The astronomical device is used for measuring the distant stars and determining stellar positions and equinoxes. The navigator's sextant is used to "take a sight" meaning to determine the distance between any two visible objects to calculate a position on a nautical or aeronautical chart. The sun can be sighted at solar noon or the North Star Polaris at night can be used in the Northern hemisphere to determine latitude. To determine longitude and mean time, the sextant measures the distance between the Moon and another celestial object like a star or planet. This association with navigation also fits with one traditional meaning of the card having to do with long distance travel. This can be literal travel or a journey of the mind.

At the bottom of the card, the six swords form the arms of an orrery. An orrery is a form of planetarium. It is a mechanical model of our solar system, usually heliocentric, used to predict and illustrate the positions of the planets. It is sort of a mechanical clock with the planets as the hands. Here the hands of the clock are the six swords, each sword propelling one of the six planets around the central sun of Tiphareth. In this card is all the beauty of the intellect in its highest form of consciousness. According to Crowley, it is intelligence which has won to the goal. The general rulers of the sign Aquarius are Saturn and Uranus. Saturn gives discipline and Uranus gives innovation and genius. The majesty of the balanced and disciplined human mind results in the brilliant discoveries of Science. The success inherent in this card is earned and comes after effort.

The Augur: The sextant, the orrery, the spiral galaxy. *Set your course for the stars and through the journey discover the beauty of the inventive intellect.*

Deck Comparisons

The Rider Waite Smith Six of Swords shows a ferryman poling a boat across a river, pushing out as if setting off on a journey. The boat carries six upright swords and a cloaked figure, probably female, sits next to a child. The Thoth Six of Swords has six swords arranged in a hexagram, pointing towards a rose cross made of six golden squares. In the background is a fencing diagram and Harris' stylized pinwheel shapes. The six swords of the Rosetta have the zodiacal glyphs and are arranged in an elongated hexagram. The central rose is surrounded by a unicursal hexagram, a circle squared within a diamond shaped vesica pisces, and lightning-like dendrites of the mind. Tabula Mundi shows the sextant and the orrery, instruments used to navigate the spiral galaxy. The card is the middle decan of Aquarius, Tiphareth of Air, and the decan is ruled by Mercury. Mental brilliance in balanced form takes one to new places one step at a time.

seven of swords

Lord of Futility (Unstable Effort)

Last decan of Aquarius, ruled by the Moon

Netzach of Yetzirah/Air

Trumps: Star, Priestess

Prince Scale for Netzach: Bright Yellow Green, plus the colors scales of the related trumps

SEVEN OF SWORDS
♒ FUTILITY ☽

The Seven of Swords, Lord of Futility is the final decan of the fixed sign of Aquarius, ruled by the Moon. Here it is placed in the sephira of Netzach of Yetzirah, the station of Victory in the Astral World with the element of Air. Like all unstable Sevens the card shows what is needed, or rather what to avoid, in order to achieve Victory. Here is the last decan of Aquarius, the decan of dissipation, ruled by the fluctuating and unstable Moon. Add to that the fact that it is a sword card in the sephira of Venus and its location far down and imbalanced on the Tree of Life, and the situation becomes futile; you gave up at the last minute though Victory was still in sight.

The card speaks of a long journey through the desert. Suddenly you find yourself surrounded by an army, armed with six sabers—and you have a boot dagger. Now, a boot dagger is going to cause trouble in some jurisdictions; it isn't exactly legal, or considered sporting. But a boot dagger has the advantage of stealth, and surprise evasive maneuvers are possible—if you make the effort. Will you try to talk your way out of it, or bring out the hidden dagger and take your chances?

From the Star card for Aquarius we have six geometric seven-pointed stars, one for each saber, and a central seven-pointed star called a septagram or "great heptagram" behind the boot dagger. The stars are enclosed within a larger seven sided polygon called a regular heptagram. The heptagram, as seen in the Star card, is a Thelemic symbol of Babalon. Alchemically, it refers to the seven first known planets. In Christianity, the seven pointed star is used to ward off evil. When called the Elven or Fairy Star, it represents a gateway for the Fae (whom everyone knows to be tricky).

From the Priestess card for the Moon, we see the Moon itself in the background, at the dark and sometimes blood red stage of the totality of a lunar eclipse. In a blood moon eclipse, people sometimes experience negative effects. At the physical level there can be lethargy and at the psychological level, negative thoughts especially about spiritual motifs. The moon's action of "flux and reflux" leads to vacillation and instability, and people are more prone to make poor decisions as the intellect is compromised.

Also in the foreground is a camel for the Priestess card, whose letter is Gimel, meaning camel. Your heavily laden camel has gone to its knees and given up on making it to the oasis. You are out of water, yet on the horizon dark towering storm clouds threaten rain. Are you going to give up now? It may be tempting to give up, because if you just fold you can claim you didn't really lose. But that is a weak argument.

The Augur: The kneeling camel, the blood moon eclipse, the boot dagger. *Doubt and vacillation lead to poor effort; be more clever if you can.*

Deck Comparisons

The Rider Waite Smith Seven of Swords shows a shifty looking man awkwardly carrying off five swords away from a pavilion of tents, while two swords are standing in the ground behind him. The Thoth Seven of Swords shows six swords with hilts of the planetary glyphs surrounding a seventh solar sword. The Rosetta card shows the sword of the Magus piercing the rose, surrounded by six curved swords with the glyphs of the Moon and Aquarius as hilts. Tabula Mundi's card shows a camel at the point of collapse, in a desert just before a storm and at the moment of negative eclipse. Six sabers surround a boot dagger. The card is the last decan of Aquarius, lunar ruled, and is in Netzach of Air. The cards share a theme of weak and unstable mental effort creating an atmosphere of futility.

EIGHT OF SWORDS

INTERFERENCE

II   4

EIGHT OF SWOrDS

Lord of Interference (Shortened Force)

First decan of Gemini, ruled by Jupiter

Hod of Yetzirah/Air

Trumps: Lovers, Fortune

**Prince Scale for Hod: Red-russet, plus
the colors scales of the related trumps**

The Lord of Interference, or Shortened Force, is the first decan of Gemini. (Let me take a moment here to say that poor Gemini gets three rather difficult cards for it's decans. I tried to make up for that by taking extra care with the designs.) The initial decan of Gemini is ruled by Jupiter, in the sephira of Hod, at the foot of the Pillar of Severity, in the astral and mental world of Yetzirah. Outside and sometimes accidental interference can be the cause of difficulty. The wrong thoughts have shortened one's force.

The mental airy nature of Gemini combined with the buoyancy of Jupiter, would normally be considered a positive. But in the unbalanced and low sephira of Hod, in the mental world of Swords, this does not give one an advantage. The combination of Jupiter with Gemini can mean too much force applied to trivial things. In this card the Will is being unexpectedly interfered with in the realm of intellectual contest. Jupiter does have an element of luck, as long as effort is made, yet sometimes the "luck" it refers to is actually referring to unforeseen sheer bad luck even if on a trivial level. With Jupiter here in Hod of Air, one may not see the forest for the trees; that is to say, that too much attention may be paid to small things at the expense of the bigger picture.

The related trump cards are the Lovers for Gemini and Fortune for Jupiter. From the Lovers card, we have the solar Lion and the lunar Eagle, engaged in a tangle over a bit of string. The imagery comes from an alchemical illustration called "The Battle of Sol and Luna," where opposites are engaged in conflict prior to union. Combined, the lion and eagle are components of the griffin. Together they would form a powerful guardian, but here they are working at cross-purposes. This is the alchemical phase of *Separatio*, the separation and struggle of opposing forces. It is a difficult time that demands will and determination. The Emerald Tablet says of this phase, "The Wind carries it in its belly," and the alchemists felt they were applying the Element Air in their work during Separation. Psychologically it is a time of deciding what to discard and what to integrate. One begins to reclaim parts that the rational mind may have rejected. Crystallized thoughts and blockages need to be released.

From the card of Fortune, we have the vajra-shuttle wound with thread, which tangles around the creatures as they pull against each other. The eight poniards, small but sharp daggers, are arranged in the shape of a great wheel, also as inference to the Fortune card. This dagger-wheel has sharp points facing in all directions, and is wound with the other end of the thread they struggle with. The wheel turns; the thread winds. The thread can be thought of like Ariadne's ball of twine that helped Theseus escape the Labyrinth and kill the Minotaur. Untangled it can be the guide that overcomes a trap of unconscious repression, or it can be a fruitless and half-hearted tug-of-war over a bit of string.

The Augur: The battle of Sol and Luna, *Separatio*, Ariadne's ball of twine. *The Will is interfered with in the realm of intellectual contest; there is indecision and obfuscation.*

Deck Comparisons

The Rider Waite Smith Eight of Swords shows a woman blindfolded and bound, surrounded by a fence or cage of swords in the ground. The Thoth Eight of Swords shows a lattice work formed of two long swords crossed by six smaller daggers, with a chaotic background. The Rosetta Eight of Swords shows a rose barricaded and blocked by eight swords with hilts marked with the zodiacal glyphs, with a backdrop of reddish dendrites. Tabula Mundi's card shows the lion and eagle as opposing solar and lunar forces being tangled in the ropes they interfere with. The card is the first decan of Gemini, and Hod of Air, and the cards share themes of blockage and binding.

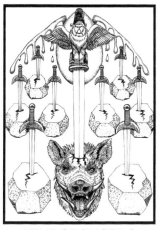

NINE OF SWORDS
CRUELTY
II ♂

nine of swords

Lord of Cruelty (Despair and Cruelty)

Middle decan of Gemini, ruled by Mars

Yesod of Yetzirah/Air

Trumps: Lovers, Tower

Prince Scale for Yesod: Very dark Purple, plus the colors scales of the related trumps

The Lord of Cruelty is the central decan of Gemini, which is ruled by Mars. It is placed in the lunar sephira of Yesod in the mental world of Yetzirah and Air. While the other Nines are all positive manifestations as can be expected in the central pillar, the Nine of Swords is the penultimate negative state of mind. The suit has degenerated almost to the point of no return, and the lunar influence of Yesod on the mind leads to pathological states where the unconscious mind takes over. It seems that negativity is inherent in the suit of Swords, and here it is about to come to fruition. Eventually the mind comes to the conclusion that all is fruitless.

Crowley makes reference to a bleak poem called *The City of Dreadful Night* in relation to this card. This is by Scottish poet James B.V. Thomson, described as a consummate pessimist suffering from depression. In the poem London is seen through the eyes of a disconsolate atheist. It is a long and despairing poem indeed. Here is a sample of just of few of its many wretched stanzas: "My soul hath bled for you these sunless years, With bitter blood-drops running down like tears: Oh dark, dark, dark, withdrawn from joy and light!" It continues "There is no God; no Fiend with names divine Made us and tortures us; if we must pine, It is to satiate no Being's gall. It was the dark delusion of a dream, That living Person conscious and supreme, Whom we must curse for cursing us with life." It goes on to curse the life we must endure if we cannot die from poison or the knife. Simply charming; this is not recommended binge drinking reading.

The related trumps are the Lovers of Gemini and the Tower for the decan's ruler, Mars. The central sword has a hilt with a winged lion, a creature of the eagle and lion combined. Over the lion's wingspan, an arching form drips poisoned blood. The blade of the sword is buried firmly in the skull of the boar from the Tower card, who screams in rage and pain. This is the anguish of the mind; the gaping mouth of madness and hunger where words cruel and despairing bring self-inflicted torture. Behind the central sword, the shape of the central element is echoed by eight of the sword-in-a-stone motifs from the Lovers card. To overcome this state of mind, the only way out is through. Pulling the sword from the stone requires an act of sacrifice; the sacrificial king. One can decide to offer no resistance to this persecution or one can offer grim and uncompromising retribution.

The Augur: The raging boar, *The City of Dreadful Night*, the Sword in the Stone. *This is the anguish of the mind, cruel and despairing, that must be overcome through mental discipline.*

Deck Comparisons

The Rider Waite Smith deck shows a person sitting upright in bed, face in hands, as if in the grips of a terrible nightmare or miasma of despair. Nine swords hang on the wall horizontally behind. The Thoth Nine of Swords shows nine vertical swords dripping blood while poison drips down behind them and chaotic forms dance. The Rosetta Nine of Swords shows a great gaping mouth with swords and curved daggers as teeth, dripping poison. Some hilts are decorated with the glyphs of Gemini, and some are phallic with glyphs of Mars. The remains of a destroyed rose are in the foreground. Tabula Mundi's card shows dripping poison and blood forming the wings of the lion of the central sword, which pierces the head of the boar like the sword within the stone. The card is the middle decan of Gemini, ruled by Mars, and is in Yesod of Air. The cards share a theme of the pain of poisoned thoughts.

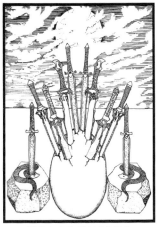

ten of swords

Lord of Ruin

Last decan of Gemini, ruled by the Sun

Malkuth of Yetzirah/Air

Trumps: Lovers, Sun

Prince Scale for Malkuth: Citrine, Olive, Russet and Black; all with Gold flecked Black, plus the colors scales of the related trumps

TEN OF SWORDS
Ⅱ   RUIN   ☉

The Lord of Ruin is the final decan of Gemini, in Malkuth of Yetzirah and the element of Air. This decan of Gemini is ruled by the Sun, but here it is matched with airy Gemini, a mutable or mutating sign in its dissipating decan. Add to this the position in earthly and heavy Malkuth, the dangling pendant on the Tree of Life, and one can see that the suit of Swords has here broken down completely. The mental qualities of Swords have culminated in the breakdown of logic and reason. Struggle and battle always eventually end in carnage. But things can be salvaged. The solar influence of the decan's ruler signifies the possibility of a new day. The light of the Sun shines upon airy ideas revealing which of them are impractical for earthy manifestation, and signals the end of delusion.

Crowley says of this card "As soon as things are bad enough, one begins to build up again. When all the Governments have smashed each other, there still remains the peasant. At the end of Candide's misadventures, he could still cultivate his garden."

The reference to Candide comes from an eighteenth century satire by the philosopher Voltaire. Candide begins in an Edenic paradise being indoctrinated with the philosophies of optimism. As the story progresses he is subjected to witness or experience horrific events one after the other: tragedy, calamity, rape, cannibalism and torture. Meanwhile his tutor constantly and ludicrously lectures that whatever life hands you it is all for the best. The humorous treatment of tragedy as Voltaire illustrates the insanity of society and government echoes the way this card often seems to be pointing to an over the top expression of woe-is-me. At the conclusion of the story, Candide is in debate with a pessimistic companion who states that "man was bound to live either in convulsions of misery or in the lethargy of boredom." It is found that the cure for the crushing boredom of existence apart from endless suffering was to be found in the toil of the garden, where man could recall the state of mastery he had experienced in Eden, and hard work left no time for philosophy and speculation.

From the Lovers card, for Gemini, we have the Orphic egg, pierced by swords cleaving and penetrating the hermaphroditic deity Phanes enclosed within. Phanes, whose name means "to bring light," was a Greek god of procreation who emerges from the cosmic egg entwined with a serpent. This is the world egg of Chronos (Time) and Ananke (Necessity or Fate). Along each side are dual sword-in-stone motifs also from the Lovers card. The swords impale the heads of the twin snakes of the caduceus from the Sun card, for the ruler of the decan. In the background, cirrus clouds obscure the face of the sun.

The Augur: Candide, Orphic egg pierced, Phanes the light-bringer. *The disruption of ruin kills logic and reason; await a new dawn.*

Deck Comparisons

The Rider Waite Smith Ten of Swords shows a man face down on the ground, his back impaled by swords. The sky is filled with dark clouds but there is light of the setting or rising sun upon the horizon. The Thoth Ten of Swords shows ten swords, some of them broken, arranged in a Tree of Life formation, with the central heart and sword of Tiphareth being destroyed. The background is filled with pinwheeling forms. The Rosetta Ten of Swords shows ten splintered and broken swords with their hilts displaying the appropriate astrological glyphs. In the background are blood red dendrite forms against a solar glow issuing from the darkness. Tabula Mundi's card shows the Orphic egg pierced and the twin snakes of the caduceus sacrificed and slain, with the sun behind shifting clouds. The cards share imagery of piercing and destruction from mental breakdown, the dark night before the dawn.

Tacere, To Keep Silent

The Disks

TWO OF DISKS

Lord of Change (Harmonious Change)

First decan of Capricorn, ruled by Jupiter

Chokmah of Assiah/Earth

Trumps: Devil, Fortune

Princess Scale for Chokmah: White flecked Red, Blue, and Yellow, plus the colors scales of the related trumps

TWO OF DISKS
♑   CHANGE   4

The Two of Disks, called the Lord of Change, is the first decan of the cardinal sign of Capricorn, which is ruled by Jupiter. It is in Chokmah of Assiah, the sephira of first force in the material world of action. With this card we have the first manifestation of the element of earth. Capricorn as the sign associated with Saturn is a sign of restriction and contraction. Yet this decan is ruled by Jupiter, the planet of abundance and expansion. Jupiter's fortune is somewhat constrained by the limiting saturnine nature of Capricorn. Yet the interplay of expansion and contraction is what drives the universe. It is a universal principal without which no engine could run and nothing could ever happen. Here the spark of Chokmah drives the internal combustion, and the expansion of gases (Jupiter) applies compression (Capricorn) to the piston. To offer another analogy, athletes know that after a muscle is stretched, it contracts. The continual treatment thusly is part of the process of muscular growth.

The card shows an hourglass, symbolic of the restrictive influence of the force of time. With the passage of time, change is inevitable. In Masonry, the hourglass is an emblem of human life and a reminder that we should make the most of it. Yet it is also a metaphor between the two halves upper and lower, heaven and earth, and the need to turn things around in order to keep a continual cycle flowing. When one side of the glass is full, the other is empty; and then we reverse it and the sands flow once again. Emptiness follows fullness and gain follows loss just as sadness follows joy, and the cycle endlessly repeats.

The hourglass is here for the Two of Disk's affiliation with the Devil card as the trump of Capricorn. What Crowley calls "the serpent of the endless band" is here suggested by a belt connecting two wheels within the sands. These wheels, from the Fortune card for the association with Jupiter, stir the sands and keep the process eternally going. One wheel is dextro and the other laevo-rotatory, keeping the flow in constant movement.

The twin peaks of the mountains in the background are those barren hills of Capricorn and Earth, and the journeys we take along our mortal path. We climb the mountains and on the other side we must descend. We focus on the climb, and achieving the goal of ascent, but the other side of the mountain contains great mystery.

The first and last trigrams of the I Ching overhang the mountains on either side of the hourglass. The first trigram, named *qián* which is alternately called "Force," "the Creative" and "god," is a dynamic force and one of the most auspicious. By asserting yourself wisely in alignment with the greater good, one achieves success. But that success can turn to failure if one is insensitive and arrogant. By doing things in the right order, one develops influence and time itself becomes the means to make potency manifest.

The final trigram of the I Ching is named *wèi jì*, "Not Yet Fording" or also called "before completion" and "not yet completed." It offers that the ever-spinning wheels of life never reach a final conclusion. Every end has the seed of a beginning, and every situation of happiness contains the possibility of sadness. Achievement can sprout from adversity. Chaos gives way to order, and order to chaos. Things are ever changing, ever evolving, and yet stay the same.

The Augur: The hourglass, the serpent of the endless band, the first and last trigrams of the I-Ching. *The forces of expansion and contraction power the engine of change.*

Deck Comparisons

The RWS Two of Pentacles shows a man on shore, juggling two pentacles in a figure eight lemniscate. The Thoth Two of Disks shows a crowned serpent, in a figure eight, surrounding a light circle and a dark circle within each of which is a yin-yang. The Rosetta shows a serpent in the same formation whose scales portray all of the trigrams of the I Ching, surrounding a solar and a lunar coin. Tabula Mundi's card has the figure eight as a band driving two wheels within an hourglass, surrounded by twin peaks and the first and last I-Ching trigrams. They all have in common a depiction of opposing forces working together in an endless band of expansion and contraction.

THREE OF DISKS

Lord of Work

Middle decan of Capricorn, ruled by Mars

Binah of Assiah/Earth

Trumps: Devil, Tower

Princess Scale for Binah: Grey flecked Pink, plus the colors scales of the related trumps

THREE OF DISKS
♑ WORK ♂

The Three of Disks, called the Lord of Work, is the second decan of Capricorn, which is ruled by Mars. Here it is placed in Binah of Assiah, the sephira of first form in the material world. Binah with the element of Earth determines the basic forms of the entire universe. It is a card of building up. This could be the building blocks of a great pyramid, the constructive work that creates material wealth, or the building blocks of DNA of which life and the body is made.

Here we have the masculine phallic nature of the Devil and the Tower, in the womb of the great mother Binah, in the physical world of the element earth. The Devil is the card of Capricorn, and the Tower is the card of Mars, and Mars is exalted in Capricorn so here is an affinity. From the combination of the Devil and the Tower, the Three of Disks inherits a towering spiral of DNA. DNA, as well as containing the building blocks of life, is a symbol of kundalini force, and the serpents of life and wisdom. The twinned serpents are also about the caduceus, the modern symbol of medicine and healing. The healing serpent in biblical times was called Nehushtan, from the Hebrew word *nahash*" meaning "to guess," and was sometimes also translated to other languages as Satan.

The DNA or twined serpent symbol was originally associated with Enki, the Sumerian creator god also known as Ea in Babylonian mythology. He was called the "one who knows" and "Lord of the Earth," the chief of the magicians. Enki was also sometimes called the serpent in the Garden of Eden. The story goes that Enki created the first human life forms from clay and blood and implanted them in his sister Ninharsag in order to create humans to be workers for the gods. Ah work; we were ever born to it.

Within the DNA spiral are three disks, with the symbols of Mercury, Sulfur, and Salt. This triplicity could correspond the three Hindu Gunas of Sattvas, Rajas and Tamas, or the three Mother letters of the Hebrew alphabet. In any case the symbolism is clear; it is the building blocks of creation. The central disk is hit with the lightning bolt of the Tower card. This is the spark of creation, the phallic explosion of conception, or the lighting flash that creates the Tree of Life, or whereby God takes on flesh. It also can symbolize enlightenment and knowledge as in loss of ignorance.

To the side, a structure is being built from bricks and mortar, work done with a trowel. On a practical level, this card is associated with employment and with builders and engineers. In Masonry, the trowel is the implement of a Master Mason. While the apprentice prepares the gross materials with the Gage and Gavel, and the Fellow Craft places them in position using the Plumb and Square, the Master Mason alone, having assured himself that all is impeccable, secures them permanently, cementing them in place with the aid of the trowel.

The Augur: The DNA spiral, the Master Mason's trowel, Enki. *Work with the building blocks of form to manifest a construction.*

Deck Comparisons

The RWS Three of Pentacles portrays three people in some sort of stone building or chapel, who appear to be discussing its construction. The Thoth deck shows the view of the apex of a pyramid, with three wheel-like disks upon a background of a frozen sea. The Rosetta Three of Disks shows a wasp building cells, and each of the three cells contains an egg with the symbols of Mercury, Sulfur and Salt. Tabula Mundi's card has the alchemical glyphs on disks at the center of twists of DNA, and the mason's tools and bricks. This is the middle decan of Capricorn, ruled by Mars, and is Binah of Earth. All of the cards share a theme of building towards manifestation of form.

FOUR OF DISKS

POWER

Four of Disks

Lord of Power (Earthly Power)

Last decan of Capricorn, ruled by the Sun

Chesed of Assiah/Earth

Trumps: Devil, Sun

Princess Scale for Chesed: Deep azure, flecked Yellow, plus the colors scales of the related trumps

The Four of Disks, the Lord of Power, is the last decan of Capricorn, which is ruled by the Sun. It is in Chesed of Assiah, the sephira of manifestation in the material world. Chesed has a Jovian influence, so here there is an abundance of power and an association with authority and law.

This decan of Capricorn is ruled by the Sun. Capricorn is a sign of industry and enterprise, and throughout history the Sun has always been a symbol of power and invincibility. Four coins are shown on the card, as in most cases power derives from wealth. The uppermost coin is engraved with the face of Sol Invictus, and the motto *Soli Invicto*, meaning "to the unconquered Sun." Sol Invictus was the official sun god of the Roman Empire, favored by emperors throughout history who engraved his motto on their coins. *Invictus* meaning unconquered or invincible was an epithet for the Roman god Apollo and the cult of Sol, and Jupiter as well which brings in the flavor of Chesed.

Also from the Sun card are the emblems of the other coins. The dual crowns come from the crowned serpents of the Sun, and crowns as the headgear of monarchs and deities are of course traditional symbols of power. However this is the last decan of the sign Capricorn, whose associated trump is the Devil. This gives the card its traditional meaning that shows that while one is firmly established materially and invested with authority and power, there is the risk of covetousness. From the Devil card, to illustrate this avaricious tendency, is the ravenous face of the Green Man like face on the Devil's belly. This portrayal of a face on the belly of the Devil was common in medieval Europe as a demonstration of his, or mankind's, appetites and their all-consuming nature. On the Devil it is located at the Manipura chakra, associated with willpower and achievement. As the face is reminiscent of the Green Man, it alludes to the Sun as the decan's ruler. Yet here the growth is more on the material plane. The Green Man guards the gate of the great divide between the kingdoms of animals and plants, and the alluring world of materiality, and the Devil card is called *the Lord of the Gates of Matter*. As this guardian here he holds the keys to the illusory paradise sought by so many: the power of wealth and treasure.

As there is something of value being guarded and perhaps hoarded, at the base of the card is a gateway between two pylons of a massive stone fortress. The pylon in ancient Egypt was a physical manifestation of the glyph for horizon or *akhet*, which depicted two hills between which the sun rose and set. Pylons were decorated with scenes emphasizing a king's authority.

The Augur: The Pylon, the Green Man on the belly, Sol Invictus. *The stability of material wealth is powerful but limiting in that it requires constant vigilence.*

Deck Comparisons

The Rider Waite Smith Four of Pentacles shows a crowned monarch holding down two coins with his feet, one on his crown, and grasping one tightly, with what looks like a city in the background. The Thoth Four of Disks shows a bird's eye view of a square stone fortress with massive corner towers showing the four elements. The Rosetta Four of Disks shows a substantial bank vault, with the glyphs of the Sun and Capricorn as dials. Tabula Mundi's card shows a fortress-like pylon guarded by a Green Man, surrounded by a diamond of disks with solar symbols of power. This card is Chesed of Earth, the last decan of Capricorn ruled by the Sun, and the cards share a theme of material wealth and guarding.

FIVE OF DISKS

Lord of Worry (Material Trouble)

First decan of Taurus, ruled by Mercury

Geburah of Assiah/Earth

Trumps: Hierophant, Magus

Princess Scale for Geburah: Red flecked Black, plus the colors scales of the related trumps

FIVE OF DISKS
♉   WORRY   ☿

The Five of Disks, Lord of Worry is the first decan of the fixed sign of Taurus ruled by Mercury. Here it is placed in the sephira of Geburah of Assiah, the station of Severity in the Material world of Earth. These are the chains of materiality (Taurus) that bind the mind (Mercury), in the harsh and disruptive world of Geburah in the suit of Earth. This brings anxiety over material things.

We see the mixing board and turntable of the Magus abandoned, smoking, and locked up. The front of the mixing board has the letter Vau, the letter Beth, and an inverse pentagram, symbolizing the decan and symbolically nailing down the house of the mind in a disruptive way. The letter Vau means nail, and affixing the above to the below. Here the nail is a constricting force, that locks the mind up. The letter Beth means house and is associated with Mercury and mental quicksilver, and the inverse pentagram signifies the fifth sephira of Geburah and the also the triumph of matter over spirit. The turntable has as its axis a massive nail with one broken record getting all the play, and four more just like it just waiting for your mental loop to replay. In place of the Sun and the lemniscate, the Magus' altar now has the heavy elephants of the Hierophant. The elephants are a symbol of great strength and perseverance, yet in this case how are you using that steadfastness? It is said elephants never forget, but some things are best left forgotten. All you can think about is material trouble, the same old tune.

Behind the altar, the massive pillars of the Hierophant stand forebodingly draped in chains that block your passage. The four Kerubic beasts have all been replaced with the bullish head of Taurus. In place of the keyhole doorway of the Hierophant, a fifth bullish head has appeared as a massively heavy and ornate padlock and door knocker.

In ancient China, padlocks were first used by the wealthy and were considered a status symbol of affluence. But in modern symbolism padlocks are indicative of something that is suppressed and locked up, or repressed psychologically, and dreaming of a lock represents that you fear you cannot get what you desire. Keys however are symbols of the solution and resolution of the blockage. You may note that the Magus' table here has the disk and the wand present, but the sword and the cup are missing. We don't have good mental control over the emotional element, in this case, of the feeling of lack and the fear of loss. However in the place where those implements stood there is now a key, unfortunately being held down by an elephant. But it is only a small elephant, which may be a figment of your imagination.

The Augur: The broken record, the padlock, Nail versus Key. *Resolve to use intelligence to stop the replay of material mental anxieties.*

Deck Comparisons

The Rider Waite Smith Five of Disks shows two crippled beggars, trudging through the snow past the lighted stained glass window of a church. The Thoth Five of Disks shows five gear-like disks arranged in the shape of an inverse pentagram. The disks bear the four elements and at the lowest point of the pentagram the fifth disk has the black egg of spirit. The Rosetta Five of Disks shows a steam punk style machine, with five round gauges each bearing bad news: pressure is too high, you are still on the clock, gas is on empty, RPMs are pegged, and the odometer is about to turn over while smoke is pouring from a vent. In the lower right hand corner there is a switch though; you could turn it all off if you chose to. Tabula Mundi's card shows Mercury's DJ station playing broken records, bound in chains and locked. This is Geburah of Earth, the first decan of Taurus ruled by Mercury, and here the mind is disrupted by thoughts of material anxiety and bound by lack.

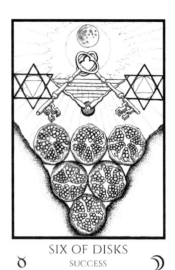

SIX OF DISKS

Lord of Success (Material Success)

Middle decan of Taurus, ruled by the Moon

Tiphareth of Assiah/Earth

Trumps: Hierophant, Priestess

Princess Scale for Tiphareth: Gold
Amber, plus the colors scales of the
related trumps

SIX OF DISKS
SUCCESS

♉ ☽

The Six of Disks, Lord of Success is the middle decan of the fixed sign of Taurus ruled by the Sun. It is placed in the sephira of Tiphareth of Assiah, the station of Beauty and harmony, with the element of Earth. The decan's ruler is the Moon, which is exalted in the sign, and the sephira of Tiphareth is that of the Sun, a natural pairing. The card shows the fertile valley of Taurus' middle decan enclosing six pomegranates in an inverted triangle, suggesting the symbol of the Earth element. The trumps associated with this decan are the Hierophant, and the Priestess; another natural pairing of the two who sit between the pillars in their tarot portrayals. In pre-Golden Dawn decks, these were the cards of the Pope and Popess.

From the Priestess card, the disks are shown portrayed as pomegranates. Pomegranates have long been associated with prosperity, fertility and abundance. Islamic legend has it that every pomegranate contains one seed from the pomegranate of Paradise and Muslims revered them as symbols of beauty and instructed women to eat them to conceive beautiful children. In India, the pomegranate is the fruit of Lord Ganesha, the remover of obstacles. To the Zoroastrians, they symbolized the perfection of nature. The calyx of the pomegranate is said to be the inspiration for the shape of crowns of the monarchy.

The word pomegranate comes from the Latin *pomom* for apple, combined with the word *granatus*, meaning seeded. It has been suggested that the pomegranate was actually the "apple" that Adam and Eve consumed in the Garden of Eden. This can be seen in the progression from the Six of Disks to the Seven of Disks which illustrates the garden after the fall. This, as well as the pomegranates association with the Persephone myth, speaks to this card's transient condition from the influence of the Moon. The Six of Disks is thus just a stop at the station of success in the cycle of abundance.

Above the disks we see the Priestess' lyre with six strings. The lyre here is both the silver lunar bow of the Priestess as Artemis, and also associated with the golden lyre of her brother Apollo the Sun god, as this is the sphere of solar Tiphareth. Symbolically the lyre is also associated with music and harmonics, and thus the harmony of this sephira.

The Hierophant contributes the two keys crossed over the lyre bow. The two keys, crossed over the triangular lyre, mathematically represent the number six as two times three. The six is also the number of equilibrium, beauty and harmony, and can be represented as the perfect number within the pyramid of pomegranates stacked as $1 + 2 + 3 = 6$.

Keys have been a symbol associated with the Hierophant and also with the Priestesses or sacerdotes of Ceres as the insignia of the mystical office. Ceres, being a goddess of agriculture, fertility and abundance, is an equivalent to Demeter. The name Ceres comes from the root *ker*, meaning to grow, which is also the root of words like kernel, bringing to mind the pomegranate once again.

In the Mysteries of Isis the key was a hieroglyphic of the opening or disclosing of the heart and conscience. The crossed keys are a taller variant of the Saltire or solar cross, a variation the Egyptians associated with the corner stars of Orion and with Sirius the Dog Star, and thus Osiris and Isis. The keys of silver and gold are said to show the balance between the subconscious and conscious. These crossed keys of silver and gold are the keys of earth and heaven, or the keys of Solomon's temple.

The Augur: The keys of the sacerdotes, valley of pomegranates, bow & lyre. *The keys to the fertile valley offer appreciation of life, beauty and abundance.*

Deck Comparisons

The Rider Waite Smith Six of Pentacles shows a man with scales, handing out alms. The Thoth Six of Disks shows six planetary disks in a hexagon formation surrounding a central sun with the rose cross at its center. The Rosetta Six of Disks shows six disks with honeybee workers surrounding a hexagram crystalline form with a Queen bee at the center and a background of filled honeycomb. Tabula Mundi shows pomegranates stacked in a feminine fertile valley. The lyre and crossed keys surmount them, with the Sun and Moon behind. This card is the middle decan of Taurus, ruled by the Moon, in the solar sphere of Tiphareth of Earth. The cards show the balance of this sphere, giving the bounty of Earth.

seven of disks

Lord of Failure (Success Unfulfilled)

Last decan of Taurus, ruled by Saturn

Netzach of Assiah/Earth

Trumps: Hierophant, Universe

Princess Scale for Netzach: Olive flecked Gold, plus the colors scales of the related trumps

SEVEN OF DISKS

☿   FAILURE   ♄

The Seven of Disks, Lord of Failure is the final decan of the fixed sign of Taurus, ruled by Saturn. It is placed in the sephira of Netzach of Assiah, the station of Victory with the element of Earth. Success has been thus far unfulfilled. What is needed to achieve Victory in the material plane of Earth, is toil through effort and endurance. The state of Man.

The trumps associated with this card are the Hierophant, of the letter Vau meaning nail, and the Universe, of the letter Tau meaning cross. Symbolically, this is evocative of crucifixion. One is bound and fixed to the entire material universe of creation. Both trumps show the four Kerubim, the tetramorphic elemental guardians in the form of the lion, bull, eagle, and man. These creatures are the embodiment and living energy of the Tetragrammaton and rulers of the fixed signs of the Zodiac.

The card shows an interpretation of a diagram of the Tree of Life after the fall of man; the expulsion of Adam and Eve from the Eden of the Six of Disks. In the initiatory grades of the Hermetic Order of the Golden Dawn, a similar diagram is shown to the candidate for the Philosophus grade of 4 = 7. It shows in a glyph the teaching proper to the grade upon entering Netzach.

The story goes that before the fall, Malkuth, or Eve, had supported the two pillars of Light and Darkness. Eve was tempted by the fruits of the Tree of Knowledge whose branches lead upwards to the seven lower sephiroth and down into the Kingdom of Shells. When she reached for the fruit and grasped knowledge for humankind, she left the pillars unsupported and the Sephirothic Tree was shattered. With mankind's attainment of sentience, the great red dragon of seven heads and ten horns, once asleep within Malkuth, now awakened. The seven heads of the dragon rose up and consumed the seven lower Sephiroth, and the dragon grew an eighth head which was Leviathan desecrating the four rivers of Eden and spewing the Infernal Waters into Daath. YHVH Elohim placed the four letters of the holy name, the Kerubim, between the devastated garden and the Supernal Eden. Malkuth was cut off from the Sephiroth and linked with the Kingdom of Shells. Adam and Eve were banished and fell from the garden of paradise, condemned to Saturnian mortal toil and labor. It became necessary that a second Adam should arise to restore the system, and be crucified on the four armed cross. Yet to do so, he must descend to the lowest, Malkuth, and be born of her.

Saturn's restrictive influence upon the fertility of Taurus is one of blight and spoilage. The promise of success has not come to fruition. Leviathan is an emblematic token of a great obstacle to be overcome. The fall of man is a state likened to the "dark night of the soul," in which temptations arise to abandon the Work. To conquer the dragon representing this mind state, and thus achieve Victory, one must both accept reality and persevere.

The Augur: The Tree of Life after the Fall, Leviathan, crucifixion. *So far success is unfulfilled: the state of Man is toil through effort and endurance.*

Deck Comparisons

The Rider Waite Smith Seven of Pentacles shows a man leaning on a scythe, looking somewhat dispiritedly at a tree bearing seven pentacles. The Thoth Seven of Disks shows seven leaden coins arranged in the malignant geomantic figure Rubeus, amongst black and blighted vegetation. The Rosetta Seven of Disks also shows the disks in the figure Rubeus, with the central disk bearing the head of the Minotaur, surrounded by disks of the labyrinth and a maze of cracked earth. Tabula Mundi's card shows the Tree of Life after the Fall, with Leviathan uncurling from Malkuth and separating the seven lower sephiroth from the upper. This card is the last decan of Taurus, ruled by Saturn, and is unbalanced Netzach of Earth. The cards share a theme of enduring though earth has been blighted.

EIGHT OF DISKS
ⅠⅡ○   PRUDENCE   ☉

EIGHT OF DISKS

Lord of Prudence

First decan of Virgo, ruled by the Sun

Hod of Assiah/Earth

Trumps: Hermit, Sun

Princess Scale for Hod: Yellowish-
Brown flecked White, plus the colors
scales of the related trumps

The Lord of Prudence is of the initial decan of Virgo which is ruled by the Sun. Here it is in the sephira of Glory called Hod, in the material world of Assiah. While it is true that Hod is low down on the Tree, there is a good deal of compatibility between the various elements of the card. Hod gives the influence of Mercury, and Mercury is both the ruler and the exaltation of the sign of Virgo. Mercury is also companion to the Sun, the ruler of this particular decan of Virgo, and the Sun is compatible to earthy Virgo, as it is a necessary component of the fertility of earth. The sun warming the Earth is a passive receipt; earth in its stability needs to do nothing at all in order to benefit from the warmth of the sun. Thus the card is one of prudence, of sowing the seed and waiting, of saving for a rainy day and accumulating interest, and of guarding one's resources. With the Eight, one has learned from the errors of the Seven that things take time and care and cannot be rushed. With this care and labor comes fruitfulness. All in all it is a positive card, though there is some possibility of hoarding and being overly careful in regard to small matters, a trait of the sign of Virgo.

The related trump for this card is the Hermit, for Virgo. The Hermit's staff is topped by an egg. Virgo is Yod, the secret seed of life, and here we see a nest with eight eggs that have been fertilized and are now being warmed by the Hermit's lantern. Symbolically the lantern is that which lights ones path, and also the spark of life. It also has to do with diligence and intelligence, appropriate for the combination of Hod (Mercury), and the Sun. The card speaks of wise discernment and aptitude in material matters. In India, the lantern is associated with the festival of Divali and symbolizes knowledge. Divali honors Lakshmi, for wealth and prosperity, Ganesha for ethical beginnings, Saraswati for learning, and Kubera who symbolizes treasury, book keeping, and wealth management.

The combination of the Sun and Virgo suggests husbandry both of crops and of animals, as well as engineering. If one has ever raised birds from eggs, one knows that they need to be carefully tended, and kept warm and safe from predators. While they take time to mature to fruition, there is not much else one must do; the maturity happens on its own. But while one is waiting, there is not slacking, there is care and patient craftsmanship, and one must build and prepare for the hatching. The decan is ruled by the Sun, and thus from the Sun card we see that the flame within the lantern is actually the Sun, giver of life, depicted surrounded by the geometrical twelve pointed form from the card.

The Augur: The lantern, the nest egg, the festival of Divali. *Guard the nest, warm the eggs and create fruitfulness through intelligence, diligence, and prudent cultivation.*

Deck Comparisons

The Rider Waite Smith Eight of Pentacles shows a craftsman seated on a workbench in the process of constructing a disk, with seven others he has created displayed around him. The Thoth Eight of Disks shows a great and twisting stalk of a plant, with eight flowers that look like they will bear fruit. Each shaded by a leaf curling above it. The Rosetta Eight of Disks shows a twisted plant stalk with eight branches. Each holds a nest containing one egg, and at the top, a great horned owl shades them and protects them. The sun is above and the plant's roots form the glyph of Virgo. Tabula Mundi's card shows the Sun at the center of the Hermit's lantern, warming a nest of eggs. This card is Hod of Earth, the first decan of Virgo ruled by the Sun. The cards all share themes of patient cultivation.

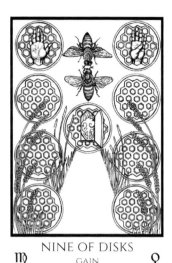

Nine of Disks

Lord of Gain (Material Gain)

Middle decan of Virgo, ruled by Venus

Yesod of Assiah/Earth

Trumps: Hermit, Empress

Princess Scale for Yesod: Citrine, flecked azure, plus the colors scales of the related trumps

NINE OF DISKS
GAIN

♍   ♀

The Lord of Gain is the central decan of Virgo, which is ruled by Venus. It is in the sephira Yesod, called *Foundation*, of the middle pillar, in the material world of Earth and Assiah. This decan contains the exaltation of the sign Virgo, at 15 degrees, and has the beneficial influence of Venus, who seems to be pleased in the lunar realm of Yesod. Earthy Virgo is also happy to be in this stable foundational position. This is a very good card for all material matters; luck is with you and now the harvest has come in. This is the penultimate state of the suit of earth, and all is plentitude and satisfaction due to the good management of the Eight.

The related trumps are the Hermit for Virgo, and the Empress for Venus, ruler of the decan. From both the Hermit and the Empress, we have a wheat field, synonymous throughout history with times of harvest and prosperity. The Hermit is the card of Yod, meaning hand, and the hand is shown on the egg at the top of his staff. At the top of this card, two of the disks also show hands, counting up to nine. Nine is the highest number of the single digits, and thus represents finalization and fruition. Man spends nine months in the womb before being born, and Persephone spends nine months above ground giving fruitfulness to the earth. As three times three, nine is a number of fertility. By showing us nine fingers, the card reminds us that nine is a number of attainment and accomplishment. We are being asked to count our blessings. Crowley calls Venus in the suit of Disks "reckoning up its winnings."

The bees of the card are also creatures under the astrological rulership of Virgo, in the sense that they are small creatures engaged in diligent behavior. At the top of the card two bees are engaged in the "bee dance" transferring nectar and pollen along with a message of where the flowers to gather them can be found. They speak to each other of abundance and its location, so that the hive may prosper.

From the Empress card for Venus, the disks are shown as round sections of honeycomb. This is a popular way for beekeepers to package honey as getting the bees to fill the round frames requires less labor for the keeper and thus gives more profit. If one has tasted comb honey one knows that there is nothing more delicious and sweet. Honeycomb is symbolic of the harvest of all of the efforts of the bee, and the resultant sweetness. This is mainly on the material and physical level, but can also be spiritual gain. C.C. Zain in *Ancient Masonry* states that "The hive proper denotes man's physical body. The honeycomb signifies that which is interior to the physical, the astral body. And the honey is symbolical of the spiritual body, which is composed of the choicest nectars and aromas of earthly experience."

The disks are arranged in the traditional Golden Dawn arrangement described and shown in Liber Theta, with two pillars of four disks at each side, and one disk in the upper central quadrant. The central disks in this arrangement portray the heart-door of the Empress, open and welcoming. The path leads there and invites you to enter and partake of the sweetness of gain.

The Augur: The open door, the honeycomb, the counting hand. *Time to count your blessings, as luck is with you and the sweet harvest comes in.*

Deck Comparisons

The Rider Waite Smith Nine of Pentacles shows a woman of means in a fertile garden. She carries a falcon and is surrounded by grapevines loaded with fruit. The Thoth Nine of Disks shows an equilateral triangle of disks with apex upwards, surrounded by an elongated hexagram of disks. These six disks are stamped with the magical images or deities of the planets. The Rosetta Nine of Disks shows a close up view of an abacus with nine green beads on a plum colored background. The abacus is marked with the glyphs of Venus and Virgo. Tabula Mundi has the disks filled with honeycomb. A path through a wheat field leads to a door in the central disk which opens to reveal the heart filled with honey. The two upper disks show hands counting to nine. This card is Yesod of Earth, the middle decan of Virgo ruled by Venus. The cards all show gifts of abundance, where the gods are with you and you have cause to count your blessings.

Ten of Disks

Lord of Wealth

Last decan of Virgo, ruled by Mercury

Malkuth of Assiah/Earth

Trumps: Hermit, Magus

Princess Scale for Malkuth: Black rayed with Yellow, plus the colors scales of the related trumps

TEN OF DISKS
♍   WEALTH   ☿

The Lord of Wealth is the last decan of earth sign Virgo. This decan is ruled by Mercury, which also rules and is the exaltation of Virgo itself. The sephira is Malkuth of Assiah, the material world of manifestation. Malkuth is the last sephira, and this is the Malkuth of Earth, the final world. Thus this card is considered the final card of the minor arcana, much as the Universe is the final trump and the Princess of Disks is the final court. What was begun with the Ace of Wands here reaches its climax and culmination, or in other words, the Pure Will inherent in Kether (represented by the Ace of Wands) and expressed in the Magus (card of Mercury and the path from Kether to Binah) is now brought to material form. This is the sum total of the Great Work, and the point at which the cycle can regenerate and begin again.

Crowley says of the card that "Therefore, in it is drawn the very figure of the Tree of Life itself." Tabula Mundi demonstrates this with a rendition of the Tree as Adam Kadmon, the "Primordial Man." Adam Kadmon is said to exist in Kether. From Adam Kadmon and the divine will of Kether, the Four Worlds descend and emerge, each as a letter of the divine name, from the very tip of the thorn of the Yod.

The related trumps of the card are the Hermit and the Magus. From the Hermit card, we have the symbolism of the Yod, shown here at the forehead of the winged helm at Kether. Also from the Hermit, the ten sephiroth are seen as descending into the stone stairwell in the ground. This is symbolically earth and the descent into matter. But also in the more mundane sense, this can be seen as a vault, with the sephiroth as coins of wealth and prosperity either descending and accumulating in the vault, or rising in order to be used. For wealth can only accumulate for so long until it becomes dormant and inert; it requires the intelligence of Mercury to give it purpose beyond pure material aggregation.

The various elements of the Magus card give the emblematic forms to the sephiroth and body of Adam Kadmon. In the place of Kether, is the Magus' winged hem accented by a central Yod. Anthropomorphically, there is correspondence between the Tree of Life and the human body. The sephiroth form the body of Adam Kadmon, and Kether is the crown and the head, while Chokmah and Binah are the cerebral hemispheres of the brain, here shown as the left and right sides of the helm. The Supernals in this sense are the mind of the figure. *Chesed* and *Geburah* correspond to the right and left arms, *Tiphareth* to the heart, *Yesod* to the genitals, and *Netzach* and *Hod* to the right and left legs. Note that depictions of the figure face into or are seen as if stepping into the Tree — when viewed from the front the sephiroth have to be flipped around the middle pillar. In this card all of the depictions on each of the coins or emanations take the appropriate parts from the Magus, with the exception of Tiphareth at the position of the heart, which takes the Yod-like flame from inside the Hermit's lantern. Thus the Supernals show the front and sides of the Magus' winged helm. Chesed and Geburah as the arms of the figure are marked with the disk and the galaxy the Magus holds. Yesod is marked with the Mercury symbol from the "wand" on his table at the level of his genitals. Netzach and Hod have the combined and interchanged depictions of the sun and solar lemniscate from the front of the mix table. This echoes the Thoth deck's depiction of a solar symbol at the level of Hod, of which Crowley comments "These disks are inscribed with various symbols of mercurial character except that the coin in the place of Hod (Mercury) on the Tree is marked with the cipher of the Sun. This indicates the only possibility of issue from the impasse produced by the exhaustion of all the elemental forces." Malkuth appropriately then shows the four worlds from the bottom of the Magus' table, here in circular form joined at the sphere of Malkuth. Symbolically they form the quartered circle, a symbol of Malkuth. This is in total a glyph of the Great Work, the Summum Bonum and realization of True Will.

The Augur: Adam Kadmon, the descent and ascent, the Vault. *This is the pinnacle of success and the culmination of will in the material world — give your wealth inner and outer purpose beyond mere accumulation.*

Deck Comparisons

The Rider Waite Smith Ten of Pentacles shows an old man seated at the arched gate of a village, surrounded by family and dogs, with ten pentacles in a Tree of Life formation. The Thoth Ten of Disks shows ten golden coins in a Tree of Life formation on a background of violet coins. The golden coins are marked with various Mercurial symbols except for Hod which has a solar symbol. Malkuth is shown as the largest and heaviest coin. The Rosetta Ten of Disks is pictorially much like the Thoth, except the golden coins have other Mercurial elements and are looped together in the manner of Chinese coin clusters given out to symbolize and increase wealth. The tenth coin is larger than the rest and dangles free from the string in the position of Malkuth, ready to drop down out of the picture and into the new cycle. Tabula Mundi shows the ten disks as a Mercurial and Solar Adam Kadmon, poised above an entrance to a vault in the earth. This card is Malkuth of Earth, the last decan of Virgo ruled by Mercury. The cards all share a depiction of material culmination.

The Quartered Circle of the Memory Palace

The Court Cards

"The combination of these four types of face and being
represents the Created Universe, a complete and eternal entity,
Man in fact, the Microcosm; and this is the first formula of the
mystical explanation of the enigma of the Sphynx."
"Do you now understand the Enigma of the Sphynx?
. . . Yes, you know that the Sphynx refers to Man.
But do you know that the Sphynx is one and alone, and remains unchanged,
while as to man—is not each one a Sphynx of a different synthesis?"

Eliphas Lévi

The court cards represent Man. Like the Sphinx, Man is composed of the four elements, though in Man they are divided and unbalanced while the Sphinx is the perfected Man, whole and with the elements in symbiotic relationship. The Four Powers of the Sphinx bring Man closer to perfection as Magus. These powers are To Will (*velle*), To Dare (*audere*), To Know (*sciere*), and To Keep Silent (*tacere*). By attaining and using the Four Powers of the Sphinx, the Adept attains the Fifth Power, To Go (*ire*). This is the indwelling of Spirit and the realization of the god within, Kether in Malkuth. The four powers of the Sphinx are the means by which Man becomes God. The Sphinx is associated with Malkuth, the Princesses, who are us. Thus each of the four powers has been assigned to one of the four Princesses. These powers bring Kether to Malkuth, the Princesses as the Thrones of the Aces.

Wheels within wheels, the court of the Tarot calls to mind Ezekiel; "Now as I looked at the living beings, behold, there was one wheel on the earth beside the living beings, for each of the four of them." Thus the court cards can be represented by a circle divided by a cross, spirit divided by YHVH. This cross divided circle is a Tabula Mundi, a picture of the world, symbol of the Universe, and ultimately Malkuth, the sphere of our material world. The tarot court cards are all about division by fours:

- The Divine Name: Yod-Hé-Vau-Hé
- The four courts: Knight, Queen, Prince, Princess
- The four worlds: Atziluth, Briah, Yetzirah, Assiah
- The four elements: Fire, Water, Air, Earth
- The four suits: Wands, Cups, Swords, Disks
- Thunder, Lake, Wind, Mountain
- The four Kerubim
- Will, Love, Reason, Action
- Velle, Audere, Sciere, Tacere
- To Will, To Dare, To Know, To Keep Silent
- Regulus, Antares, Fomalhaut, Aldebaran

This four-by-four arrangement divides and recombines the world into the manifest sixteen court cards. Tarot is a complex and faceted world in which Four is an important number. Yet it works in combination with Three and with Ten. Threes and fours; this is a model that repeats in the zodiacal groupings and the triplicities and quadruplicity of sephiroth groupings on the Tree of Life.

Three of the four courts, the Knights, Queens, and Princes, and thus twelve cards, are each given ownership of the qualities of a 30° segment of the 360° circle of the Zodiac. Thus these cards are associated with three cards each of the decanic minor arcana. They each have primarily the first two decans of one sign of the suit's element as part of their visible nature, plus they pick up the last decan of the preceding sign in a contrary element which supplies a shadow part of their psyche. This arrangement makes them complex, as real people are, and is said by this intermingling of elements to bind the elements of the world and keep them from separation. I think of it as picking up a stitch which makes the binding stronger linking together the signs.

The sign that each court is attributed is chosen so that the three Gunas are in balance. The three Gunas (Rajas, Sattva, Tamas) are components or divisions of *Prakriti*, Sanskrit for "Nature." *Prakriti* corresponds to the Princesses. The Knights, which are Cardinal, Sulfuric, and Rajasic in nature, pick up the last ten degrees of a Fixed sign and are assigned the first twenty degrees of a Mutable sign. The Queens, which are Fixed, Salty, and Tamasic in nature, pick up the last ten degrees of a Mutable sign and are assigned the first twenty degrees of a Cardinal sign. The Princes, which are Mutable, Mercurial, and Sattvic in nature, pick up the last ten degrees of a Cardinal sign and are assigned the first twenty degrees of a Fixed sign.

As we can deduce, the natures of each court are determined by the three decans of which the card is composed. Study of the minor arcana card for each

THE SPHINX

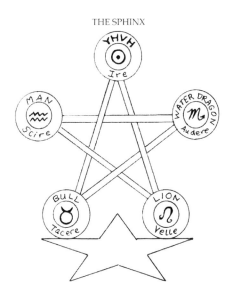

Modified version of Diagram 8. from the Book of Thoth, *the description reads: This diagram represents the four Kerubs who are about the throne of the Almighty; they show the central zodiacal signs of the four Elements, Leo, Scorpio, Aquarius, and Taurus. The Kerubic sign in any Element exhibits the most powerful and balanced form of that Element. Attached to these are the names of the four Virtues of the Adept, those which enable him to overcome the resistance of the elements; they are: to Will, to Dare, to Know and to Keep Silence. By the harmonious exercise of these, the fifth Element of Spirit is formulated in the being of the Adept. It is the god within, the sun, which is the centre of the Universe from the human point of view, with its own particular virtue, which is to Go. The essential characteristic of the godhead is this faculty of Going: the free movements of space and time and all other possible conditions. In the Egyptian hieroglyphic system, this faculty of going was represented by a sandal strap, which represents by its hieroglyphic form the crux ansata, the Rose and the Cross, which in its turn gives the formula of Love.*

of the three decans will yield much about their attributes. Some astrological knowledge will enhance your understanding of the courts, though even contemplation of the trumps associated with the astrological signs would be sufficient.

As mentioned, the three Gunas of Rajas, Sattva, and Tamas are divisions of *Prakriti,* Sanskrit for Nature. *Prakriti* corresponds to the Princesses. Therefore each Princess rules one-fourth of the zodiac, or a quarter of the heavens around the North Pole, centered above the Kerubic (Fixed) signs. Where the other court cards oversee a sector of the year and thus rule a section of Time, the Princesses rule a sector of Space. The Princess of Wands for example, rules the 90° segment of the zodiac centered over the Kerubic fire sign Leo. As we mentioned earlier, the Aces being the Point or hub of the Zodiacal Wheel, the Aces are the pole. Thus the Princesses form the thrones of power of the four Aces. The Princesses as thrones of the Aces contain the courts and suits just as the Aces contain their suit and courts. This description of the Princesses as "thrones of the Aces" reminds us that they are the ultimate receptacle for all of the potential of the suit inherent in the Ace, and that through them, the lowest world of Malkuth is connected to the highest world of Kether. They are our inborn potential.

It is helpful to keep in mind that the court cards relate to the four letters of the divine name YHVH, and to recall the Qabalistic fairytale of the four characters, and the mythologies of the Dying God. Ultimately they all exist in Kether, but have separated fourfold. Until they reunite, the following story replays endlessly.

Once there was a Knight who rode forth swiftly, and met a great Queen. They united in marriage, temporarily becoming one. The Knight in his passion shot forth his seed, and then slept. The Queen, receiving this seed, became reflective, for she had conceived. She was delivered of twins, the Prince and the Princess. The Prince was seen as having the best qualities of his two parents, and was thus given the greatest and most central part of their Kingdom to rule. The Princess however was most misunderstood, and was banished; exiled to the lowest part of the world. The Prince never forgot her, and longed to be reunited. The Princess however, being so far from home, forgot who she was and slept for a long time. One day, she woke, and discovered that the Prince remembered and longed for her and had ridden forth to meet her. They were united in marriage, becoming the new King and Queen. The King shot forth his seed, and then slept . . .

This is the story of how the Princess "awakens the eld of the All-Father" or the Yod of the Old King. "Eld" is an archaic term for an age of the world, olden days, and for old age. Thus the Princess is the created thing and holds the key to the renewal of the cycle, in which one world proceeds to the next.

The Knights are the Father, and correspond to the Yod of the fourfold name, and the element of Fire. Their force is that of will; swift, inflaming, and initiating. Thus they are portrayed upon horseback, in full armor. On the Tree of Life they correspond to Chokmah, though as the Yod, they begin in Kether though they are not conscious of it. They are the first motion, and first force; the line that extends from the point, and the thrust of the first phallus. They are masculine and potent, but their male force is transient, expending itself quickly.

The Queens are the Mother, primal Hé of the divine name, and the element of Water. As the givers of form to the force initiated by the Knights, they are steady and receptive; abiding and reflecting. They incubate and gestate the seed, ordering and regulating what the Knight has started. Thus they are shown seated upon thrones, reflective and considering, and also armored. On the Tree of Life they correspond to Binah. They are counterpart to the Knight and exist as part of the Supernal triad above the Abyss.

The Princes are the Son born of the love of his Supernal parents, the combination of Fire and Water yielding the intellectual element of Air. The Knight's first urge and the Queen's receptivity to his advances has resulted in the birth of the Prince, the Vau of the fourfold name. On the Tree of Life they correspond to Tiphareth, and provide a connection through which we can contact divinity. The Princes are the Holy Guardian Angel that we, as the Princesses, must unite with. As the heir of the Supernals, the opposing parental influences of force and form have here reached equilibrium. The main decanic cards of the Prince are also those of opposing forces, either side of two extremes. He inherits some of the swiftness of his father, though less transient, combined with the endurance of his mother, though more yielding. Thus the Princes are shown armored and borne upon chariots, being both rapid and enthroned. The power of the Prince is only valid if founded on and responsive to the two opposing forces within him. The Princes, as the Kerubic signs, are also carrying the powers of the four Royal Stars in four directions. They bring them to the Princesses, who must awaken and unite with the Prince in order to wield them.

The Princesses are the most enigmatic and yet most important of the courts; for they are us. They reside in Malkuth on the Tree of Life. The Princesses are the Daughter, the Hé final of the divine name, and the element of Earth, which holds within it the three other elements combined. They consolidate and materialize the three preceding forces. The Princess is permanent and yet volatile, stable and yet erratic. Liber Theta calls her "an inertia of irresistible momentum"; such an enigmatic, evocative, and beautiful phrasing. Crowley says they show the materialization of the element, yet also the re-absorption of the Energy, and "they are thus at the same time permanent and nonexistent. An audit of the equation o=2." [23] Thus the Princesses are portrayed as Amazons, and stand firmly of themselves, wearing little armor. The power of the Princesses must come from the harnessed forces of the others. If she is manifest as the Daughter of Chokmah

23   *Book of Thoth* pg 150

(Will) and Binah (Love) and betrothed to Tiphareth (Beauty) then the temple (Kingdom) has been rightly built and she is the Throne for the Force of Spirit, and a mighty material force. "Woe unto whomsoever shall make war upon her, when thus firmly established!" [24] While they have no zodiacal attribution, they represent, according to Crowley, those powerful and compelling "elemental people whom we recognize by their lack of all sense of responsibility." The Sphinx is associated with Malkuth, and to the Princesses are assigned the four powers of the Sphinx: *Velle, Audere, Sciere, Tacere*. To wield the powers they must awaken and symbolically join with the Princes.

When creating the court cards, I consulted the traditional Golden Dawn descriptions of their posture, attire, crest and equipment as described in both Book T and Liber Theta. Please consult Liber Theta for one of the best descriptions of the attitudes and attributions of the court cards. When studying the court cards, it will be helpful to consider their three related minors, as well as the trump that corresponds to their main astrological sign from the first two decans of their suit's element, and the trump of their shadow sign, from the last decan of the sign preceding.

The cards are labeled with their elemental nature. To illustrate, let us look at the suit of Disks. The Knight of Disks is labeled "Fire of Earth." There is no actual Fire element in the card, only Earth. But it is the fiery part of Earth, the part that is of mountains and earthquakes but also the warmth and fertility that sparks life. The Queen of Disks is labeled "Water of Earth." It can be said that she is the "watery part of Earth" but that could be confusing as there is not an element of water in the Queen of Disks, only Earth. It is more appropriate to consider that she uses her powers of Earth in a watery or receptive and reflective way. The Prince of Disks is then "Air of Earth," the air that has resulted from the union of the fire and water of his parents. Yet he is ultimately of the airy part of the element of Earth, and thus it is that he uses his practical powers of Earth in an airy or intellectual way. The Princess of Disks, as Earth of Earth, is the ultimate fruition of not only the element of Earth but of the entire sequence, the true final Hè of the divine name.

The chapters on the court cards list the related Minor and Major Arcana cards each is associated, with the secondary or shadow cards listed parenthetically. The courts are also associated with a hexagram of the I-Ching. In general, in the system of the I-Ching Knights and Wands are *Thunder*,

---

24   "Woe unto whomsoever shall make war upon her, when thus firmly established!" is
        from Book T. I love saying that. Coincidentally, the four words "I love saying that"
        mean, Will-Love-Logos-Which Is.

Queens and Cups are *Lake*, Princes and Swords are *Wind*, and Princesses and Disks are *Mountain*. Thus these four hexagrams are linked to the court cards that are the ultimate expression of the elements; the court cards Fire of Fire, Water of Water, Air of Air, and Earth of Earth.

These court cards are denizens of what I call the Memory Palace of the Tarot. The Memory Palace is a mnemonic device first used by the ancient Greeks and Romans. It is also known as the "method of *loci*," Latin for places. It is a memory enhancement technique that uses visualization and imagination to organize and recall information. Tabula Mundi has visually coded the courts to seed them with imagery from the Minor Arcana cards of the decanates they rule, similar to the way in which it coded the Minors with images of their related Majors. Thus in the Knights, Queens, and Princes you can see visual cues from the three minor cards of their decanates, and the Princesses are visibly linked to their Aces. It is recommended to study these related cards together to embed the images and their relationships in your own memory palace.

KNIGHT OF WANDS

KNIGHT OF WANDS
FIRE OF FIRE

***The Lord of the Flame and the Lightning;
The King of the Spirits of Fire***

King of the Salamanders

Fire of Fire

20° Scorpio to 20° Sagittarius

**Related minors of the decans:
(7 of Cups), 8 of Wands, 9 of Wands**

**Astrological trumps: mainly Art for
Sagittarius as the main sign of the card;
(secondarily Death for the last decan of
Scorpio as the shadow)**

I-Ching: Hexagram 51 *Thunder (Arousing)*

Book T description: A WINGED Warrior riding upon a black horse with flaming mane and tail: the horse itself is not winged. The rider wears a winged helmet (like the old Scandinavian and Gaulish helmet) with a Rayed Crown, a corslet of scale-mail and buskins of the same, and a flowing scarlet mantle. Above his helmet, upon his curass, and on the shoulder-pieces and buskins, he wears as a crest a winged black horse's head. He grasps a club with flaming ends, somewhat similar to that in the symbol of the Ace of Wands, but not so heavy, and also the sigil of his scale is shown; beneath the rushing feet of his steed are waving flames and fire.

The Knight of Wands, King of the Spirits of Fire, bears the crest of a winged black horse's head, the black horse being a symbol of strength, swiftness, power and life force. The Lord of the Flame and the Lightning bursts forth as if released from a starting gate, surrounded by waving flames. He is Fire of Fire, which is Yod of Yod; this is the card that best represents the Father, the masculine first letter of the divine name. This is the primal fire of creation and the life force, vigorous and potent, though not lasting. This Knight is proud and noble. He revels in being first to act, and act swiftly, but must succeed at first go or he has not the patience or nature to regroup and try again.

His traits are mainly that of the sign Sagittarius. Sagittarius is the ninth sign of the zodiac and its planet is Jupiter. Sagittarius says "I aim." Sagittarius is the sign of the Centaur as Archer, and its symbol is an arrow. Arrows travel, they aim, and they seek. It is a mutable fire sign and is philosophical and visionary; a transformer of ideals. At its highest expression, Sagittarius is active, ardent, expansive, jovial, honest, sincere and optimistic. Sagittarius at worst is pompous, careless, irresponsible, bigoted, violent, overly frank and prone to exaggeration. In the body Sagittarius rules the liver and the hips and thighs. The trump card associated with Sagittarius is *Art* giving the transformative powers of alchemy, the divine force that releases the arrow, and the fire that tempers.

The Knight of Wands rules from 20° Scorpio to 20° Sagittarius, which includes the constellation Hercules, who kneels with one foot on the head of Draco. Hercules was a virile divine hero, whose weapon was a club. He was the son of Zeus (Jupiter) and a mortal woman, but hated by Hera as he was yet more proof of Zeus' infidelities. He was famed for his heroic adventures including the fabled "twelve labors" he had to undergo as a result of Hera's jealousy. Hercules used strength and wisdom to overcome many monsters or moral obstacles, but ultimately is defeated, posthumously by the centaur Nessus. Nessus was killed with a poisoned arrow by Hercules for trying to steal his second wife Deianira, whom Hercules actually had taken from a river god he killed. Before dying, as revenge Nessus gives Deianira a sample of his blood claiming it would keep Hercules faithful to her. Of course Hercules fathers illegitimate children all over the world and falls in love with another woman. Deianira in desperation smears the poisoned blood on his tunic, unwittingly killing him. It is also thought that the precursor to the Greek Heracles was Gilgamesh, a Mesopotamian demi-god king of superhuman strength.

The Knight of Wands primary sign is that of Sagittarius, the first two decans of the sign.[25] The related minor arcana are the Eight of Wands, *Swiftness*, and the Nine of Wands, *Strength*. His shadow card is the Seven of Cups, *Debauch*, from the last decan of Scorpio. The Knight's shield thus has the winged sandal of *Swiftness*, the arrow of *Strength*, and the mirage cup of *Debauch*. He is armed with the bow and arrow of Art. The background of the card shows the pyramid of Death. Thus his best traits are described by

25   Note that the Knight of Wands is the significator of the author's Sun at 13 ° 49'
        Sagittarius, the 14th degree. The Sabian symbol for this degree is "A vast panorama
        of sand and time is unfolding—the pyramids and the sphinx in their glory rise
        before the eye." The Kozminsky symbol for this degree is "A human eye surrounded
        by a circle of flames."

the Eight and Nine of Wands. He has the mercurial brilliance and True Will of *Swiftness*, combined with vitality and health as well as resilience, aim, and flexibility, from the lunar influence of *Strength*. If his Will is improperly channeled, he may at times slip into the illusory swamp of *Debauch*.

The Avatar

The Knight of Wands brings *Swiftness*, *Strength*, and will-force. There may be a sudden and unexpected opportunity that must be seized swiftly and with strength and confidence. One must be resolute, yet apprehensive of the possibility to crash and burn. Correctly wielded, the outwardly extended fire energy of the Knight of Wands is that of leadership that sparks visionary genius and brings forth a new creation to the world. If his Will is not appropriately channeled it can degenerate to *Debauch*. As a person, he represents one who is confident, idealistic, energetic, adaptable and motivated. If ill-dignified, he represents brutality, cruelty, and too much force too quickly expended.

Queen of Wands

QUEEN OF WANDS
WATER OF FIRE

The Queen of the Thrones of Flame

Queen of the Salamanders

Water of Fire

20° Pisces to 20° Aries

Related Minors of the decans:
(10 of Cups), 2 of Wands, 3 of Wands

Astrological trumps: mainly the
Emperor for Aries as the main sign of
the card; (secondarily the Moon for the
last decan of Pisces as the shadow)

I-Ching: Hexagram 17 *Following*

Book T description: A CROWNED queen with long red-golden hair, seated upon a Throne, with steady flames beneath. She wears a corslet and buskins of scale-mail, which latter her robe discloses. Her arms are almost bare. On cuirass and buskins are leopard's heads winged, and the same symbol surmounteth her crown. At her side is a couchant leopard on which her hands rest. She bears a long wand with a very heavy conical head. The face is beautiful and resolute.

The Queen of the Thrones of Flame bears a crest of a winged leopard's head, the leopard as a symbol of her feminine mystique and controlled transformation. She sits reflectively upon a wide throne surrounded by steady flames as opposed to the wavy and volatile flames of the Knight. She represents the watery part of Fire, and thus channels her creative fire inwardly in ecstatic meditation, shown by her lowered lids. She is Hè primal in relation to Yod. This is the fiery feminine, the receptacle that draws in and gestates the True Will initiated in the Knight. She embodies the nature of the Scarlet Woman, the sacred feminine flame. She radiates the calm authority of one with true inner power and is capable, decisive and generous, though she can also be vain, self-satisfied and tyrannical. She is quick to take offense and can be vengeful without justification. Crowley says of the extent of her vengeful nature "when she misses her bite, she breaks her jaw!"

Her traits are mainly those of the sign Aries. Aries is the first sign of the zodiac, the sign at the horizon or ascendant[26], and is cardinal fire. Aries says "I am." It uses its pioneering, martial energy "to boldly go where no man has gone before." Aries is the sign of the Ram, and like the ram, Aries is impulsive and headstrong. As an archetype it is at best courageous, vital, dynamic and confident, and at worst can be infantile, selfish, warlike and impatient. In the body, Aries governs the head. The Emperor is the trump card associated with Aries, giving a masculine drive to order.

The Queen of Wands rules from 20° Pisces to 20° Aries, and includes the constellation Andromeda. Andromeda was the daughter of King Cepheus and Queen Cassiopeia. As a result of her mother's hubris in claiming Andromeda was more beautiful than the Nereids, Poseidon sent Cetus the sea monster to inflict divine punishment on the kingdom. Andromeda was chained to a rock and offered as a sacrifice or divine marriage to the monster, but was ultimately rescued by, and married by, Perseus.

The Queen of Wands primary sign is that of Aries, the first two decans of the sign. The related minor arcana are the Two of Wands, *Dominion* and the Three of Wands, *Virtue (Established Strength)*. The Mars decan gives her the masculine qualities of courage, boldness, fierceness and ambition, while the Solar decan gives warmth, power, dignity and nobility of purpose. The crook and flail from the Two of Wands are displayed behind her as a reminder of her dominion, authority and resolve. From the Three of Wands, a Thrysus wand with a large conical head suggestive of the rites of Bacchus is planted in the foreground. Her shadow card is the Ten of Cups, *Satiety*, for the last decan of Pisces, and is hinted at by the poppy pod in the mouth of the leopard of her crest. Thus her fantasy of oblivion, satiation, and the surrender of her control could lead to her undoing.

The Avatar

The Queen of Wands brings the qualities of *Dominion* and *Virtue*, steady progress towards a goal, power, courage, and command. She is the sanctifying and anointing fire. Correctly wielded her inwardly reflective fire energy brings business success and magnetic personal attraction. Her danger is in surrender and *Satiety*. As a person the Queen of Wands is a regal and powerful leader, kind and generous unless opposed, and bearing great magnetism. If ill-dignified she is vengeful and autocratic, imperious and oppressive, and quick to take offense.

---

26   The ascendant is the sign on the eastern horizon, beginning of the first house of the zodiac, the time of sunrise and the vernal equinox, and associated with the body, the mask, and the lens or filter through which the world is seen from within and viewed from without.

Prince of Wands

The Prince of the Chariot of Fire

Prince and Emperor of the Salamanders

Air of Fire

20° Cancer to 20° Leo

Related Minors of the decans:
(4 of Cups), 5 of Wands, 6 of Wands

Astrological trumps: mainly Lust
for Leo as the main sign of the card;
(secondarily the Chariot for the last
decan of Cancer as the shadow)

PRINCE OF WANDS
AIR OF FIRE

I-Ching: Hexagram 42 *Increasing*

Book T description: A KINGLY Figure with a golden, winged crown, seated on a chariot. He has large white wings. One wheel of his chariot is shewn. He wears corslet and buskins of scale armour decorated with a winged lion's head, which symbol also surmounts his crown. His chariot is drawn by a lion. His arms are bare, save for the shoulder-pieces of the corslet, and he bears a torch or fire-wand, somewhat similar to that of the Zelator Adeptus Minor. Beneath the chariot are flames, some waved, some salient.

The Prince of the Chariot of Fire bears the crest of a winged lion's head, showing his regality and kingly judgment. As he is the result of the union of the King and Queen, he is shown borne in a chariot, drawn by a lion through a field of waved and salient flames. He represents the airy part of Fire, the expanding and spiritualizing of the element that thus brings the mental qualities of reason to the primal will force. His is the consciousness that steers the fire force though the fixed nature of the Kerubic Lion. He has all of the virile potential of his father combined with the steadying reflective lucidity of his mother. As the Vau of the world of Atziluth, he is the channel and cmissary between our inwardly reflected consciousness and our spiritual creative will. This was Perdurabo's court card for the degree of his ascendant, and of it he says "He is always fighting against odds, and always wins in the long—the very long—run."

His traits are mainly of the sign Leo, the fifth sign of the zodiac ruled by the Sun. Leo says "I will." It is the sign of the lion, and its symbol represents the lion's mane of hair. Leo is a fixed fire sign, regal in nature, romantic, attention seeking, boastful and dramatic. It is a vigorous, creative sign which at best is generous, creative, romantic, warm and broad-minded. At its worst Leo is prideful, pompous, drama-seeking, overbearing and autocratic. In the body, Leo rules the heart and spine. Its trump card is *Lust* giving passion and vitality.

The Prince of Wands rules from 20° Cancer to 20° Leo, including most of the constellation of Leo Minor, the Little Lion, or lion cub that follows Leo Major. The brightest star in Leo Minor is called Praecipua meaning "chief." The Chinese included our Lesser Lion with the Greater Lion in their still greater Dragon mounting to the highest heavens, and in yet another figure, the State Chariot. The constellation Leo Major's alpha star is Regulus, the Little King, also called Cor Leonis, the Heart of the Lion. This is one of the four Kerubic Royal Stars, the Watcher of the North that carries the power of Velle, to Will, to the Princess.

The Prince of Wands primary sign is that of Leo, the first two decans of the sign. The related minor arcana are the Five of Wands, *Strife*, and the Six of Wands, *Victory*. As the child of the King and Queen, he inherits and reconciles these two opposing forces. Like all the Princes, he is the connecting force between two extremes. Thus he contends with pressure and conflict, the tension of *Strife* from the constricting influence of Saturn upon Leo, yet achieves *Victory* and acclaim as a joyous climax to his struggles, through vigilance and the expansive nature of Jupiter. From the Five of Wands, *Strife*, we see in the background the pressurized volcano erupting, indicating the forces of tension seeking release. Yet the winged lion's head of his crest wears the laurel leaf crown of *Victory*, the eventual reward for his dauntless courage and acuity. His shadow card is the Four of Cups, *Luxury*, shown as the scallop shell and pearl on his chariot. This is the last and lunar decan of Cancer, showing his love of pleasure and emotional high points.

The Avatar

The Prince of Wands brings *Strife* and *Victory*, and uses the power of reason to triumph in the struggle of life pursuits. He enjoys the *Luxury* of emotional highs, and brings vitality and drama, and when he appears one may be the focus of attention. There is a lust for life and the ecstasy of the fulfillment of true Will. As a person, he is generous and proud, willing to give patronage, virile and swift, self confident and joyful. If ill-dignified, he is overly prideful and self aggrandizing, cruel, intolerant, contemptuous and dogmatic.

princess of wands

The Princess of the Shining Flame;
The Rose of the Palace of Fire

Princess and Empress of the Salamanders

Throne of the Ace of Wands

Earth of Fire

0° Cancer through 30° Virgo, *centered on*
the Fiery Kerubic constellation Leo

Related Minor: Ace of Wands

PRINCESS OF WANDS
EARTH OF FIRE

Astrological trumps: Chariot, Lust,
Hermit; *centered on Lust*

I-Ching: Hexagram 27 *Nourishment (Jaws)*

Book T description: A VERY strong and beautiful woman with flowing red-gold hair, attired like an Amazon. Her shoulders, arms, bosom and knees are bare. She wears a short kilt reaching to the knee. Round her waist is a broad belt of scale-mail; narrow at the sides; broader in front and back; and having a winged tiger's head in front. She wears a Corinthian-shaped helmet and crown with a long plume. It also is surmounted by a tiger's head, and the same symbol forms the buckle of her scale-mail buskins. A mantle lined with tiger's skin falls back from her shoulders. Her right hand rests on a small golden or brazen altar ornamented with ram's heads and with Flames of Fire leaping from it. Her left hand leans on a long and heavy club, swelling at the lower end, where the sigil is placed; and it has flames of fire leaping from it the whole way down; but the flames are ascending. This club or torch is much longer than that carried by the King or Queen. Beneath her firmly placed feet are leaping Flames of Fire.

The Princess of the Shining Flame, Rose of the Palace of Fire, has a winged tiger's head as her crest, the tiger being a symbol of willpower, fiery sensuality, and courage. As Earth of Fire she is Hè final in relation to Yod. The Princess of Wands is the throne of the Ace of Wands, *Root of the Powers of Fire*, and is thus the spiritual fire of the Yod manifest as Hè final of fire in the perfect physical vehicle to sustain it. She is the ultimate receptacle of the element of fire, where things of the element of fire such as passion and will are given form. The original Will has been expressed; the Great Work complete and in action. She is the earthy part of Fire, the potent and irresistible fuel that is compelled to burn; the pristine and living flame of the soul. She is pictured as one with the mighty trunk of the Ace. She is standing before a Tabernacle or altar of incense ornamented with ram's horns and a blossoming rose, for she celebrates the rites of Spring and is the rose at the heart of the palace of flame. Her helm is plumed with the Yod-like flame of Kether and she is surrounded by a corona or crown of light. Around her are leaping flames.

The Princess rules the quadrant of space from 0° Cancer through 30° Virgo, centered on the Fiery Kerubic constellation Leo. Leo says "I will." The Princess of Wands has the first of the four powers of the Sphinx, *Velle*, To Will or the power of Will. Her primary astrological trump is *Lust*. This gives her the characteristics of vitality, vigor, and daring. She is all-consuming, insatiable, passionate, enthusiastic and aspiring. She has seductive appeal. Crowley says of her "The force of her character imposes the impression of beauty upon the beholder." Her secondary trumps are the Chariot and the Hermit. The Chariot shows that she is a vehicle of the will, and the Hermit confers upon her the purity and sanctity of a vestal virgin and actions rightly taken. The fires of the spirit are incarnate. This is the creative impulse that sets things in motion and shows spontaneous combustion; the living flame of will.

The Avatar

The Princess of Wands brings lust for life, passionate avowal, sudden desires, adventure and action expressive of Will. With her power "To Will," creative and spontaneous inclinations are set in motion. As a person she possesses much sexual charisma. She is ardent and ablaze, brilliant, enthusiastic, daring and impassioned. She fans the flames of desire and attracts much sexual attention. Yet her spontaneous ignition can be childish and fickle, provoking passion without offering commitment. If ill-dignified she is superficial and volatile, theatrical, arrogant, reckless, domineering, and vengeful.

KNIGHT OF CUPS

KNIGHT OF CUPS
FIRE OF WATER

The Lord of the Waves and the Waters;
The King of the Hosts of the Sea

King of Undines and Nymphs

Fire of Water

20° Aquarius to 20° Pisces

Related Minors of the decans:
(7 of Swords), 8 of Cups, 9 of Cups

Astrological trumps: mainly the Moon
for Pisces as the main sign of the card;
(secondarily the Star for the last decan
of Aquarius as the shadow)

I-Ching: Hexagram 54 *Marrying Maiden*

Book T description: A BEAUTIFUL, winged, youthful Warrior with flying hair, riding upon a white horse, which latter is not winged. His general equipment is similar to that of the Knight of Wands, but upon his helmet, cuirass and buskins is a peacock with opened wings. He holds a cup in his hand, bearing the sigil of the scale. Beneath his horse's feet is the sea. From the cup issues a crab.

The Lord of the Waves and the Waters has a peacock with opened wings as his crest; the peacock is a symbol of transcendental experience. The peacock here is also symbolic of the brilliance of water in its active phase, how it sparkles and fluoresces. The Knight rides a white steed through churning waves of the sea. He is the fiery part of Water, or the forceful, powerful aspect of the element. His waters are rains and gushing springs and the alchemical power of solution. The Knight of Cups combines the creativity of fire with watery receptivity; thus he is artistic and gifted with divine inspiration. Like Parcival who sought the Grail, the Knight of Cups seeks redemption through purity and renunciation. But the energy of Knights is fleeting; his waters do not run deep, and his nature is passive. His will is concentrated upon the vibrations he receives.

His traits are mainly of the sign Pisces, the twelfth and final sign of the zodiac. Its modern planet is Neptune, and its traditional planet Jupiter. Pisces says "I believe." Pisces is the sign of dual fishes, and it's symbol represents two fish swimming in opposite directions. Like Pisceans, the fishes dreamily circle, and it is not clear what direction they are moving in. Pisces is a mutable water sign and is otherworldly, amiable, compassionate and empathetic. At best, Pisces is psychic, kind, imaginative and mystical. At worst, Pisces is deceitful, deluded, escapist and weak. In the body Pisces rules the feet and the immune system. The Moon is the trump card associated with Pisces, giving Pisces the ability to plumb the unconscious depths.

The Knight of Cups rules from 20° Aquarius to 20° Pisces, including the greater part of the constellation of Pegasus. Pegasus was the divine winged stallion sired by Poseidon the sea god upon the Gorgon Medusa, spontaneously born from her blood when Perseus beheaded her. *Pegasus* is from the *pēgē*, meaning spring or well. Wherever he struck his hooves, a spring of inspiring waters burst forth. One of these was the Hippocrene, sacred spring of the Muses whose waters gave poetic inspiration.

The Knight of Cups' primary sign is that of Pisces, the first two decans of the sign. The related minor arcana are the Eight of Cups, *Indolence*, and Nine of Cups, *Happiness*. His shadow card is the Seven of Swords, *Futility*. The peytral, or chest armor shield of the horse, thus bears mnemonic imagery from the three minors. From the Eight of Cups, *Indolence*, we see the figure head of the abandoned ghost ship, indicating stagnation, placidity, and the loss of heart and darkness of soul that occurs in the creative process. The Nine of Cups, *Happiness*, provides the hand-serpent offering the large end of the wishbone. This is the emotional expansion when creativity is fulfilled. From the Seven of Swords, *Futility*, is the collapsed and overburdened camel kneeling. This is the danger that passivity can lead to the will-force being squandered, and to the loss of sacred vision.

The Avatar

The Knight of Cups brings artistic inspiration and receptivity to divine will. There is a tendency to the amiable passivity of *Indolence* and yet there can be the transcendental *Happiness* and emotional fulfillment that comes from creative impulse being followed. If that inner spark is not nurtured and he loses heart, *Futility* is the result. As a person, the Knight of Cups is creative and inspired, graceful and pure, soft and receptive; passive unless enthusiastically roused. If ill-dignified he is overly sensitive, shallow, stagnant, brooding or apathetic, and lazy.

QUEEN OF CUPS
WATER OF WATER

QUEEN OF CUPS

The Queen of the Thrones of the Waters

Queen of Nymphs and Undines

Water of Water

20° Gemini to 20° Cancer

Related Minors of the decans:
(10 of Swords), 2 of Cups, 3 of Cups

Astrological trumps: mainly the Chariot
for Cancer as the main sign of the card;
(secondarily the Lovers for the last
decan of Gemini as the shadow)

I-Ching: Hexagram 58 *Lake (Joyous)*

Book T description: A VERY beautiful fair woman like a crowned Queen, seated upon a throne, beneath which is flowing water wherein Lotuses are seen. Her general dress is similar to that of the Queen of Wands, but upon her crown, cuirass and buskins is seen an Ibis with opened wings, and beside her is the same bird, whereon her hand rests. She holds a cup, wherefrom a crayfish issues. Her face is dreamy. She holds a lotus in the hand upon the Ibis.

The crest of the Queen of the Thrones of the Waters bears an ibis with open wings. The ibis is a waterfowl and alchemically symbolizes the lunar forces and cycles of time, the realms of duality, and successful transmutation. As a variety of stork it also signifies the maternal instinct. The Queen sits with her skirts pooled about her like water, gazing at her reflection in the river waters below. She is Water of Water, which is also Hè primal of Hè primal, and thus the fitting representative of the Mother, the second letter of the Divine name. The watery part of water is its receptivity and reflection. She is veiled in light and it is hard to look upon the truth of her, for she reflects and mirrors the viewer.

Her traits are mainly that of the sign Cancer, the fourth sign of the zodiac, at the nadir,[27] with the Moon for its planetary body. Cancer says "I feel." It is the sign of the crab or crawfish, and its symbol resembles crab claws or some

---

27 The nadir is the bottom of the horoscope, the time of midnight and the summer
     solstice, and is associated with the home and the nurturing parent.

say breasts, the part of the body Cancer rules along with the womb. The breasts are a clue to the nurturing and maternal nature of the sign. Cancer is a cardinal water sign, and like the crustacean, it is hard on the outside for protection of its soft interior. Cancer at best is protective, caring, intuitive and imaginative; at worst Cancer is moody, overly sensitive, and clingy. The Chariot is the main trump card, giving the maternal qualities of containment and gestation, as the bearer of the Grail. The crayfish raises a claw from the cup, symbolic of the protective shell of enclosure.

The rules from 20° Gemini to 20° Cancer. The constellation of Cancer includes M44, a cloud-like cluster of stars in the heart of the Crab called the Beehive Cluster, known in classical times as *Praesepe*, meaning "the manger." These stars once marked the position of the Sun at the June solstice, and Mesopotamian lore thought they marked the gateway of incarnation. In the Egyptian tradition, Cancer was the dawn solar god Kheprhi, a personification of the scarab of life, rebirth, and fertility. Castor and Pollux are also nearby. These were the twin sons of Leta, one fathered by her mortal husband and one by Zeus in the guise of a swan. In Egypt, these stars were seen as a pair of sprouting plants.

The Queen of Cups primary sign is that of the first two decans of Cancer. The related minors are the Two and Three of Cups, *Love* and *Abundance*. Her shadow card is the Ten of Swords, *Ruin*. From the Two of Cups we have the twinned bees, the Venusian indicators of the sweetness of *Love* and fertility. From the Three we have twinned lotus or lily pads as their reflection. This decan gives her the Mercurial powers of prophecy, and the joy of the fecundity of the union of two that results in three. The Ten of Swords provides the background of the card, the light broken by cirrus clouds, disrupting her serenity and reflection. The light reveals which of her ideals are impractical for manifestation, and signals the end of delusion. But this is a disruptive force of the serenity of her pure intuition.

The Avatar

The Queen of Cups brings *Love*, nurturing, *Abundance*, and fecundity. It is a time of intuition, prophecy, and dreams. If the inner world is divided, there can be disharmony and the disruption of *Ruin*. But such is foreign to her nature. As a person, she is imaginative and feminine, guided by her own depths. She mirrors, reflects, and attracts others by penetrating the mists of the unconscious and dissolving boundaries. As such much depends on the forces surrounding her. If ill-dignified, she is not willing to take responsibility for another, and has no character of her own but a reflection of every passing impression.

prince of cups

PRINCE OF CUPS
AIR OF WATER

The Prince of the Chariot of the Waters

Prince and Emperor of Nymphs and Undines

Air of Water

20° Libra to 20° Scorpio

Related Minors of the decans: (4 of Swords), 5 of Cups, 6 of Cups

Astrological trumps: mainly Death for Scorpio as the main sign of the card; (secondarily Adjustment for the last decan of Libra as the shadow)

I-Ching: Hexagram 61 *Sincerity*

Book T description: A WINGED Kingly Figure with winged crown seated in a chariot drawn by an eagle. On the wheel is the symbol of a scorpion. The eagle is borne as a crest on his crown, cuirass and buskins. General attire like King of Wands. Beneath his chariot is the calm and stagnant water of a lake. His armour resembles feathers more than scales. He holds in one hand a lotus, and in the other a cup, charged with the sigil of his scale. A serpent issues from the cup, and has its head tending down to the waters of the lake.

The Prince of the Chariot of the Waters bears an eagle as his crest. As he is the result of the union of the King and Queen, he is shown borne in a chariot, drawn by an eagle above a lake with rippling waters. The eagle is the highest form of the sign of Scorpio, representing exultation above matter. The eagle can see into the waters with miraculous clarity, and as Air of Water the Prince of Cups uses reason to plumb the depths of the soul and emotions. He is above all a philosopher with clear vision, a bridge between intuition and reason. The currents and fluidity are representative of the airy part of water, the wave-like fluctuations of the serpent of Scorpio and transformative life energy. As the result of the union of the fire of Yod and the water of Hè primal, in the element of water he also presents as steam. Steam is at once both powerful catalytic energy and etherealization of water.

His traits are mainly those of the sign of Scorpio, the eighth sign of the zodiac whose inner planet is Mars, sharing this planet with Aries, and also having Pluto as its outer planet. Scorpio says "I desire." Scorpio is the sign of the Scorpion, and its symbol has the pointed barb of the scorpion's tail or an upright sexual organ. Both seek to prod or sting you and find out where you are sensitive. It is a fixed water sign and is secretive and potent. At its best, Scorpio is deep, magnetic, tenacious, passionate and willful. At worst it is jealous, vengeful, obsessive/compulsive, vindictive and unforgiving. In the body Scorpio rules the sexual and eliminative organs. Death is the trump card associated with Scorpio, and is linked with the letter Nun, meaning "fish." According to Crowley this Princes' wings are ephemeral or tenuous like steam, so here they are shown as the delicate webbed wings of a flying fish.

The Prince of Cups rules from 20° Libra to 20° Scorpio. The constellation *Scorpius*, the Scorpion, contains the alpha star *Antares* which means "rival of Aries." This is the heart of the Scorpion and one of the four Kerubic Royal Stars, the Watcher of the West that carries the power *Audere*, to Dare. In Egypt the stars of Scorpius were seen as a serpent.

The Prince of Cups primary sign is that of Scorpio, the first two decans of the sign. The related minor arcana are the Five of Cups, *Disappointment (Loss of Pleasure)*, and the Six of Cups, *Pleasure*. As the child of the King and Queen, he inherits and reconciles these two opposing forces. He has a sustained passion for life and death, pleasure and loss, passion and pathos. From the Five of Cups, the eagle of his crest clutches the desiccated fish of *Disappointment*. From the Six of Cups he inherits the *Pleasure* of soaring above the waters, and we see the sun-sparkled lake from the card in the background. His shadow card is the Four of Swords, *Truce (Rest from Strife)* and from that card we see the vajra between the scorpions on the front of his chariot. But rest is not the way of Princes, and thus "Truce" represents him in a state of emotional exhaustion and debilitation.

The Avatar

The Prince of Cups brings a time to be a hero of emotional explorations. One knows oneself, and the polarities ranging between *Disappointment* and *Pleasure*. A Prince is not inclined toward *Truce* in between these options, unless the life force is exhausted, as he prefers the intensity of emotional extremes. As a person he is secretive and artistic, ardent and torrential, secretly desirous of power and control. On the surface he appears calm, while underneath he is intensely passionate. If ill-dignified he is evil, ruthless and without conscience, and cannot be relied upon to work for the common good.

Princess of Cups

PRINCESS OF CUPS
EARTH OF WATER

The Princess of the Waters;
The Lotus of the Palace of the Floods

Princess and Empress of the Nymphs and Undines

Throne of the Ace of Cups

Earth of Water

0° Libra through 30° Sagittarius, *centered on the Watery Kerubic constellation Scorpio*

Related Minor: Ace of Cups

Astrological trumps: Adjustment, Death, Art; *centered on Death*

I-Ching: Hexagram 41 *Decreasing*

Book T description: A BEAUTIFUL Amazon-like figure, softer in nature than the Princess of Wands. Her attire is similar. She stands on a sea with foaming spray. Away to her right a Dolphin. She wears as a crest a swan with opening wings. She bears in one hand a lotus, and in the other an open cup from which a turtle issues. Her mantle is lined with swans-down, and is of thin floating material.

The Princess of the Waters, Lotus of the Palace of the Floods has the open-winged swan as a crest. The swan is a symbol of grace and beauty, purity and transformation. In Greek tradition, the Swan is the symbol of the Muses. Socrates wrote that the swan would only sing it's most beautiful song just before it died, leaving us with the phrase "swan song." The swan also has erotic connotations as Aphrodite, the Goddess of Love, had a swan-drawn chariot. The earthy part of water is its crystallization and powers of creation. As Earth of Water she is the daughter Hè final in the world of her mother Hè primal, the embodied soul in relation to the higher soul.

The Princess of Cups is the Throne of the Ace of Cups. *Root of the Powers of Water*. Thus she is the ultimate receptacle of the element of water, where things of the element of water such as love and creativity are given form. She is pictured as an undine forming and rising from the waters of the great shell cup of the Ace of Cups, with the Moon from the card behind her. She lifts the lotus in recognition of her title as *Lotus of the Palace of the Floods*.

The Princess rules the quadrant of space from 0° Libra through 30° Sagittarius, centered on the Watery Kerubic constellation Scorpio. Scorpio says "I desire." The Princess of Cups is given the second of the four powers of the Sphinx, *Audere*, To Dare or the power of Love. Her primary astrological trump is *Death*. This gives her the characteristics of transformation from low to high, as she imagines herself fluidly shape shifting through many forms, each part of her nature. Her secondary trumps are *Adjustment* giving her discernment of ethical action, and *Art* for her powers of healing and idealization.

The Avatar

The Princess of Cups brings a longing for divine union and exploration of the soul. One acts in response to intuition to embody ideals. With her power "To Dare," love and inspiration are given form. As a person she is helpful to others and rarely obtains stature in and of herself. She is dreamy, kind, imaginative, and fearless if roused. She appeals to others on the emotional level. If ill-dignified she is selfish, pleasure seeking, and deceptive.

KNIGHT OF SWORDS
FIRE OF AIR

KNIGHT OF SWORDS

The Lord of the Winds and the Breezes;
The King of the Spirits of Air

King of the Sylphs and Sylphides

Fire of Air

20° Taurus to 20° Gemini

Related Minors of the decans:
(7 of Disks), 8 of Swords, 9 of Swords

Astrological trumps: mainly the Lovers
for Gemini as the main sign of the card;
(secondarily the Hierophant for the last
decan of Taurus as the shadow)

I-Ching: Hexagram 32 *Enduring*

Book T description: A WINGED Warrior with crowned Winged Helmet, mounted upon a brown steed. His general equipment is as that of the Knight of Wands, but he wears as a crest a winged six-pointed star, similar to those represented on the heads of Castor and Pollux the Dioscuri, the twins Gemini (a part of which constellation is included in his rule). He holds a drawn sword with the sigil of his scale upon its pommel. Beneath his horse's feet are dark-driving stratus clouds.

The Lord of the Winds and the Breezes has a winged six-pointed star similar to those represented on the heads of Castor and Pollux, the twins of Gemini called the Dioscuri. Part of the constellation of Gemini is contained in the sector he rules. The mother of the Dioscuri was Leda, wife of the King of Sparta, who was also the mother of Helen of Troy and Clytemnestra, both of whom had roles to play in the Trojan War. The King of Sparta fathered Castor, but Pollux was fathered by Zeus, who took the form of a swan and who seduced Leda. The Dioscuri were venerated as helpers of humankind and held to be patrons of travelers and of sailors in particular, who invoked them to seek favorable winds. They were also associated with horses and huntsmen, and intervened at the moment of crisis, aiding those who honored them. The Knight of Swords is the fiery part of Air, or Yod relating to Vau. This is the spark of ideas necessary for evolution and civilization, the winds of change through science and intelligence. The creative fire is channeled through the intellect, making him a force of great brilliance and command, though cool and imperious. This is the violent motion of air, the attacking winds of the tempest that bring down the heavens. Crowley calls Fire of Air "the extended flame of the mind" and "the True will exploding the mind spontaneously."

His traits are mainly those of the sign of Gemini, the third sign of the zodiac. Its planet is the airy aspect of Mercury. Gemini says "I think." It is the sign of the twins, and its symbol represents two figures standing side by side, emphasizing its dualistic quality. What do two figures do when they find themselves side by side? Talk, and hopefully communicate. Gemini is an air sign, mercurial and mutable in nature. It is social, flighty and intellectual. Gemini is restless, witty, intelligent and adaptable at best, and cunning, fickle, superficial and shallow at worst. In the body Gemini rules the hands, arms, bronchial passageways and lungs. The Lovers is the trump card associated with Gemini, whose letter is Zain meaning sword. This is the Sword of the mind that divides; the function of the mind that creates and classifies through dualities.

The Knight of Swords rules from 20° Taurus to 20° Gemini, including not only part of the constellation of Gemini as described, but also the constellation *Auriga*. Auriga is Latin for *charioteer*, and the shape of the constellation was said to be similar to the pointed helmet they wore. Of course, being associated with Gemini, there are two charioteer stories associated with this constellation in mythology. Auriga is most frequently identified with Erichthonius, king of Athens and son of the fire god Hephaestus. Erichthonius was raised and taught by the goddess Athena, making him very clever. Erichthonius is usually credited for the invention of the four-horse chariot, the quadriga, made in imitation of the sun god's chariot, which made Zeus impressed enough to place Erichthonius among the stars. But Auriga is also identified with the story of the duplicitous charioteer Myrtilus, who with a cunning trick betrayed his King, replacing the axles of his chariot with wax in order to win the hand of his daughter Hippodameia, the horse-tamer. Myrtilus' victory is short-lived as he is in turn betrayed by the son of Hermes who had earlier aided him. Hermes, who appreciated tricks and cunning, then honored him with a position in the stars.

The Knight of Swords' primary sign is that of Gemini, the first two decans of the sign. The related minor arcana are the Eight of Swords, *Interference (Shortened Force)*, and Nine of Swords, *Cruelty*. The decan of the Eight of Swords is ruled by Jupiter. The combination of Jupiter with Gemini brings the storm, the thunder and lightning; too much force applied to trivial things. In this card the Will is being unexpectedly interfered with in the realm of intellectual contest; the wrong thoughts can shorten one's force. In the Knight's crest, the poniards, or small daggers of the Eight of Sword's dagger-wheel make up the star of the Dioscuri. The decan of the Nine of Swords is ruled by Mars. The pierced boar's head of the Nine of Swords, *Cruelty*, is the design on the peytral, or chest armor shield of the horse. The boar's head also has the horns of a bull, from his shadow card, the Seven of Disks, *Failure*. The Nine of Swords indicates his often callous brutality, coming from a place of mental distress. If especially well dignified, it can also indicate his great mental perseverance and courage. His shadow card is the force that is anathema to his nature, that of the torpor of *Failure*, the decan of Taurus ruled by restrictive Saturn. This is what his mind most fears and that which he overcompensates for.

The Avatar

The Knight of Swords brings the powers of the intellect to the forefront. One is discriminating and analytical, coolly rational, and brilliant, but can tend towards being domineering, using too much force applied to insignificant things, creating *Interference*. There is the danger of *Cruelty* and duplicity, coming from a place of mental anguish, though if well-dignified, the Knight of Swords can bring much mental discipline. As a person he is clever, cunning, scientific, assertive and astute, being comfortable with duality and contradictions. While very brave, dynamic, and intelligent, if ill-dignified he can be unreliable, deceitful, petty, malicious, and tyrannical. He is prone to change his mind to suit himself. He fears inertia and *Failure* and thus performs both great and twisted acts of mental agility to achieve clarity, without principle or scruples.

QUEEN OF SWORDS
WATER OF AIR

Queen of swords

The Queen of the Thrones of Air

Queen of Sylphs and Sylphides

Water of Air

20° Virgo to 20° Libra

Related Minors of the decans:
(10 of Disks), 2 of Swords, 3 of Swords

Astrological trumps: mainly Adjustment
for Libra as the main sign of the card;
(secondarily the Hermit for the last
decan of Virgo as the shadow)

I-Ching: Hexagram 28 *Great, Exceeding*

Book T description: A GRACEFUL woman with wavy, curling hair, like a Queen seated upon a Throne and crowned. Beneath the Throne are grey cumulus clouds. Her general attire is as that of the Queen of Wands, but she wears as a crest a winged child's head. A drawn sword in one hand, and in the other a large, bearded, newly severed head of a man.

The Queen of the Thrones of Air has a winged child's head as her crest. The face of the child is actually a cherub. A cherub (*keruv*) is like a child (*ke-ravya*), since in Babylonian Aramaic a child is called *ravya*. Cherubim are a sort of divine guard, known to guard the Ark, the holy temple, and the Garden of Eden. The name *kerub* seems to come from the Akkadian root *karābu*, which means "bless." The *karibu* are the blessed ones; they were lower level divine beings who function as supplicants, standing before the god and praying on behalf of others. The Queen of Swords is the watery part of Air, the flows and currents of the mind; the intuitive perception of patterns and ability to transmit.

Her traits are mainly those of the sign Libra, the seventh sign of the zodiac, at the descendant,[28] and its planet is the airy aspect of Venus, sharing

---

28   The descendant is the beginning of the seventh house of the horoscope, and is the
      time of sunset and the autumnal equinox, and is associated with the concept of the
      partner or other.

this planet with Taurus. Libra says "I balance." Libra is the sign of the Scales, and these are pictured in its symbol. Just like a person using a scale, Libra is concerned with beauty, truth and balance. It is a cardinal air sign, and is fair-minded, tactful and just. It is a social and harmony seeking sign. At its highest expression Libra is charming, peaceful, sociable, and easy to get along with. At worst, Libra is easily led, gullible, indecisive and frivolous. In the body Libra rules the lower back along with the kidneys and adrenals. Adjustment is the trump card associated with Libra, which links her with Ma'at, goddess of truth and the administration of law. This is the *Woman Satisfied*, and the "woman girt with a sword" who teaches the lessons of karma through cool calibration and minute adjustments of the intellect. She holds a severed head, as her sharpness cuts away the masks of illusion through the clarity of her perception.

The Queen of Swords rules from 20° Virgo to 20° Libra. The constellation *Librae*, the Scales, goes back to Mesopotamian times. The balance symbolized the equal lengths of day and night, as two millennia ago the Sun passing into Libra marked the autumnal equinox. Roman astronomers called them the scales of Justice, held by Astraea, goddess of Justice in neighboring Virgo. According to legend, Astraea will one day come back to Earth, issuing in the utopian Golden Age of which she was the ambassador. (Is this the Age of Ma'at, which follows the Age of Horus?) Crowley's sun sign degree falls here at 19°14' Libra.[29] He calls the Queen of Swords the Liberator of the Mind and says, "Such people inspire intense love and devotion from the most unexpected quarters."

The Queen of Swords' primary sign is that of Libra, the first two decans of the sign. The related minor arcana are the Two of Swords, *Peace*, and the Three of Swords, *Sorrow*. From the Two of Swords, crossed swords form the fulcrum of the scales on her throne perched among cumulous clouds. This decan is ruled by the Moon. The mind, like the moon, is subject to fluctuations, and mental flexibility results in the balance of intellectual harmony. From the Three of Swords comes her throne itself, as she sits on the tripod in the place of the Oracle. This decan is ruled by Saturn, and indicates that her wisdom comes through isolation and the suffering that perceiving the sorrowful secrets of nature can cause. Through the motto of the Pythia, *Know Thyself*, she bears witness to the darkness within. Her shadow card is the Ten of Disks, *Wealth*, and the two disks of equilibrium from that card are balanced in the pans of

---

29   The Sabian symbol for the 20th degree of Libra, Crowley's Sun, is "A rabbi performing his duties."

her scales. As this is her shadow, it shows that completion and regeneration are not her ideals; rather she prefers the continuous dance of adjustment. If she were simply to administer justice as a done deal, minus the dance and flow of the weights and balances, she would be too autocratic.

The Avatar

The Queen of Swords brings intuition, clarity, and perception of patterns. She cuts away illusions and liberates the mind. Compromise and mental flexibility bring her *Peace*, but in experiencing isolation and the *Sorrow* of solitude she can also be enlightened. Her highest way is not that of the *fait accompli* that the powers of *Wealth* can confer, for on that path she becomes tyrannical and dictatorial, losing the timeless perspective that the dance gives as she constantly weighs and balances truth against false logic. As a person, she is perceptive and graceful, intelligent and discriminating. She has freed her mind through self-determination. If ill-dignified she can be cold and cruel, micro-managing, superficial, severe and stubborn, using her considerable attractiveness in a deceitful way.

prince of swords

The Prince of the Chariot of the Winds

Prince and Emperor of Sylphs and Sylphides

Air of Air

20° Capricorn to 20° Aquarius

Related Minors of the decans:
(4 of Disks), 5 of Swords, 6 of Swords

Astrological trumps: mainly the Star for Aquarius as the main sign of the card; (secondarily the Devil for the last decan of Capricorn as the shadow)

I-Ching: Hexagram 57 *Wind (Gently Penetrating)*

PRINCE OF SWORDS

AIR OF AIR

Book T description: A WINGED King with Winged Crown, seated in a chariot drawn by Arch Fays, represented as winged youths very slightly dressed, with butterfly wings; heads encircled by a fillet with a pentagram thereon; and holding wands surmounted by pentagrams, the same butterfly wings on their feet and fillets. General equipment as the King of Wands; but he bears as a crest a winged angelic head with a pentagram on the brows. Beneath the chariot are grey nimbus clouds. His hair long and waving in serpentine whirls, and whorl figures compose the scales of his armour. A drawn sword in one hand; a sickle in the other. With the sword he rules, with the sickle he slays.

The Prince of the Chariot of the Winds bears a crest with a winged angelic head with a pentagram on its brow. "For secret symbols on my brow, And secret thoughts within, Compel eternity to Now, Draw the Infinite within." [30] The pentagram is a five pointed star, said to represent the four directions, plus above, or the four elements plus the quintessential element of spirit. It is a sacred geometry construction in which all of the parts relate to each other via the golden ratio. It is used in both invocation and protection. The

---

30   The Palace of the World, describing the spiritual aspect of the "Lesser Ritual of the Pentagram" from the Temple of the Holy Ghost by Aleister Crowley

pentagram represents the five upper sephiroth on the Tree of Life which represent pure archetypal forces: *Strength*, *Mercy*, *Understanding*, *Wisdom* and the *Crown* of transcendental splendor. It also stands for the five senses, and is thus representative of Man. The pentagram is also the diagram of the four powers of the Sphinx plus the fifth power of Spirit. As this Prince is Vau of Vau, he reminds us that the Princes carry these powers to the Princesses, or that Malkuth achieves these powers through connection with Tiphareth. The Prince of Swords is Air of Air, Vau of Vau, and thus the fitting representative of the Son, the third letter of the Divine name centered in Tiphareth, connecting all the spheres. The airy part of Air is its motion and flow, and describes the fleeting and ephemeral nature of thought. He carries a sickle representative of the planet Saturn; what he mentally creates, he simultaneously instantly destroys. His chariot is drawn by winged Fays, capriciously pulling in varied directions. This is a perfect analogy of the Buddhist term "monkey mind," the inconstant, restless, uncontrollable nature of thought. This Prince is purely intellectual, whose mind overflows with ideas and ideals. He is rational and clever, but does not relate his ideas to practical effort and can thus sustain any conceivable argument. Crowley says these natives are "indifferent to the fate of a contrary argument advanced two minutes earlier, impossible to defeat because any position is as good as any other" and that they have enormous potency, "as if an imbecile offered one the dialogues of Plato." [31]

The traits of the Prince of Swords are mainly those of the sign of Aquarius. Aquarius is the eleventh sign of the zodiac, and its ancient planet is Saturn; it shares it with Capricorn. Its modern planet is Uranus. Aquarius says "I know." Aquarius is the sign of the Water-Bearer, and its symbol is suggestive of waves of both water and of electricity, and also suggests light or thought waves. Aquarians are telepathic and shocking. Aquarius is brilliant, humanitarian and revolutionary. It is a fixed air sign and is unique, individual and inventive. At best Aquarius is progressive, futuristic, original, loyal and selfless. At worst it is detached, aloof, distracted, fanatical and contrary. In the body Aquarius rules the calves, shins and circulatory system. The Star is the trump card associated with Aquarius, and from the Star he gets his idealism and vision.

The Prince of Swords rules from 20° Capricorn to 20° Aquarius. The constellation Aquarius is depicted as a figure pouring water from a jug into the *Fluvius Aquarii* , the River of Aquarius, onto the Royal Star Fomalhaut, from

---

31   *Book of Thoth* pg 163. I find this incredibly amusing as the degree of my ascendant falls here.

the Arabic *fum al-hawt* meaning "mouth of the (southern) fish." Fomalhaut is one of the four Kerubic guardians, the Watcher of the South that carries the power *Sciere*, to Know. In ancient Egypt, the figure was associated with the blue skinned Nile God Hapi, who distributed the waters of Heaven from his urn symbolizing a fount of good fortune. Later European representations associated the figure with Ganymede, whose name means "rejoicing in virility." The son of the King of Troy, Ganymede was the most beautiful youth alive and thus was chosen by Zeus to be forever young as the bearer of the cup of divine nectar.

The Prince of Swords primary sign is that of Aquarius, the first two decans of the sign. The related minor arcana are the Five of Swords, *Defeat*, and the Six of Swords, *Science (Earned Success)*. As the child of the King and Queen, he inherits and reconciles these two opposing forces. The first decan is ruled by Venus, who in combination with Aquarius gives an idealistic and humanitarian nature, but prone to weakness from pacifism and lack of grounding. Yet the Venusian influence indicates one who gets much enjoyment from exercise of the intellect. The second decan is ruled by Mercury, giving brilliance, innovation and foresight, with much flexibility of mind. The shadow card is the Four of Disks, *Power*, from the last decan of Capricorn. This rigid application of authority is contrary to his nature, but in times of weakness he slips into this mentally domineering and uncompromising role.

The Avatar

The Prince of Swords brings an onrush of ideas and innovations; the challenge is holding on to them. He is idealistic and visionary, highly intellectual and clever. This Prince is altruistic and humanitarian, but an excess of passivity and pacifism can lead to *Defeat*. He earns success with the application of *Science*, using his intelligence and considerable flexibility of mind. In times of exhaustion, he clings to the rigidity of *Power* and can become unyielding. As a person, he is brilliant, inventive, theoretical, humane, and progressive. If ill-dignified he can be harsh, disdainful, plotting, erratic, and unreliably passive, building castles in the air and fluctuating between lack of commitment to any argument or fanatical devotion to a whim.

Princess of Swords

The Princess of the Rushing Winds;
The Lotus of the Palace of Air

Princess and Empress of the Sylphs
and Sylphides

Throne of the Ace of Swords

Earth of Air

o° Capricorn through 3o° Pisces,
centered on the Airy Kerubic
constellation Aquarius

Related Minor: Ace of Swords

Astrological trumps: the Devil, the Star,
the Moon; *centered on the Star*

I-Ching: Hexagram 18 *Remedying*

Book T description: AN AMAZON figure with waving hair, slighter than the Rose of the Palace of Fire. Her attire is similar. The Feet seem springy, giving the idea of swiftness. Weight changing from one foot to another and body swinging around. She is a mixture of Minerva and Diana: her mantle resembles the Aegis of Minerva. She wears as a crest the head of the Medusa with serpent hair. She holds a sword in one hand; and the other rests upon a small silver altar with grey smoke (no fire) ascending from it. Beneath her feet are white clouds.

The Princess of the Rushing Winds, Lotus of the Palace of Air, has as a crest the head of Medusa with serpent hair. The name Medusa comes from the Greek word for "guardian, protectress." She was a Gorgon, from ancient Greek word gorgós, meaning terrible or dreadful, that comes from the Sanskrit word "garg" which is a guttural sound similar to the growling of a beast. The Gorgons were three sisters with hair of venomous snakes. Looking at their flashing eyes was said to turn one to stone. In ancient Greece, the *Gorgoneion* was a stone carving of Medusa's head placed above doorways and used as an apotropaic amulet to ward against evil. The Medusa head design also was used by Athena as an aegis on an animal skin mantle, and sometimes on a shield. The Aegis implied divine birth or protection; doing something "under someone's *aegis*" means doing something under the protection of a powerful, knowledgeable, and benevolent source. The Princess of Swords is the earthy part of Air, smoke, and she represents the wrath of the gods and the influence of Heaven upon Earth. She has the power of settling controversies, and is stern and avenging. Hers is the grounded action taken in response to Idea. Her battle is on the astral level; she is the warrior of the mind. She battles to liberate herself from delusion.

The Princess of Swords is the Throne of the Ace of Swords, *Root of the Powers of Air*. Thus she is the ultimate receptacle of the element of Air, where things of the element of air such as thought and idea are given form. She is pictured in motion, whirling, through the smoke of the city of the pyramids beneath the crown from the Ace of Swords.

The Princess rules the quadrant of space from 0° Capricorn through 30° Pisces, centered on the Airy Kerubic constellation Aquarius, and thus her primary astrological trump is *The Star*. This gives her the power of the star maiden, the infinite view. The motto of the sign Aquarius is "I know," and *To Know* is her power, the third of the four powers of the Sphinx and that of Reason, corresponding to Kerubic Air. Her secondary trumps are *The Devil* and *The Moon*. These cards surrounding her center are the *Gates of Matter* (Devil) and the *Flux and Reflux* (Moon). The Devil was the god who protected humanity and gave the gift of knowledge. On the path of the Moon the seeker has to rely on the three lower senses: touch, taste and smell. Thus the Princess is poised between the conscious and unconscious realms, using discernment to peer though the veils.

The Avatar

The Princess of Swords brings a battle for insight, to slash through the smoke of delusion and act with decisive vision. It is a time for action in response to idea, as there is connection between the astral and material worlds. It may be a time of settling controversies, and avenging wrongs. One uses clear perception for self-realization. Her power "To Know" will liberate the mind. As a person, she is volatile and impulsive, insightful and sharp. She is clever and strategic, dexterous in the management of her affairs. If ill-dignified, she is destructive and quarrelsome, and displays a low form of cunning.

KNIGHT OF DISKS

The Lord of the Wide and Fertile Land;
The King of the Spirits of Earth

King of Gnomes

Fire of Earth

20° Leo to 20° Virgo

Related Minors of the decans:
(7 of Wands), 8 of Disks, 9 of Disks

Astrological trumps: mainly the Hermit
for Virgo as the main sign of the card;
(secondarily Lust for the last decan of
Leo as the shadow)

I-Ching: Hexagram 62 *Exceeding*

KNIGHT OF DISKS
FIRE OF EARTH

Book T description: A DARK Winged Warrior with winged and crowned helmet: mounted on a light brown horse. Equipment as the Knight of Wands. The winged head of a stag or antelope as a crest. Beneath the horse's feet is fertile land with ripened corn. In one hand he bears a sceptre surmounted by a hexagram: in the other a Pentacle like that of the Zelator Adeptus Minor.

The Lord of the Wide and Fertile Land bears the winged head of a stag as his crest. The stag is a symbol of strength, masculinity and virility. Stags grow antlers in the spring, symbolic of birth, renewal, and the return of life. The antlers fall off in the fall symbolic of death, introspection and hibernation. Thus the stag reminds us of the cycles of the renewal and growth of nature. Its antlers have a solar connotation, as they represent the expanding rays of the sun. The Knight of Disks is the fiery part of Earth, its warmth and ability to produce life in conjunction with the sun. This is the Yod of Earth, or the seed of the generative force of the land. His horse, a "shire horse, solidly planted on all four feet, as was not the case with the other Knights."[32] He is the King one with the land; it is the story of the sacrificial King that starts the sequence of YHVH in the material world.

His traits are mainly those of the sign of Virgo, the sixth sign of the zodiac. Its planet is the earthly aspect of Mercury, sharing Mercury with

32   *Book of Thoth* pg 164

Gemini. Virgo says "I analyze." It is the sign of the Virgin, and its symbol is said to represent the sexual organs protected by crossed legs. Like its glyph, they are seeking to create and preserve perfection. Virgo is a mutable earth sign, meticulous in nature, and is associated with agriculture, health and food production. At its best Virgo is discriminating, modest, diligent, efficient and dutiful. The worst qualities of Virgo are expressed as criticism, anxiety and pickiness. In the body Virgo rules the nervous system and the digestive tract. The Hermit is the trump card associated with Virgo, whose letter is Yod. This gives the Knight of Disks a link to the secret seed, from which all things descend. He is an aspect of the Hermit, the solitary bearer of the solar light.

The Knight of Disks rules from 20° Leo to 20° Virgo including the magnificent star Spica, alpha star of the constellation Virgo. Spica is a star of considerable beauty because it is a binary, or double star, of two stars larger than our Sun. It marks the ear of corn in the maiden's left hand. An Egyptian Coptic title was *Khoritos*, "Solitary," as Spica was such a notably brilliant star in an otherwise poorly lit area of the sky. This seems to also fit well with his association with the Hermit, the solitary wanderer.

The Knight of Disks' primary sign is that of Virgo, the first two decans of the sign. The related minors are the Eight of Disks, *Prudence*, and the Nine of Disks, *Gain*. On his shield, from the Eight, we see the nest of eggs, symbolic of his cultivation of life, ideas, and people. This decan is ruled by the Sun, which is contained in the lantern that warms the eggs. This indicates the light of intelligence, careful planning, and patient cultivation. The Nine of Disks contributes the counting hand of Yod, carefully tracking and nurturing the blessings of the harvest and the sweetness of the hive. The shadow card is the Seven of Wands, *Valour*, which contributes the snarling face of the tiger. This is the hidden side of his nature that may yearn to go on the offensive and display a more valiant and tiger-like demeanor. His though is a quieter path, and valorous behavior though admirable would take away his greatest strength, that of patient and capable development.

The Avatar

The Knight of Disks brings a coming focus on *Prudence*, shepherding something material towards a state of *Gain*. This takes intelligence and attention to detail. It takes time for these material creations to develop. It is not a time for the heroism of *Valour*; it is a time to experience procreative powers and patient cultivation. As a person he is hard working, taking great care with his projects and not rushing them along. He is diligent, but not particularly prone to courageous action. If ill-dignified, he is dull, plodding and materialistic.

QUEEN OF DISKS

The Queen of the Thrones of Earth

Queen of Gnomes

Water of Earth

20° Sagittarius to 20° Capricorn

Related Minors of the decans:
(10 of Wands), 2 of Disks, 3 of Disks

Astrological trumps: mainly the Devil
for Capricorn as the main sign of the
card; (secondarily Art for the last decan
of Sagittarius as the shadow)

I-Ching: Hexagram 31 *Influence
(Attraction)*

QUEEN OF DISKS
WATER OF EARTH

Book T description: A WOMAN of beautiful face with dark hair; seated upon a throne, beneath which is dark sandy earth. One side of her face is light, the other dark; and her symbolism is best represented in profile. Her attire is similar to that of the Queen of Wands: but she bears a winged goat's head as a crest. A goat is by her side. In one hand she bears a sceptre surmounted by a cube, and in the other an orb of gold.

The Queen of the Thrones of Earth bears a winged goat's head as her crest. The goat is a sure footed climber; dignified, independent and persevering. It has associations with fertility and lusty behavior though Pan, God of Nature, the satyr with the hindquarters, legs, and feet of a goat. The goat is also associated with Baphomet, the Goat of Mendes, whose binary elements represent the sum total of the universe—light and darkness, male and female, good and evil. In Book 4, Crowley calls Baphomet "the Androgyne who is the hieroglyph of arcane perfection . . . He is therefore Life, and Love. But moreover his letter is *ayin*, the Eye, so that he is Light; and his Zodiacal image is Capricornus, that leaping goat whose attribute is Liberty." She is the watery part of Earth, or its internal waters that nurture and drive seeds to grow. Her passivity is fertility; this is the card of Mother Nature. She gestates the seed, or Will, put forth by the Knight of Disks.

216

Her traits are mainly of the sign Capricorn, the tenth sign of the zodiac, at the zenith,[33] and its planet is Saturn. Capricorn says "I use." Capricorn is the sign of the Sea-Goat, and its symbol is supposed to suggest a goat with a fish tail. Goats are climbers, and so are Capricorns. It is a cardinal earth sign and is ambitious, disciplined and persevering. At its best, Capricorn is enduring, responsible, cautious, clever and hard working. At worst, it is pessimistic, cold, striving, rigid and overly conservative. In the body, Capricorn rules the bones, knees, joints and teeth. The Devil is the trump card associated with Capricorn, and his titles are the *Lord of the Gates of Matter* and the *Child of the Forces of Time*. From the Devil, the Queen of Disks gains the ability to take the long view, as the goat upon the zenith. The Queen of the Thrones of Earth sees and manipulates the forces of matter and time for her own benefit. Crowley comments that she "represents the ambition of matter to take part in the great work of Creation."

The Queen of Disks rules from 20° Sagittarius to 20° Capricorn, including the constellation *Aquila*, the Eagle, another indication of her lofty view as the eagle sees best from great heights but has poor near vision. Aquila was the eagle that carried and retrieved Zeus' thunderbolts. Zeus sent his eagle to punish and torment Prometheus for the crime of giving fire to humankind. In another myth, Aquila represents Aphrodite disguised as an eagle, pretending to pursue Zeus in the form of a swan, so that Zeus' love interest, the goddess Nemesis, would shelter him. Zeus later places the images of the eagle and the swan among the stars in commemoration. The alpha lucida star of Aquila is *Altair*, the twelfth brightest star in the sky. Altair takes its name from the Arabic word for "flying eagle" *al-nasr al-ta'ir*, and was also known as the eagle to the Babylonians and Sumerians. Thus it represents the entire constellation. Altair forms one apex of the Northern Hemisphere Summer Triangle, along with the alpha stars of Cygnus, the Swan, and Lyra, the Lyre. Ptolemy considered Altair to give strong passions, indomitable will, a dominating character, influence over others, and a keen penetrating mind.

The Queen of Disks' primary sign is that of Capricorn, the first two decans of the sign. The related minors are the Two of Disks, *Change (Harmonious Change)*, and the Three of Disks, *Work*. From the Two of Disks, the decan ruled by Jupiter, we see the hourglass behind her throne. Within Saturn's glass, the wheels of Jupiter churn the sands of time, the forces of expansion and contraction that drive harmonious material change. The disk in her lap is

---

33   The zenith is the midheaven or highest point of the zodiac, the time of noon and
      the winter solstice, and associated with the outer persona, the career and the
      disciplinary parent.

divided into three internal disks, each containing one of the three alchemical elements Mercury, Sulfur, and Salt, from the Three of Disks card. These are building blocks with which she does her *Work*. This decan is ruled by Mars, the received spark within her that she nurtures, and the power and force of the builder. Her shadow card is the Ten of Wands, *Oppression*. This last decan of Sagittarius is ruled by Saturn. The hammer and pick of the card are hidden in her crest, symbolizing the destructive powers of tyranny. While this is not her primary nature, if from her elevated position she becomes despotic and overbearing she runs the risk of sacrificing all she has worked for.

The Avatar

The Queen of Disks listens within and brings the possibility of completing the cycle of gestation. With her fertility she is bringing forth something material to fruition. Through the expansion and contraction inherent in *Harmonious Change* she achieves goals and a lofty position. With her great capacity for *Work*, she strives for and manifests security, building structures of life and wealth. If in her striving she embodies the force of *Oppression* and becomes tyrannical, she may abort all that she has gestated. As a person she is ambitious, earthy, matriarchal, practical, grounded and sensual. If ill-dignified she is severe, debauched, obtuse, unstable, and dogmatic.

Prince of Disks

PRINCE OF DISKS
AIR OF EARTH

The Prince of the Chariot of Earth

Prince and Emperor of Gnomes

Air of Earth

20° Aries to 20° Taurus

Related Minors of the decans:
(4 of Wands), 5 of Disks, 6 of Disks

Astrological trumps: mainly the Hierophant for Taurus as the main sign of the card; (secondarily the Emperor for the last decan of Aries as the shadow)

I-Ching: Hexagram 53 *Developing Gradually*

Book T description: A WINGED Kingly Figure seated in a chariot drawn by a bull. He bears as a crest the symbol of the head of the winged bull. Beneath the chariot is land, with many flowers. In the one hand he bears an orb of gold held downwards, and in the other a sceptre surmounted by an orb and cross.

The Prince of the Chariot of Earth bears the head of the winged bull as a crest. The bull is a symbol of stability, earth-shaking strength, and procreative powers. It is symbolic of wealth, as wealth was once measured in stock of cattle, and as in modern times it is a term for an upward swing of the stock market. It also is associated with perseverance, endurance, and stamina as well as the fighting charge. In ancient times the cult of the bull was very important, as the bull sired the milk and meat-giving cows and pulled the plow that broke and seeded the earth. The bull also has an ancient association with spring, as in Sumerian times the New Year was at the vernal equinox, and Taurus was the rising constellation. The Sumerian deity Gugalanna was the Bull of Heaven sent to punish Gilgamesh for his rejection of the sexual advances of Inanna. In Egyptian times, the bull god was Apis, a fertility god of grain and herds, chosen because it symbolized the pharaoh's courage, virility, strength and fighting spirit.

The Prince of Disks is the airy part of Earth, or the mind inclined towards practical pursuits. His is the consciousness that steers the Air of Reason though the fixed nature of the Kerubic Bull. He has all of the potent potential of his father combined with the steadying practicality and passive viewpoint of his mother. As the Vau of the world of Assiah, he is the channel between meditative thought and material action. He brings his intellectual power to bear upon the pragmatic, slowly and unwaveringly.

His traits are mainly those of the sign of Taurus, the sign of the bull associated with the earthy side of the planet Venus, sharing Venus with Libra. Taurus says "I have." It is a sensual earth sign, fixed in nature. As the second sign, it plows and fertilizes the lands that Aries has discovered. The symbol represents the head and horns of the bull. Like the bull, Taurus is grounded, patient, strong and stubborn. At its best it is tactile, reliable, fertile, and voluptuous—and a fine judge of quality. At worst, it is a sign of plodding, stubbornness, greed and sloth. In the body, Taurus governs the throat. The Hierophant is the trump card associated with Taurus, and thus further connects him to Vau of the Holy Guardian Angel. From the Hierophant, The Prince of Disks inherits the ability to work upon the inner being, seeking truth, and to persevere until contact is made with the spiritual nature.

The Prince of Disks rules from 20° Aries to 20° Taurus, including the constellation of *Perseus*. Perseus was the son of Zeus upon mortal Danaë, daughter of the King of Argos. The Delphic oracle had made a prophecy that the King would be killed by Danaë's future child, and so he locked Danaë in a bronze chamber open to the sky. Zeus came to her in a "shower of gold" and impregnated her, and thus Perseus *Eurymedon*, the far-ruling, was born. Perseus becomes the first hero, defeating many monsters and fulfilling many quests. His most famous exploits were the killing of Medusa and the rescue of Andromeda from the sea-monster Cetus. Also in this section of the Zodiac is the constellation Taurus, The Bull, whose alpha star is *Aldebaran*, from the Arabic *al-dabarān*, which means "the follower." The star got this name because it appears to follow the Seven Sisters of the Pleiades cluster. Aldebaran is a giant reddish aging star, the fiery Eye of the Bull and the 13th brightest star in the sky, and one of the four Royal Stars as the Watcher of the East, carrying the power *Tacere*, to Keep Silent.

The Prince of Disks primary sign is that of Taurus, the first two decans of the sign. The related minor arcana are the Five of Disks, *Worry (Material Trouble)*, and the Six of Disks, *Success (Material Success)*. As the child of the King and Queen, he inherits and reconciles these two opposing forces. The first decan is ruled by Mercury, the planet of intelligence bringing a tendency to grind the mental gears over material concerns. But ultimately he endures and applies his mind towards proper accounting. Balancing this is the second decan ruled by the Moon, which is exalted in Taurus and gives adaptability to shepherd earthly phenomena to a fertile and successful conclusion. His shadow card is the Four of Wands, *Completion (Perfected Work)*. This sense of perfection and completion, however positive a conclusion, would undermine his strength. It is his mental anxiety that leads him to continuously apply his thoughts towards making improvements, which brings him success.

The Avatar

The Prince of Disks brings the forces of reason applied to the increase of matter. With great energy and fortitude, he brings thoughts towards fruition. By applying the positive nature of *Worry* over material troubles, he strives to perfect and improve things, and with perseverance and adaptability, he ultimately brings the abundance of material *Success*. Reaching *Completion* undermines his gift, which is to continually strive towards improvement. As a person, he is competent and capable, responsible and steadfast, hardworking and predictable. Though seemingly somewhat plodding and dull, his intellect is strong and adaptable. Like a bull in the ring, he is slow to anger but violent and wrathful once stirred. If ill-dignified he can be insensitive and lacking in empathy, selfish, stubborn, and greedy, and making little effort beyond his scope.

PRINCESS OF DISKS
EARTH OF EARTH

Princess OF DISKS

The Princess of the Echoing Hills;
The Rose of the Palace of Earth

Princess and Empress of Gnomes

Throne of the Ace of Disks

Earth of Earth

0° Aries through 30° Gemini, centered
on the Earthy Kerubic constellation
Taurus

Related Minor: Ace of Disks

Astrological trumps: the Emperor,
the Hierophant, the Lovers; centered
on the Hierophant

I-Ching: Hexagram 52 Mountain (Stillness)

Book T description: A STRONG and beautiful Amazon figure with rich brown hair, standing on grass or flowers. A grove of trees near her. Her form suggests Hebe, Ceres, and Proserpine. She bears a winged ram's head as a crest: and wears a mantle of sheepskin. In one hand she carries a sceptre with a circular disk: in the other a Pentacle similar to that of the Ace of Pentacles.

The Princess of the Echoing Hills, Rose of the Palace of Earth, has as her crest a winged ram's head. The ram is the symbol of Aries, and the stone of Aries is the Diamond, a connection with Kether. At first glance one might find this association with Aries as a crest confusing, as it is only a secondary quadrant of hers. But it is a symbol of the renewal of spring over winter, the connection between the end and the beginning, similarly calling to mind the "double Mars" repeating planetary ruler in the zodiac wheel of the decanates. It is symbol of the masculine within the feminine. One may note that the shape of the womb is the shape of a ram's head. This is a hint of her creative power and force. Khnum, the ram-headed Egyptian creator god, was said to have formed the entire Universe from a single egg. The ram's head is also an inverted pentagram, the five pointed star of man, the significance of which will be seen when we review her relationship to the four powers of the sphinx. She wears a mantle of sheepskin; as the guardian of mankind's flocks she shows us the way. The Princess of Disks is the throne of the Ace of Disks, *Root of the Powers of Earth*. We see her standing sensually upon the rolling hills of the Earth Ace, with the disk of Babalon behind her. She is Earth of Earth, final Hè of final Hè, the ultimate receptacle of not only the Ace of Disks but also the entire court sequence. She is the last of the court cards and the connection with Yod of Yod, the Knight of Wands. Thus in the perfection of her expression of the Will of Heaven done on Earth, she awakens the eld of the All-Father, the old King, renewing the entire cycle. She is the temple rightly made, ready and receiving the spark of the Yod, impregnated by Will, conceiving all potential.

The Princess rules the quadrant of space from 0° Aries through 30° Gemini, centered on the Earthy Kerubic constellation Taurus, and her primary astrological trump is *The Hierophant*. This gives her the power of wisdom, and she is thus the connector of the above to the below. "To Keep Silent" is her power, the final of the four powers of the Sphinx and that of Action, corresponding to Kerubic Earth. The motto of the sign Taurus is "I Have," and what she has is the most profound power of all – that of the synthesis of all four powers. You may recall her crest is a ram's head, which is also the five pointed star of the five senses, the inverted pentagram. The pentagram is symbolic of man, and its inversion shows the physical world poised over the spiritual, just as she is ready to descend from the Earth plane to renew the cycle. She is mankind, she is the Sphinx, and the four upper points are the four powers of the Sphinx: to *Will*, to *Dare*, to *Know*, and to *Keep Silent*. In her silence she has united the four elements and awakens the fifth power, that of Spirit, the god within and the power *To Go*. By uniting the four elements the adept acquires the fifth virtue and realizes the reconciliation of the lowest with the highest to become God. Her other two trumps are *The Emperor* for Aries, giving her both the Kingdom and the King, and *The Lovers*, whereby they are united.

The Avatar

The Princess of Disks brings the ultimate fruition of Will and the possibility for both fulfillment of one's potential and the renewal of a cycle. Her power of Earth, "To Keep Silent" and thus take Action in the material world allows for the synthesis of all of the other elemental powers, which combine to awaken the fifth power, "To Go." This reconciles the lowest with the highest and connects us to Spirit. She is pregnant with all possibility. As a person she is kind and generous, steady and industrious, sensual and womanly. If ill-dignified she is dissipated, bewilderingly erratic and wastes her inherent potential.

Kether is in Malkuth

The Card Back Design

The entirety of the card back design is a glyph of the concept that Kether is in Malkuth. One will notice with use and contemplation the myriad ways this is illustrated. In *The Book of the Law*, Crowley introduces the Word of the Aeon, *Abrahadabra*, as signifying the Great Work accomplished. Malkuth is the Ten, the circle and the point, the One and the Zero, and *Abrahadabra* is a symbol of the "establishment of the pillar or phallus of the Macrocosm . . . in the void of the Microcosm." The infinitely small and atomic yet omnipresent point conjuncts infinite space; Ra-Hoor-Khuit or Horus is born. Crowley's *Magick in Theory and Practice* states "The Microcosm is an exact image of the Macrocosm; the Great Work is the raising of the whole man in perfect balance to the power of Infinity." It speaks of transmuting the Many into One. Malkuth is the destination of the original emanation in Kether. It receives all above it and gives form to the other emanations, thus it is also the connection to Kether above as well as below. The Ace proceeds to the Ten. The Knight proceeds to the Princess, who in turn awakens the eld. The Fool ends up at the Universe, transmuted, and the journey begins again.

A symbol of Malkuth is the circle divided fourfold, which is also a symbol of the Universe, as the original impulse that began in the Fool has extended in the four directions; the four elements, the Rose and the Cross, the Tau cross of expansion. Recall the enigma of the Sphinx, that Man is the Microcosm and the Sphinx is Man. In the Sphinx, the four elements, or the powers of the four Kerubic beasts, combine to make a fifth of unity, *To Go*, just as the four corners of the card can combine as wallpaper [34] into one tree and its reflection, connected at the Gate of Tears and surrounded by four Kerubic beasts.

Malkuth is the *Kingdom* and Kether is the *Crown*. We peer down through the Crown of Kether at the four ritual implements, as a reminder of the four powers of the Sphinx: *To Will*, *To Love*, *To Know*, and *To Keep Silent*. In their unification, we connect to Spirit, and the power *To Go*, the meaning of the name of God. The astrological counterpart of the power *To Go* is the Sun, in the center of the four Kerubic signs, seen here as the small point in the circle at the center of the card. It is thus that Crowley calls the Sphinx the true symbol of the Great Work under the law of Thelema, "the Completion of the True Man as the Reconciler of the Highest with the Lowest." [35]

---

34   Recall Oscar Wilde's last words about his wallpaper: "One of us has To Go."
35   Aleister Crowley, Liber Aleph Vel CXI, *The Book of Wisdom or Folly*, pg 152

A Spread

The Riddle of the Sphinx

It is said that Hera sent the Sphinx to guard the entrance to the Greek city of Thebes. The Sphinx asked a riddle of travelers to allow them passage. There are two riddles that she reportedly asks. The first is more well known: "Which creature has one voice and yet becomes four-footed and two-footed and three-footed?" She strangled and devoured anyone unable to answer. Oedipus solved the riddle by answering: Man—who crawls on all fours as a baby, then walks on two feet as an adult, and then uses a walking stick in old age. There was a second riddle: "There are two sisters: one gives birth to the other and she, in turn, gives birth to the first. Who are the two sisters?" The answer is "day and night" as both words are feminine in Greek. Night and Day, Nox et Lux; but there is yet another. Michael Maier in his 1617 book, the Atalanta Fugiens, states that the solution to the Sphinx's riddle is the Philosopher's Stone:

Sphinx is indeed reported to have had many Riddles, but this offered to Oedipus was the chief, "What is that which in the morning goeth upon four feet; upon two feet in the afternoon; and in the Evening upon three?" What was answered by Oedipus is not known. But they who interpret concerning the Ages of Man are deceived. For a Quadrangle of Four Elements are of all things first to be considered, from thence we come to the Hemisphere having two lines, a Right and a Curve, that is, to the White Luna; from thence to the Triangle which consists of Body, Soul and Spirit, or Sol, Luna and Mercury. Hence Rhasis in his Epistles, "The Stone," says he, "is a Triangle in its essence, a Quadrangle in its quality."

This spread considers the four directions as the four elements, the four letters of the divine name, and the four powers of the Sphinx. After invoking Hru, and shuffling, the first four cards are drawn from the top of the pack. In the North, as the first card, Velle, To Will, is placed. This is the spark or first force, the father of the situation, and the primal beginnings and first stirrings. Consider things of the element of Fire such as life force, creativity, passion, and the force of Will. This is the Wand you wield. The next card, placed in the West, is Audere, To Dare. This is the power of Love, and the first form, the mother where the spark of will that has been received now gestates. Consider things of the element of Water such as love, conception, joy, fertility and the emotions. This is the Cup where things are conceived. The third card, placed in the South, is Sciere, To Know. Here is the power of Reason, of thought. This is what has been created from the prior two cards, the son of the primal parents of Will and Love. Consider things of the element of Air. This is the Sword that your intellect has invoked. The fourth card, placed in the East, is Tacere, To Keep Silent. This is the power to take action in the material world, and is the combination and culmination of the other three cards, the daughter. Consider things of the element of Earth such as materiality, and incarnation. This is the Disk of discernment you are

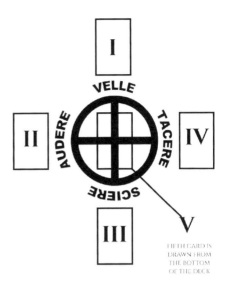

given. The fifth card is drawn from the bottom of the pack. This is the fifth power, Ire, To Go, the unification of all the four combined as the holy name. Consider it a message from Spirit.

To expand this spread one can draw four more cards from the top of the pack, placing them around the circle to show the forces that influence the first four cards, either helping or hindering each of the four powers according to elemental dignity.

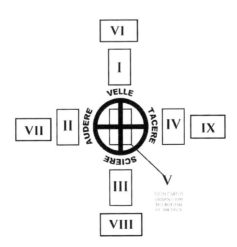

Another Ride on the Wheel

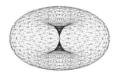

The Tarot illustrations in this book come from the Tabula Mundi Nox et Lux edition, or the black and white pen and ink drawings. *Nox et Lux* translates to "night and day" or "Dark and Light," and I hope it has made some of the invisible, visible.

Light breaks down into color. After the publication of *Book M:Liber Mundi*, I will begin the process of painting the rest of the full seventy-eight card deck with colored inks for release in a future year. The coloring will follow the traditional color scales of the Golden Dawn. This will be the *Colores Arcus* edition, meaning "colors of the rainbow." Note that the rainbow is a symbol of the Art card. The arrow of Sagittarius pierces the rainbow—the paths on the Tree of Life that spell QShTh, meaning bow or rainbow. Sagittarius is the trump of my solar sign, the middle decan, and colors are my *Strength*. Sagittarius looks forward, never back. I am looking forward to it, and I hope you are too.

After that, ever onward, I hope that Fortune is with me, as I take another ride on the wheel.

> Do what thou wilt shall be the whole of the Law.
> Love is the law, Love under Will.
> ~ Aleister Crowley, year 1904

> Dilige et quod vis fac. (Love and then what you will, do.)
> ~ Augustine of Hippo, year 407

א ל

Untangling the Nots

An Anti-Biography

M.M.Meleen is Not:

- A member of any occult order, unless it has a membership of One
- A graduate possessing any degrees, collegiate or fraternal
- A learned scholar of anything in particular
- An exhibitor of artworks in any major galleries or museums in cities around the world
- A student of any prestigious art school
- An expert on the Western Hermetic and Mystery traditions

Know Naught!

Appendix

The solar barge and the side view of a wormhole. See the Death card.

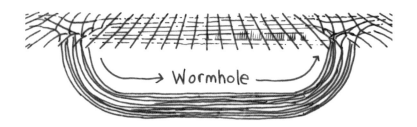

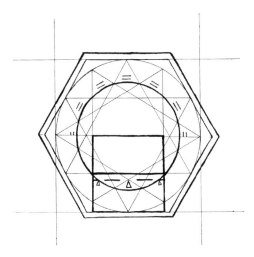

Layout of Robert Fludd's Memory Theatre, which Frances Yates suggests may be a plan based on the layout of the lost Globe Theatre. Adapted from Yate's The Art of Memory *pg 358; compare to Sun card, which is a mnemonic for the signs, planets and suits of the decans.*

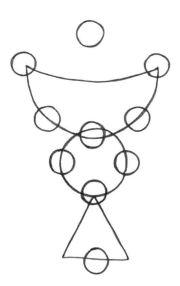

The Cup of the Stolistes; on the Tree of Life, it embraces nine of the Sephiroth, exclusive of Kether. Refer to the Ace of Cups.

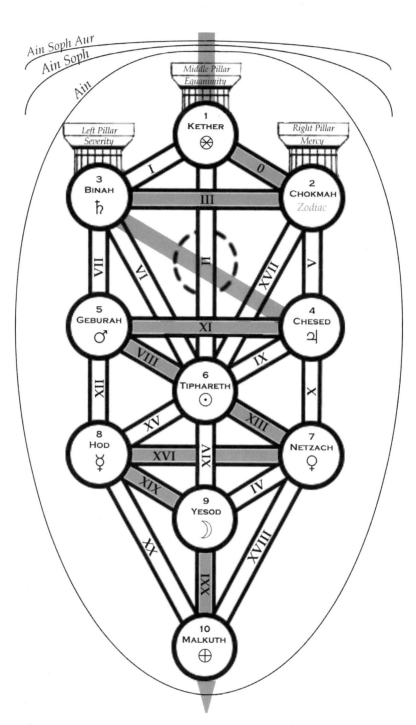